The Secret DJ

First published in 2018
by Faber & Faber Limited
Bloomsbury House
74–77 Great Russell Street
London WC1B 3DA

Typeset by Ian Bahrami
Printed in the UK by CPI Group (UK) Ltd, Croydon CR0 4YY

© The Secret DJ, 2018

The right of The Secret DJ to be identified as author of this
work has been asserted in accordance with Section 77 of the
Copyright, Designs and Patents Act 1988

A CIP record for this book
is available from the British Library

ISBN 978–0–571–33448–3

2 4 6 8 10 9 7 5 3 1

Contents

Acknowledgements   vii
Introduction   ix

A-SIDE

Chapter 1   A Night in the Day of   3
Chapter 2   One Thousand Hotels   36
Chapter 3   'Cos She's the Taxman   69
Chapter 4   Von Ryan's Express!   102
Chapter 5   O.P.U.L.E.N.C.E. – How to Survive
in NYC   120
Chapter 6   Redacted   149

B-SIDE

Chapter 7   We Are Not Your Friends   153
Chapter 8   From Ibiza to the Norfolk Broads   172
Chapter 9   Festival of Shit   213
Chapter 10   The Man Who Disappointed Himself
to Death   232
Chapter 11   Happy as a Bastard on Father's Day   256
Chapter 12   There Are Some Mountains High
Enough   269

Epilogue   295
Glossary of Terms   301
Index   305

Acknowledgements

Thanks to:

Our tech friends at Hornsey Research and their amazing Secret DJ jukebox app.
My family, if I still have one after they read this.
Duncan J. A. Dick, editor of *Mixmag*. It's all your fault.
Jez, Tim and Keith from REDACTED, without whom . . .
Ben and Julian at L.A.W.
Lee at Faber & Faber.
Justin Robertson.
Bill Brewster.
Ransom Note and Boiler Room.
REDACTED at REDACTED and everyone there.
Paul REDACTED, who gave me my first break.
Ian Bahrami for his painless, swift editing.

To all the people who know exactly who I am and are doing the right thing by engaging in a great big SHUSH.

. . . and to the Tour Manager. Gone somewhere, but certainly never forgotten.

    Certainly not now anyway.

Introduction

I have had an interesting life, and unlike a lot of my peers I have made copious notes along the way, perhaps in the full knowledge that much will be forgotten. I certainly never set out to be 'a DJ'. No one did in the 1980s, unless you wanted to get on the radio and dubiously close to children. Then it was literally to be a 'Disc Jockey', a radio term about a radio job. Sure, 'Mobile DJs' existed and we all had the school disco in the 1970s, but even if you took the thing out of the radio studio and into a church hall, the DJ still spoke between the records as if he were on-air – something, I *still* have to explain to old folks, that just doesn't happen any more. One thing they do understand is how much more important a record was back then. People would sit in a room together in silence and listen to a record with reverence. The idea of 'background music' was unheard of. Compared to today even 'easy listening' was paid attention to rapturously (the clue is in the name). It was as crazy as the idea of making reality TV that isn't designed to be watched. Imagine a time when there was nothing digital in the home and the domestic sound system meant more to many people than the rarer television. Most of the first-generation DJs you revere come from a time when very little came in through the eye and everything that mattered entered your ears. Today the job is very much about a deep love of the self, instead of the music. Music itself has been devalued almost to the point of zero. It is merely fuel for the careers of DJs, the soundtrack to something, not a thing in itself; 'content' for your totally awesome life, and disposable content at that. I come from a time when it was everything, rather than nothing. It was an object, a highly fetishised totem that didn't come to you and wasn't available all that regularly. You had to leave the house and find this thing, using nothing but your physical senses. I don't say this to alienate young readers – I owe you everything! Every week I work for you. It's just by way of context, to help you understand. This book is for you, after all.

For me, like I imagine many others, music was a connection to something ephemeral and deeply glamorous that happened to other people *very* far away. Many of the very successful can be born into an industry, either directly to industry parents or in a major city where the industry is conveniently located. Some of us, however, watched from such a remove that it was *comical*, somewhere radio waves barely reached, never mind the latest vinyl or current clothing fashions. But for all of us it started with radio empowering nerds. Wherever you were. However nerdy. If you are younger than me, just replace the word 'radio' with 'internet'.

The Swinging Sixties and modern dance music have much in common. Both started as a counter-culture and both were in large part protest movements. They were driven by a love of music and centred around 'the rave'. Drugs, lights and sounds were the church. Staying up all night was what it was all about. However, the 1960s have been incredibly well documented, maybe even a tad over-glamourised. Indeed, it could be said the northern soul or punk or heavy-metal scenes have received almost as much reverence and documentation as modern dance music. The dance music scene has lasted *far* longer than any other – thirty years rather than a mere decade – but has enjoyed very little coverage other than a couple of frankly awful films and a handful of books. I'd like to redress that a bit. I'd like to see more. Because dance music is simply fucking huge, mate. It's big. It's larger than Jupiter's codpiece. It's the world's biggest youth movement bar none, and unlike its grandfather, the 1960s, it's *still* getting bigger. America stuck its flag in the '60s as if the decade never happened anywhere else, and now they have finally arrived at the rave. Again they are claiming it for themselves, long after the rest of the world. But Hollywood feature films and huge global magazine sales are just the tip of the iceberg amid the vastness of the dance scene. A newcomer might be forgiven for thinking it started very recently in the US. Indeed, many believe that to be the case. It's simply not true. We've been raving hard since the Second Summer of Love in 1988, and we're *still* at it.

My aim is to tell the true story of DJing, to be an authentic voice speaking from and to this scene, to give hints and guide newbies on their pilgrimage and to tell it as it really is. It is *my* story, however. For that I am both sorry and unapologetic. It's the only story I know. I'm no statistician, fetishist or collector. I'm just a working DJ. So, in the absence of knowledge and an education, the only way I can be an authority is to present my experience. It's all I have.

It's not an instruction manual or a history book. Shall we just agree to call it a cautionary tale that may illuminate? Just for the record, I *could* write a manual, OK? Yeah, and it would be amazing. Totally. But a book can't instruct upon something as simple and intuitive as playing records. House music is a *feeling*. Anyway, you just want the rock 'n' roll dirt, don't you? *Naughty*.

A-SIDE

Chapter 1

A Night in the Day of

17.00 hrs

You are *always* ready to leave. You are in a constant state of readiness. You can be ready to travel in the time it takes to put your shoes on, pick up last week's tunes and walk out the door. An international DJ works every weekend. All year round. Midweek too sometimes. This time the tour manager is late. I call him 'tour manager', but he's my best mate and I'd recently convinced my agent he should have the title. He's driven me to lots of places on home turf but this is his first time in an official, titular capacity. And his first one overseas – Ibiza, rather unsurprisingly. It's always Ibiza in the summer months.

As the appointed time comes and goes it's clear the flight is going to be missed. Before now I'd never missed a gig. There isn't much to this job. Turn up, play records, get paid, leave. It's not rocket science. My mate arrives for his debut as tour manager two hours after the flight has left. He is wearing a T-shirt that has 'SACK THE FUCKING TOUR MANAGER' written on it in large friendly letters. He'd realised he'd missed the window of opportunity after my forty-third angry text, so rather than rush he'd spent the time constructively, getting a novelty T-shirt printed up at a tourist kiosk on the way over. He'd misread 17.00 as 7 p.m. On his first day in the job. Style. Where I come

3

from, once you get a nickname it sticks for life. He would be known as Tour Manager for evermore.

He bursts in the door, a blur of amphetamine enthusiasm as usual. 'Sack the fucking tour manager!' he bellows, gesticulating madly at his unmissable chesty slogan. 'I'm ready for you this time, you cunt! You will never push me in the pool.'

On every occasion we'd been in Ibiza together I'd managed to push him in a pool. He had to be fully clothed – and ideally carrying costly valuables of the non-waterproof variety. It had become a ritual. He'd even suggested I got him this job simply to be able to humiliate him across the globe. This was, of course, absolutely ridiculous and entirely factual. Missing the flight, however, was 'a problem'.

21.45 hrs

In times of difficulty you call your agent. Bigger agencies have people who deal specifically with logistics and travel. Missing a flight was an easy fix. Holiday flights to Ibiza tend to leave almost hourly in the summer. The cheap ones are always at crazy times in the night. We are in luck. The last one to Ibiza tonight would be boarding not long after the soonest we could feasibly get to departures. Airports at night are always bleak and populated entirely by lunatics. Your ordinary citizen is not used to the heady combo of being out late and about to go on holiday. It works on their brain like a chisel. They freak out. DJs are not on holiday, we are going to work, only really, really far away in the middle of the night. Only the top DJ dogs go to work on anything but the cheapest flights. With a destination like Ibiza, there is no choice but to ride the cheap seats, especially if, thanks to your insane hiring policies, you've missed the better-quality flight already. Even if you have some sort of frequent-flyer thing, airports close down 99 per cent of anything useful at night, and you tend to end up part of a gaggle of barking, chanting, aggressively drunk holidaymakers, all en route to their yearly two weeks away from their lives. While you are on your way deeper into yours.

Is there anything more fearsome than five hundred drunken teens and adults-who-should-know-better about to go on holiday? The nearest I can think of is sitting in a longboat among pre-pillage Vikings. The gear marks you out. Back then it was two gigantic flight-cased record boxes that few other occupations could boast as hand luggage. 'Yes, DJ here, look at me!' These days every Tom, Dick or Harriet uses some sort of DJ-esque luggage accessory. However, just ten years ago you could easily be the only DJ in the entire airport, never mind on a flight.

Tour Manager is, as usual in dull moments, off doing some pointless drug-fuelled task at relentless intensity while blithering and yelping. I'm trying not to look like a DJ, while surrounded by hundreds of clubbers. I'm failing. They tend to be able to smell a DJ, never mind see one. I'm not trying to avoid them out of arrogance; I'm just really not in the mood today. They are at an insane pitch of hyper-excitement about their annual blowout, while this is your weekly commute over decades. They are out of their minds on alcohol and ecstasy, while you are trying to do a crossword. The loudest one is an American (unusual for Ibiza at the time) with a voice so penetrating it makes the perfume samplers on the shelves of the nearby duty-free shop rattle. She is blonde, blandly pretty, and is doing an amazing job of being louder than five hundred really loud people.

'OMIGERD, YOU'RE A FUCKING DJ, MAAAN! WAIT, I KNOW YOU! OMIGERD, OMIGERD!'

I know most red-blooded fellows won't mind at all when a young halfwit attempts to communicate by waggling their bits in your face. But some days you'd just rather do the crossword. Oh, you wouldn't? OK, come back to me when you've been at it thirty years and we'll talk then. Being 'on' all the time is not an option for a travelling entertainer. It will drive you insane. It is as inevitable as the tide. I should also add that these days I have more grace under pressure. Then again, you had to be there. She was next-level annoying: drunk and evangelical about it, and the Princess of Shoutington was the sort who always got exactly what she wanted, and quick.

'WHERE ARE YOU PLAYING, DUDE!? CAN WE GET ON THE LIST? THERE'S ONLY LIKE TWENTY-FIVE OF US! IT WILL BE TOADALLY AWESOME! DRINK SOME FUCKING PUNCH, MAN. IT'S LIKE FULLY LOADED WITH MDMA, DUDE.'

'Sure. I can sort you out if you get me a list of names. Can we do it when we land? I really don't want a drink. I'm kind of working, not really here to party.'

'FUCK YOU, MAN! YOU SHOULD BE NICER TO PEOPLE WHO PAY TO SEE YOU!'

'But you're not paying to see me sit in this chair reading! I'm off duty, please.'

'HEY, YOU GUYS! *HE JUST WANTS TO BE ALONE.* BOO HOO, BOO HOO.' (Cue much laughter and bugging me whenever the opportunity arose for the next two hours.)

'Amazing tits. You will never throw me in the pool, by the way,' says a familiar Scots voice from the side. I tell him never to call me that again. Then we commence the ritual of waiting as far away as possible from the gate in order to be absolutely the last people to board, demonstrating to the world and mainly ourselves that we are waaaay too cool to stress about where to sit on such a short flight and that we do not queue EVAH. Naturally we end up in horrible seats right in the middle of the pack of loons. They start in on their drugs in earnest once we take off. The thing about rock 'n' roll, which I have been around all my adult life, is that bad behaviour is OK if done with style, but it is an unwritten law that you leave civilians out of it. The thing about dance music culture, and maybe even society in general, is that every deeply deluded one of us thinks we are stars. It's the beautiful glow around the dark heart of it, the best and the worst part. Never writ more large than when big gangs of rabid mongs are boshing gear in front of civilian families.

Ketamine. In the early days it came in bottles lifted from vets. On the label it said: 'For use with domestic felines and sub-human primates only'. That's a *warning*, not an invitation, kids. You can tell it's mainly ketamine and cocaine as the volume starts to go up, up and UP and the coherence goes down, down, down, until some of them are just lowing like cattle. It's quite a scary noise. It's the sound of stupid.

I have earplugs. Occupational tools. I feel it's rude to put them in while in the company of Tour Manager. I turn around to see him in the thick of the kids. Happy as a sandboy. Flirting disastrously with my bleach-blonde nemesis. As doomed to failure with her as only a fifty-two-year-old man who looks like he's from the Old Testament can be.

Don the plugs. Don them!

Ibiza, 23.30 hrs local time

The aircraft doors open. The cold, recycled, corporate, germ-filled air is sucked out and the warm, fuzzy wall of heat hits you hard as you step onto the stairs and descend towards the bus. Arrival is always easy in Ibiza. It may be smart policy, it may be the sheer numbers, it may just be that Ibicencos are so damn cool, but it's a breeze going in and out of Ibiza airport. No matter how jaded and tired you are it's always a pleasure to arrive and equally easy to leave. It's not just the wall of heat that hits you, the haze in the air and the mix of dust, sea and bougainvillea blooms assaults the nose too. As does the subtly constant whiff of cigarette smoke that says you are now somewhere else, somewhere that does not care all that much. Smells a bit like . . . hedonism.

Naturally a pro carries everything with them. As well as hundreds of hours of music in that bag there is, rolled absurdly tight, a full change of clothes, plus a miniature toolkit and shaving set, earplugs, first aid, electrical tape, spare stylus, cartridges . . . even a needle and thread. Yeah, I'm loads of fun. However, there are only two ways to travel professionally: as some sort of shambolic diva caravan, with all the attendant dramas and disasters; or as a tight, self-sufficient, no-mess expert travelling unit. I was usually the latter, but the recent hiring and firing of my crack team of one loopy aristocrat as technical assistant means I'm sliding far more towards the former.

I have the whole luggage thing down to a fine art. Tour Manager does not. While the johnny-holidays are shuffling around the luggage carousel, the pro knifes through with hand luggage only. Straight to the point, past all the nonsense and straight out. Unless, of course, your recently fired tour manager is there to render the whole process a shambling, shouty, hour-long abortion. Finally, as the magic doors slide open, we are revealed in all our glory: a tall man carrying way too much accompanied by an even taller hermit from the Dark Ages, one who rather pointedly isn't carrying any luggage at all, despite it being his job until very recently.

The arrivals gate is a sea of kids in shades, cargo pants and vests. It's always like that. All we know is that Hans is meeting us and he's a young German. This worries me, as Tour Manager still thinks it is 1943. I pull him to one side.

'Listen, you *lunatic*,' I hiss. 'Just for one moment can you attempt some sort of normality? My livelihood is at stake here. NO GERMAN JOKES. Not one. Are we clear?'

'*ACHTUNG!*' roars Tour Manager, while doing a large Nazi salute in front of a large crowd of every European nationality.

A slightly built young man immediately peels out of the crowd. He approaches us and says in flawless English, 'Ah, you guys must be here for me. I could not help but notice you.'

I'm mortified, but Tour Manager is, as ever, completely immune to his surroundings.

'I am Hans,' says the kid, extending a palm for a shake.

'I've got two as well, no need to show off,' barks His Tourmanagerness, and he walks off smartly in the wrong direction.

We finally walk out into the rich, dense air of Ibiza, load up the car and move into the night. It's possible for a working DJ to spend many years visiting Ibiza and never see it during daylight – a crime of truly epic proportions. Tour Manager owns a small club back home. When he isn't leaping about doing pointless things very quickly he's ignoring pleading texts from the venue, on a phone that he never answers. Sat in the front of the car he is visibly trying hard not to talk to Hans and instead is staring at his phone screen.

'So,' begins Hans, 'it's nice to see you, T-Man.'

'How do you know my name!?' squeaks His Tourmanagerness.

Hans merely smiles a small smile and continues driving. Then he asks, 'So, T-Man, my friend, have you ever been to Germany?'

'No, but my dad went once,' is the curt reply. Tour

Manager then turns to me and says in a really loud stage whisper, 'I think this Kraut fancies me.'

I am definitely panicking about the situation at this point. Hans isn't just a driver sent to pick us up. He's one of the promoters of the event and I'm working for them for the first time, and quite possibly the last. At this rate Tour Manager is going to cause an international incident before we've even got to the venue. I have to admire Hans for his diplomacy and am boiling mad with rage at the behaviour of my compatriot. Luckily we're coming to a halt at our destination.

'I am so, so sorry about him. He's old,' I apologise weakly as we disembark from the car and gather the luggage.

Hans embraces me and proclaims, 'Thank you so much for bringing him!'

'No! I apologise unreservedly!' I reply hurriedly. 'He's a bit eccentric. Technically I *had* to bring him as he is the tour manager.'

Hans seems to find this very amusing and replies, 'No, don't apologise. I think he is the funniest man in the world. Did you know I was working at his club last night?'

'What!?'

Like many promoters and club workers, Hans is also a working DJ in his own right. Unlike us he's able to function in many roles, efficiently and with no fuss, over many borders and time zones. It transpires that just the previous evening, two thousand miles away, Hans had been the guest DJ and Tour Manager had been the host. His Tourmanagerness literally has no recollection of the previous night at all. He certainly paid no regard whatsoever to the minor players in it, meaning anyone else at all but himself.

'Yes. I was playing at his club last night. He is even wearing the same clothes. It is a funny surprise to bring him here.'

Apparently T-Man had been exactly the same combination of barking and deeply inappropriate, spouting anti-German epithets non-stop and referring constantly to World War II. Which, rather amazingly, Hans found amusing.

Christ. A German with a sense of humour. I really must be in Ibiza.

00.00 hrs

As we arrive at the appointed hotel with Hans it becomes clear that it isn't up to muster. In the parts of Spain they like to keep foreigners in, they basically add a star to the international hotel star system. A five-star is a four, a four a three, etc. The entrance takes us towards reception, and as we pass a row of shrubs I use my entire bodyweight to charge at Tour Manager, pushing him completely off his feet, through the bushes and straight into the pool.

'YOU MASSIVE GAPING CUNT!' he screams as he surfaces. He doesn't even take in any air. It's as if a dolphin's blowhole could swear.

Phone, watch, luggage, wallet – all ruined. In record time too. Like all hairy creatures he has a way of looking extra sad and small after being submerged. I feel, however, that after 'Hansgate' he actually deserved it for once.

I have to up our game. 'If it's any consolation, your

Tourmanagerness,' I say, 'we're fucking this gaff right off and going to Es Vive. On me. Hans, would you mind giving us a lift?'

Ibiza is a tiny island with hundreds of hotels. A very smart Brit had worked out that a slight bump upwards in luxury and service and a nod towards DJs and more affluent clubbers would elevate his hotel. Mixing this with a Miami-esque art deco look cemented Es Vive as the place to be. 'Boutique hotel' became a phrase long after this place finished inventing it. We walk from the street towards the reception of the most rock 'n' roll hotel on the island and almost crash into our loud, blonde friend from the flight, who is now without her entourage of Viking raiders.

'YOU'RE SOMETHING OF A DICK, SECRET DJ!' she yodels at welding volume.

'Maybe she's right, you know,' I muse thoughtfully as I push Tour Manager one-handed into this new pool for a record-breaking second time. People on high-grade amphetamines are easy targets. They just aren't very observant.

Hans backs away, carefully.

01.30 hrs

No matter how insane the schedule there is always a small oasis of calm. The law of averages demands it. Even the most rabid of rock 'n' rollers spend time doing nothing, if only by accident. Dinner is usually your last chance to enjoy your only slice of normal pie. I eat like a champion. Tour Manager eats nothing at all as it means he would have to stop talking. Hans is equal parts amazed and appalled. But this pocket of normality is fleeting, as now it's time to get involved.

If you're in the Old Town – or Dalt Vila, as it's known – and especially if you're old school, it's down to the port for *chupitos* and gak. The port of Ibiza at night is an Arabian bazaar of smells, sights and sounds, and it's always thick with people. We don't really have the luxury of time, but for veterans it's a tradition to show your face on the strip. You've not arrived until you've been to the Rock Bar, paid your respects and drunk a measure of the local firewater. Hans is sufficiently experienced to know that this isn't a request. It's an obligation.

Dalt Vila glitters in the Mediterranean night, dominating the bay, as is its purpose. Its cubist spires, visible from most of the southern part of the island, are a clarion call to the night creatures to come out and worship. It's like a deep valley, with the vessels of the super-rich and the vast cruise ships on one side and solid bricks of ancient history on the other. The port itself hums like a plucked string with energy and promise. It's the starting gate for the nightlife. If you're wealthy enough not to be forced to buy your club tickets months in advance, this is where you come to decide where to go, to gossip about which of the hundreds of events that evening is the one to be seen at. The clubs and promoters know this and seek to influence the decision. Their solution was to organise outlandish parades up and down the port like a tiny boutique carnival. Between the goggling civilians a gaggle of beauties of every persuasion would march holding banners, *banderas* and placards, and always dressed according to some ridiculous sexual theme. Ibiza settled on the 'sex sells' theory of marketing decades ago and never bothered to tweak it. It's an angle the notorious Manumission played out to the extreme. Speaking of which, there's Johnny the Dwarf, roped in to yet another parade and singing for his supper. An almost imperceptible shrug, a knowing wink, 'Drink later?' and the flecks of true colour in the beige circuit move on down the strip. Of course, the parades are banned now, like all interesting things, in the spirit of the new global puritanism.

Ninety per cent of the perambulators are tourists who have no idea that this one bar is special and the haunt of celebrities, or that the next is strictly for Italians looking to score hashish; that this one is owned by that mega-club, or that that one is a front for Serbian organised crime. To outsiders they're all the same and all equally intimidating, so they keep walking, some looking scared, some amused. It's like a reverse zoo, with those of us ensconced in our seats and stools viewing the merchandise filing past. We earned these front-row seats over decades. The strip in the port is the airport carousel made large, its luggage as dull and tired as it is sometimes exotic and rich. All Ibiza is here and even Tour Manager's eccentricities are eclipsed by it.

Even though we have no time for leisure the ceremony has to be acknowledged with a single shot of Hierbas in the Rock Bar. When the booze hits the throat you are transported back through a string of pasts to the Domino Bar, the Moors, further even to an officer of Carthage guarding warships in the bay at night. Hierbas, ancient aniseed doom. The chilled, unique flavour of Ibiza rolls through your inner core. It's like being mugged gently by an old friend. Salute the fallen and the present.

Then it's back into the waiting car and a visibly nervous Hans.

03.00 hrs

It can be tough getting through a busy venue's door. There's certainly an unusual amount of commotion this time. From a distance, it looks like the gatekeeper did not have his door under control. Up close this proves an understatement. The exterior is a vast car park, the club a series of walls and awnings like a mock-rustic stone ship adrift in a junkyard sea. This is Ibiza. The idea of an orderly queue is utterly alien to at least four of the dominant nationalities, and an unruly mass is pressing against the entrance. It's a well-dressed slow riot. Kwowser, an old friend and something of a professional 'picker', was supposed to be the doorman in charge. That very day, through mutual contacts, he'd landed a trial period working on this very door. He'd been out there a week already, and I'd been looking forward to seeing how things were working out.

He is curled up just in front of the club, having, I later discovered, treated himself to a few high-powered chunks of MDMA, *far* stronger than is usually available back in London. Knowing him well, I begin to worry, as some of the security people move to wake him. Having done a lot of doors Kwowser is neither a small man nor afraid of a bit of casual violence. He is also half German. One of the owners of the venue is stood behind security looking very unamused.

Both halves of him are German. Just in front of Kwowser, trying to navigate the scrum, is a German film crew, here to film the evening and interview the proud owner. Kwowser is prodded awake by security, upon which, hearing German spoken, he screams '*ARSCHLOCH!*' at all the Germans in the area, which means everyone important. This is far more insulting in German than its strict translation into another language would suggest. It leaves the owner somewhat lost for words. When he finally finds them, they bring about the termination of Kwowser's extremely brief tenure there, as well as ordering his immediate ejection from the grounds, never to return. It takes four security men to drag him away.

Hired, fired and barred for life all in one day. Nice going, Kwowser. I am strangely proud.

To the clubber the door is everything. It's the portal to the temple. To the pro it is just an inefficient and overcrowded entrance. You squeeze past the bottleneck of chaos, go through the inner doors, enjoy a brief decontaminating shower of welcome air con and then the dense soup of sound and darkness closes in. It's a fictional atmosphere, a constructed 'other' where we go to be someone different, somewhere else. Your pupils spasm and flex to try and compensate for the sudden pitch-darkness. There's a moment of disorientation in a black tunnel and then the lights explode to match the sonic assault. The press of bodies and sensory overload never cease to short-circuit the senses. It's something that's best eased into, if possible.

Unfortunately that isn't possible. On this occasion I'm late. Which doesn't mean I've missed the actual time I was scheduled to start. That rarely happens. Being late means arriving too close for comfort, with no time to settle in, relax and get a feel for what has come before. You're effectively shoved onstage, blinking at the lights in the darkness. You hold your boxes and bags over your head. You barge, push, squeeze and shout your way through. No one pays attention to anything. They're all in little worlds of their own. They're concentrating on experiencing the bigger picture and always, ALWAYS facing the DJ booth. Rapt. Away. The booth is the pulpit, the lectern from which you address the faithful. I always dread the DJ booth shift change, one ego handing over to another. It's a higher state of awkwardness. It works both ways, for incumbent or arriviste. Amateurs make an entrance, pros keep the vibe. Wankers hog the booth, pros make a smooth transition. Nice people say hello, nasty ones frown and mumble. Have I made my point yet? Yeah: don't be a dick.

This bunch are not happy to see me, which is often par for the course, but it can get out of hand when there is an entourage involved. I'd arrived fifteen minutes before I was due on. For me this is very late, but to many, especially those on tight schedules with several gigs over a weekend, it is standard. Wrong, but standard nonetheless. My intuition suggests that if there are signs of the incoming DJ being late, the incumbent might get a little thrill from thinking that he can perform for longer. Then, when the next DJ does in fact arrive just in time, there is crushing disappointment. That's one explanation I have for the wall of animosity that can greet you. Then there's just plain envy, or hangers-on 'supporting' their hero by deciding to hate you. Maybe they've met me already. Who the fuck knows?

I spent decades as the warm-up. It requires superior skill. It will eat your ego alive if you are ambitious. The trouble with the mega-clubs is that often the guys on before are not regular hard-working residents, they are stars in their own right. 'Stars'. Yeah, I know. Ridiculous, isn't it? Still, it's real.

So you sheepishly navigate the glaring hostility. You meekly squeeze past those who are not meant to be in your working space. You make yourself as small as possible. It's bad form to make a fuss and cast a shadow over someone else's limelight. At this point some sort of help would be useful, but that's the tour manager's job and I'd sacked him ten hours ago. Anyway, he was currently resembling a furry grey lighthouse, scouring the venue for women with a 360-degree lechery beam. He was gone. He'd lived a good life, died and gone to T-Man heaven. I wrestle the kit through the phalanx of derision and turn to find the usual mountain of bags, coats, purses, computers, cloaks, hats, furs, phones and general detritus clogging every space available. The correct form is to make space for an arriving DJ, but this was a sit-in, occupied territory. It wasn't going to happen without a fight.

DJs always know when their time is up. We count it down, pace our work to match the time frame. Come ten or fifteen minutes to the hour, with your time nearly up, you start looking out for the next guy. You begin tidying your bits and packing up. Five minutes to and you are unplugging your headphones. As a consideration, if the next guy is stressed or needs to breathe you might ask politely if he would like you to 'play one more'. It's a courtesy. Or he may ask it of you first. There is usually some sort of exchange, 'the old booth shuffle', I call it, like getting changed on the beach under a too small towel – a slightly embarrassing necessity. Sometimes the previous DJ does not look up, does not acknowledge you are there, hides in the pantomime of 'being in the zone'. Then you know you are in for trouble. You're being punished for something. It may be just for being in a better time slot than them. It may be that they don't think you are as good as them 'artistically'. It may be drugs or insane ego. Maybe they've had a shit day. You just have to deal with it.

I wrestle the bags in past the aggro. Look for a space. None. Bend down, pull back some coats to make room and – HOLY SHIT! – a face is revealed in the baggage. I jump in the air in cartoon shock. Seriously? You've made a little fort in the coats so you can do drugs? Unreal.

There are nerves. Ask many DJs if they suffer from them and they will say no, but show me one of those and I will show you a liar. On the surface I am calm. I feel calm, I exude calm. I need a shit, though. I always do just before. This is how I know the nerves exist. My conscious mind tells me I have been doing this for decades, that there is no fear. But my guts know different. Things are accelerating, the pace quickening. The dude wants to play longer? Fine. I need the toilet.

The one thing any DJ will tell you is they wish they had their own bathroom. For some strange reason the toilets and the booth are always at opposite ends of a venue. Back into the fray, senses now stretched taut. You appear to the throng like a lunatic, pushing and stressing your way through like an angry King Canute. Something in the eyes tells them you are all business, and the Red Sea parts. Get to the toilets and, of course, the gents are like a swamp. Borderline *Deliverance*, geared only towards the swift sniffer, useful for nothing much other than catching something nasty. It doesn't matter anyway 'cos as usual you sit down and can't go. It's all in your mind. You try, fail and then need to go again by the time you get to the door. Does this seem ridiculous? Have you ever performed solo in front of two thousand souls? It's part of the radiation of being late. The stressy atmosphere in the booth. In some part, a brown ritual. You catch yourself in the mirror, shake your head in bemusement. Cold water on the face. What a ridiculous pantomime.

Now it's with a certain grim determination that you move back through the throng and up to the booth to take your place. It's yours now. No time for fragile egos and boundary waltzes. Stride straight into the booth. Bark at the hangers-on to make way. Ask them politely to leave. Ignore the evil glares. Tap the DJ, who's studiously ignoring you, on the shoulder and gesture at your watch. He knows he's had his extra fun. Time to go, son. Some people, unbelievably, have even paid to see me in particular (still can't get my head around that part). It's as automatic as tying your laces. Bags open. Tunes out. Reset the system from the guy before, monitors always set to ear-bleed in his excitement. Bring down the gain levels to normal. Catch the sound guy's eye. He's happier now. You've been working subconsciously all through the last thirty minutes of the previous DJ's set. What would dovetail nicely with his sound? The temptation to fuck it all off is there, to slam on the brakes, change the vibe, switch off all the lights to announce yourself, sound the dickhead's fanfare. Sometimes you have to. Not tonight, though. He was hard work but his music wasn't, and it's easy to find a couple of openers to match his vibe. Maybe it was all your stress? But it's not about you or him. It's about them out there. All of them. And they are very happy right now. It's your job to continue that.

Settle in? Sometimes it takes an hour, but once you are comfortably at the controls and the bad vibes have left the booth you finally relax. This time I'm lucky. Sometimes the previous DJ and his entourage are always in your peripheral vision, staring at you venomously for the duration. Thankfully not this time. It's time to look up (you'd be surprised but some DJs never look up from their work once to read the room). It's time to make the connection. The sea of bobbing heads is always there, a little like a choppy ocean. And like being on an ocean once you grasp the wheel you suddenly seem to focus on it intensely. Now you are in the moment. Time stops. A record that is clearly marked as nearly ten minutes long appears to pass in moments. Your five senses each reduce to a tunnelled-down version. The pressure of two thousand eyes demands your own focus. Like reading a score you are simultaneously in the moment and also two or three tunes ahead. Audio chess with a worthy opponent.

It's a little like swimming. You are adrift in a shimmer of blurred light and totally enveloped in sound. There is always a rhythm, of course, the beat of your legs in the current. The *one, two, three, four* is as natural as breathing.

There is no thinking. You just know. Have you ever tried too hard at something physical, a sport or a game? Have you noticed how you are never better at it than when you are not thinking at all? It's that. The lights are too much and close down your vision. You barely focus on anything apart from the tunes themselves, and even then it's fairly intuitive. You know exactly where the one you want is. You break the surface now and then to focus on individuals, and they lock eyes with you. You know you're doing it right. Occasionally the connection breaks and you make a change to compensate. But not tonight.

I see DJ colleagues with lists. I see them with computers and colour-coded wallets of CDs. I see them with USB sticks and frowns of concentration. I also see some who just float. I'm one of those. I'm not there. In my darker times I curse myself for not being more 'professional' about it all, but even when I try it all falls apart, melts away in the heat. It's a thing I do, and do well. I try not to question it. The subconscious plays a big part. Anyone who truly *lives* a thing properly has anxiety dreams about it. You try to do your thing in the dream, and you can't. If you're ever at a loss about what it is you're good at, what it is that you actually *do*, ask your dreams. I dream of being up there and there's a fault with the equipment, a simple everyday technical fuck-up. But the crowd doesn't know. They think it's you (this happens for real too). But everyone has an anxiety dream some time. This is mine. It is how I know I am a DJ.

There is a flow. Of that there is no doubt. It is a by-product of the whole. The party is everyone and each

23

person pitches in, yourself included. These big gigs are a breeze mainly because every soul in there sincerely wants them to be. When it's working it's a real high. All hyperbole aside, it just happens and you are part of something special. If you're an idiot, you try to claim authorship. Rainmakers[*] are a real problem. You can see why they do it, though.

Just as you are lost in it all there is a tap on your shoulder. There is nothing like someone blagging their way into your reverie to break the mood. But it's an occupational hazard, and part of being a professional is to deal with it with a measure of grace. Pro booths are supposedly inaccessible, but then again, it depends on who you are when it comes to access. You can feel them before you see them in your peripheral vision. We call them 'booth wankers'. They aren't happy unless they are in there next to the DJ, soaking up adulation by association, like a deluded lizard basking under a sun lamp in a basement. It happens from top to bottom. They can be crackheads or billionaires. My own view is they are fine. Whatever turns you on. Give me enough room to turn around to reach my tunes and move my elbows, and you'll hear no complaints. Don't talk to me, please. DON'T TALK TO ME. I'm at work. I'm also in a state of reverie. Break my vibe and you break the vibe for everyone. Doesn't matter what I want, though – that won't stop it happening.

'HEY! HEY, DUDE, GREAT SOUNDS. Have you got that one that goes UMPHT-UMPHT, WAKKA-WIK, HRFT-HRFT, DANK-DANK?'

***

[*] See the Glossary of Terms.

Does anyone really say 'sounds'? Is he kidding? No, he's not kidding. Thing is, I know exactly what tune he means. DJs are like dentists. They can understand you perfectly with both hands shoved wrist-deep into a numb mouth. Over the years you develop a weird ability to decipher the ridiculous noises people make when requesting, even when you don't want to. I'm a pro. I always nod and smile. Engage. Sometimes that is all they want – for the crowd to see them talking to you. The request is just a thing to do to get them in the booth. Bad DJs hate it. HOW DARE someone approach them!? *Tranquilo*, dude. Be a pro, deal with it.

That doesn't mean nightmares don't happen.

Mad Girl used to get up in my face every time I played in my home town. When I was there to see my folks I happened to see her while out shopping and saw she worked in a high-fashion ladies clothes shop. Every cell in my body wanted to kick the doors of the shop in and shout at the top of my lungs right in her ear, 'EXCUSE ME, DO YOU HAVE ANY 1980 MILITARY UNIFORMS? I NEED A LIEUTENANT'S BLUES. ANY AIGUILLETTE IN GOLD? NO? WHAT ABOUT FLIPPERS? GOT ANY FLIPPERS? NO!? SERIOUSLY!? WHAT ABOUT SNORKELS THEN? I MEAN, IF YOU DON'T HAVE FLIPPERS YOU MUST HAVE SNORKELS!? NO? ARE YOU FUCKING CRAZY? IF YOU DON'T, THEN I WILL LEAVE AND SO WILL ALL THE OTHER CUSTOMERS. NO ONE HERE LIKES YOUR SHIT DRESSES. HEY, TELL YOU WHAT, LET ME LOOK AT YOUR STOCKROOM AND SEE

IF THERE IS ANYTHING I LIKE. WHAT DO YOU MEAN, NO? YOU'RE SHIT AT YOUR JOB THEN. I'M LEAVING!'

Yeah, that's what I wanted to do, but I didn't. This guy in my ear right now is a saint compared to most. I even play the tune for him. Yeah, even do the job I'm paid for. Some days it all comes together and even the intruders are easy. Time was I used to look down on playing records. I came from playing in bands. DJing was something we did for fun before or after the band played. After so long doing it I've come to realise that like a lot of things that look easy, it isn't. Not to do it well. Everyone can run but not everyone is an Olympic sprinter. Everyone can breathe but only a few are free divers. To be internationally good at something takes decades of experience, and there's always room for improvement. It is something, though, to *hit that groove*, when everyone is in on it. Without the party you are just an unplugged flesh jukebox shouting into an empty canyon. When it's good it's a perfect storm of many factors. After all the palaver, tonight was a good one.

06.00 hrs

Two hours pass like twenty minutes. The final epic tune is played. The 'One more!' chant. The one more is dutifully played. You should always end on time. There's other people working here tonight who want to go home. Don't keep them twenty minutes longer just for your ego. House lights up. Sound off. The people file out. Some things should never be seen in the cold light. The club's empty space now looks bleak. Ten minutes ago the place was a wonderland of sound and light. Now it's a dirty, empty barn. Sometimes you just stand around like a goon. Lost. Grinning. A ghost haunting the scene of its last mortal triumph. You're at your most vulnerable here. Your soft underbelly is exposed. You say yes to everything. You're high as a kite. You drank continuously during the last two hours but barely noticed. As soon as you step out of the booth every gill of booze hits you like a hammer. The adrenaline takes it for you. The buzz is impossible to shake. I've tried everything over the years and the only thing you can do is let it all happen. These days the money thing is all done electronically in advance. On this night we were still at the stage of going back into the bowels of a club to get paid in cash by someone extremely sobering. The beating heart of a venue isn't the brightly lit stage, it's the sweaty little office. The biggest clubs employ artist-relations people. I'm being led into the deepest recesses of the place by one of them. It's possible he's called Warren. We go through kitchens they never use, with racks upon racks of barrels and crates of drinks sold at insane prices, weaving through corridors and stairwells until we reach the nerve centre. The boss is sat in his throne. It's the German owner from earlier who had Kwowser fired and barred. I'd recommended Kwowser to him. I'm in no fit state to deal with this. I have to though, if I want my money. Hans is there too. Both look very serious.

'Did you notice we had the new CO_2 cannons installed?' asks Hans.

I reply that I have, though I haven't seen them in action. The boss turns then and in his thick, lugubrious Bavarian accent says, 'No, ve have not turned on ze gas yet.'

My face is a mask of horror. I blurt out, 'No, no! It's more of a "jet". In English I would say "jet" instead.'

There is a pause and then both of them roar with laughter. Shit. Even when they are joking the Germans do not mess about. Heavy.

07.00 hrs

The flow of a club is like the opposite of a bank. It's so hard to get stuff in but very easy to get out once they are done with you and you've given them all your money. Despite the labyrinthine ways in and through to the bowels of the club it seems the exit is just a step out of the office. You push some huge fire doors and a savage blast of light and heat denotes it is daytime and steaming hot again. You know you should go to the hotel. You want to, but it isn't going to happen. You've tried and failed too many times. It's not just the high you are on from performing; your body clock has been flipped over. The flight is some hours away. Better to carry on rather than pace around a room on your own. By some odd osmosis, a location for those willing to carry on is always found. Certainly in Ibiza. Hans drives us to a strange and dreary dive that is clearly some sort of brothel. Ibiza has been party central for a very long time, but underneath all the glitz it has a rather seedy underbelly.

We weave through the sad and tired-looking fading Latinas, nod to the two ancient locals sat on stools and emerge out the back onto a *terraza* complete with plastic lobsters in fishing nets, false palm trees and rattan – plus a couple of hundred quadra-spazzed, panda-eyed veterans of the previous night. It's a buzz you can almost touch. It's great talking to people after the isolation of the booth. A crowd may cheer you but sometimes it's better, more real when an actual person thanks you afterwards. It's not you they were cheering back there anyway. It's the music. It's the whole. If you think it's you, well, that way madness lies. So it's great to meet the other people from last night. In a way you were one of them, though denied any contact. The boy in the bubble. Mad faces and grinning loons come at you from all corners. Even if you don't think the night revolves around you, many of them do. And if someone had a bad night, it's your fault too. It's so easy in these moments to lose perspective, to believe the hype all around you. I sometimes do.

Then the high subsides and the physical fatigue starts to encroach. Now it really is too late to go back to the hotel and get anything more than two hours bad sleep or some lonely masturbation. It's about now you start to think, 'Fuck it,' and you do a little something 'just to avoid the crash'. Everyone has their own species of excuse, their personal arsenal of stupid. Stay awake for twenty-two hours travelling and working and then tell me about tired. Talk to me about bad decisions then. It's inevitable after a time. As the drugs marry the exhaustion in the Vegas of your guts it all becomes so familiar. It makes sense suddenly. Everyone stops seeming weird, needy and distant, and you remember they are your people.

'What's your name? What are you on? Where you from?' is the litany of the afterhours. The false economy of friendship-from-a-bottle. We believed it wholeheartedly for a while in the 1980s. We still do in these moments. There is a weird sense of triumph in the air: that we *made it*, that we know the world is just waking up and yet somehow we are still here. We're the emperors of everything right now, glittering idiots spouting golden nonsense. I laugh at my own thoughts. We play on words badly in several languages we've never learned. There's a lot of laughing. Always a lot of that. If ever there was a situation where the combination of volume, incoherence and exhaustion means no one communicates at all, it's right here. The deep irony is everyone thinks there's meaning, and even depth, but there's none at all. Just people quacking and barking absolute drivel. When sober these things make me feel old, as redundant as a fat reference book weighing down a groaning shelf in the age of Google, as obsolete as a rusty swing in a playground, but this is my world. And I love it.

Then you are playing records again, just to keep going. While you're at the controls everyone is kind of holding you up, willing you forward. Everyone is talking a foreign language, especially the ones from your own land. This is when those who can afford to miss their flight home will do so with relish and glee. A fulcrum moment. It's the Switzerland in the war of common sense, the neutral moment when you either pull the cord and leave, or stay on and willingly weave your wobbly way into the unknown with people you've only just met. You manage to stagger to the hellish bathroom. A small epiphany is squeezed out. This is what it's all about, innit? This is a binary decision about who you are. Are you player or the played? Are you about beards, limited editions, internet arguments, vinyl-only, television, burgers and smartphones . . . or are you about genuine adventure? Do you subscribe to the constant propaganda of the Hollywood *Übermensch*, with their vacuous smiles and artificial teeth? Or do you understand and participate in human reality? We live in a time of sexy everything. I've seen sexy zombies, sexy newsreaders, sexy furniture and even sexy politics. Nothing is sacred except the right to be obscene and untouchable. During my lifetime the world's become morally bankrupt, and I've been vilified for being averagely righteous. It's a poor state of affairs when our drug-addled idiots are taking the moral high ground. I'm on my own in a room full of random internal questions, surrounded by a random parliament of extreme characters from all over the globe. It feels like home.

Then you make the biggest mistake of the last twenty-four hours. You ask Hans the time.

13.00 hrs

Panic stations. WHOOP WHOOP. No sign of Tour Manager. Your flight is in two hours. Hans is in no state to drive. You bid genuinely fond farewells and try to navigate the blinding Ibiza siesta time, humping your bags that now weigh several tonnes along empty boiling concrete. Why your brain told you it would be easy to find a cab is a surprise to you. The same brain that was making clever-ish observations to you not long ago in a toilet is nowhere to be seen. You're now in hell, the hammer of the sun pounding on the anvil of your face. You're the only person for miles around. There are no cars at all during siesta time, never mind taxis. You black out. Trudge. Black out. TAXI! There is a God. He drives a cab and picks up lost idiots. Knowing your set was very late you didn't leave anything in the hotel so you wouldn't have to go back there afterwards. You've misplaced your aristocrat, however. Best go and check. You get there and see him unconsciously entertaining the entire hotel. Holidaymakers lunching in swimwear are all staring agape at the older gentleman dressed head to foot in a fine black three-piece suit lurching about the buffet like a mad sweating crow.

Creep. Hide. LUNGE. Push Tour Manager in the pool. But your heart just isn't in it. All the holidaymakers stare as if I am Satan himself. People grab their children and pull them away. Red-skinned tubes of meat part wherever I turn. Shocked faces. Don't they realise *he's* the weird one?! How can they know that his notable ancestor fought privateers and pirates, and the reason I always push His Tourmanagerness into the pool is a reference to the fact that his ancestor sank for his country? Well, that's today's reason anyway. The fact he has to go and change out of his dripping finery makes the whole thing a bad idea and all the funny has left. Tour Manager is staying on, he decides. He'd like to spend a few days here on dry land once I'm gone, he explains. By now I'm a staggering, heavily perspiring wreck. Even without the drugs and booze, anyone would be after so long awake in such heat. I don't have the time or inclination for a shower. When you get to this point, any kind of normality breaks the spell that's keeping you upright and exhaustion creeps up and mugs you. All you can do is keep going. The real danger here is using drugs simply for that, as an occupational tool to make it through. Not today, though. Maybe tomorrow. Perhaps a shower is a good idea after all, so you use the expensive hotel room for the first time, for approximately fifteen minutes in total, too fucked-up to feel the shame. That comes later.

☊

Without knowing how, you are suddenly sitting like a rigid plank in a taxi, knowing that even being maniacally scrubbed cannot hide your squirming interior and the mad look in your eyes. No wonder the Spanish hate you and your kind. No wonder the Germans laugh at you and the French frown. But you've done it so long it's all like cotton wool. By the time you're dropping bits of everything, everywhere, you just wear the whole shambles like a shaggy coat. May as well own the situation. No point being uptight at airport security. You have nothing to hide. You might as well be naked for all the good it would do to try and pretend you're not a mess. They've seen it all a thousand times. The X-ray machine is scanning you for SHAME. The uniformed eyes beam disappointment and pity. Good riddance to you.

Things like waiting are easy in this state. Nothing waits as well as a corpse. You couldn't sleep even if you wanted to. Your body has no idea what is going on and can't perform any kind of function without extreme persuasion. The holidaymakers are quiet too. They always are when leaving.

Many are as whacked-out as you are. Some are worse. It's not even a comfort that they're leaving you alone. You just wish you could be home. It's almost painful how badly you want the next few hours to disappear. The flight is almost pleasant, like being in a tin womb. You look at a paragraph in your book and realise you've looked at it more than fifty times and not grasped a word or even realised you're doing it. How many drinks of water can you possibly ask for without looking like the world's worst cactus? People are definitely avoiding you. You are a dehydrated Bermuda triangle. You are degradation, exhaustion and paranoia. That's something to declare right there.

17.30 hrs

Customs are a laugh. You are literally so spent that you always arrive back about half the weight you were when you left, defying all the laws of physics in the process. However, you still chant 'I AM NORMAL, I AM NORMAL' in your head all the way through the green channel, even though you are 100 per cent legal. You have a train ticket back already paid for at a reasonable price, or you could pay a king's ransom for a cab to go door to door. Despite always hating yourself later for it, you go to the cab stand. You've spent nearly half what you earned last night, and it was only handed to you a few hours ago. Ninety minutes later you are tearing your luggage to pieces looking for your keys. You crash into your room. You always make up the bed so it's all nice when you get back. You immediately throw up on it.

Nice.

Oh, I forgot to mention: the Ibiza gig was on a Sunday night. I'd already done a gig in Kuala Lumpur and a gig in London on the Friday and Saturday. In three days I'd have to prepare to do it all again. And again the week after. And every week thereafter. This was my zenith, the summit of nonsense. I didn't know it at the time, but it would be downhill all the way from here. In a few years I would be taking meth daily, living on a mountain sharpening knives, and my best friend would be a dog. But for now I was just glad to get through the glorious peaks and soul-destroying valleys of another working weekend. And finally to get some sleep.

Chapter 2

One Thousand Hotels

There is an ancient adage, which I just made up, that 'DJing is mostly airports and hotels'. You can read that phrase in two ways: one is that airports and hotels are inherently amazing, deeply exciting things; or you can see them as homogeneous examples of soul-crushing banality. As we will discover, it's all directly proportional to your level of exposure. Nothing anyone does all day, every day is awesome. The job can't keep being fun, and neither can you. Cold DJ fact.

Ibiza was last week. I'd arrived back in London for an important event. At this point in rave history the major labels were desperate to have a large piece of the pie. Venal, hungry and paranoid, they were lost for a while, not knowing where raving came from. Naturally they had to *own* it, lock and stock. Part of this was down to the need for them to have 'dance hits'. Major labels call themselves a business, but they're insanely unprofitable, utterly uncertain, totally rudderless and completely ignorant. They simply hang around waiting for something to happen and then pounce on it like a bushwhacking spider, pump it full of poison and then leave it hanging to get nice and ripe so they can gorge on it at their leisure. I was a chubby, happy little fly.

Sign. Record. Deal. It was actually a dream of my youth, but part of being ripe for a good plucking is your innate delusion that it's all there just for you. An inevitability. Justice. Your pay-off for being born awesome. I know – 'What a dick.' That's what the labels think too.

My reckless desire for a record deal was compounded with other factors. The best way of dealing with always being tired and in the wrong country at the wrong time is to be perpetually out of your mind. Honestly, you don't even have to be really hardcore. Most travellers constantly self-medicate with alcohol, pills and caffeine in order to deal with the shocking effects of sleeplessness and time-zone dilation. You can be a stumbly mess just by using occupational amounts of legal helpers. Of course, the real solution is exercise and endorphins, but really? That comes much later. If you survive the learning process, that is.

Are there more competitive places than London? If there are, there sure aren't many. Just the cost of living there is beyond the reach of most. The people who come from the city will never change that. Rebellion is something that is lacking in Londoners – they love the crumbs from their masters' tables. Their entire identity is built on the fact they are privileged Londoners, even if they personally had nothing to do with that fact other than their parents lived there. However, when the sun shines and they emerge blinking to stand in huge crowds in the middle of roads outside pubs or sunbathe on pathetically tiny strips of brown grass next to huge coughing roads . . . well, I can't help but love the place.

The Zombie Taxi is the run from Heathrow into town. The roads narrow from vast eight-lane superhighways to medieval winding cobbles over the course of a turgid, hellish ninety minutes. So much of this game is your head vibrating against steel and glass in a car, train or plane, trying to zone out as the faded colours of dying industry and bustling transit ooze by through slitted eyes. Excited as I am to be in the capital, she sure doesn't make it easy on you.

I am hardcore. No, really. Still am. I was born into it. At this point, however, I was a shambles. The walking dead. Sharp, though. It takes a lot to really dull me. I'd just done a week of flights and gigs, but nothing wakes you up like having to check in to a hotel. It's something akin to being checked out when you check in. There's a whiff of the police station or hospital about it. The key to dealing with a hotel reception desk is to achieve peak normal. If you're at a proper hotel that has any kind of professionalism, then there's *nothing* they haven't seen and, indeed, probably eyeballed this very week. If you think you are weird, then you should meet some travelling salesmen, journalists or arms dealers. However, there's something about reception that is all to do with the sense of it being a gateway. There's never the same feeling of dread with a concierge as there is with reception. The accepted way in many places is once through the door you are in. It's the door that matters. Order chocolate enemas and giraffe-skin spats from the concierge by all means, but reception is the doorman, security, head teacher, judge and jury. The clue is in the name. Not only do they receive you into their world, your behaviour is judged by what you dish out to them. They tend to prefer receiving money and courtesy wherever possible. Enough of both and you are judged well, and they will even help rather than hinder. This could be anything from the next shift being told about your wake-up call to magically finding a suitable headphone connector at 6 a.m.

'Pulling off human' is a trick you really need to learn, not only if you're an international nitwit but also if you're just a very weary normal. At the wrong end of a killer journey you need to not only hold it together at this point but avoid any possible venting. They *want* you to kick off. They love it! It breaks the monotony. Sometimes they even let you know in a sly way. You've already lost if you've engaged. Save your rage. Take it out on your agent – after all, that's their job, and one paid for directly by you. Experienced jet-freaks can switch to full-on normal faster than a pro alcoholic at a parent–teacher evening. Ironically, in a hotel, a place where service is purchased, the general onus is very much on you. My tip is always turn it around, to understand they're in charge and you're the subservient one. This goes for airline staff too. Everything goes like clockwork if you know your place. This is essential early in your stay, as later things are bound to get very weird. You need to win them over and get in credit. Rudeness and anger are the preserves of the super-rich, the ill-bred and the lower parts of the aristocracy . . . and no one wants to be like those nasty counts.

Speaking of insane aristocrats, I had just been met by His Tourmanagerness and the rest of the band outside one of London's finest hotels. You've met Tour Manager already, but now we were joined by the mighty Xenon and the enigma known only as Baccarat.

At this point in history there was a merging of the roles of producer and DJ – in essence, the making of the records and the playing of them. It has become so that the two are now one and the same. You can't be a DJ without having made some records, and you can't be a producer without offering the option of going out on the road and appearing for money. Apparently people still love music, they just won't pay for it any more. They will pay to *see* someone 'famous', though. So at this point we were a band of sorts. Xenon and I were what they call an electronic duo. Like the Sith, there's always two in these bands and they invariably take on the roles of loudmouth and nerd, together forming a whole personality. The actual distribution of tasks can be varied, but there is always one who is quiet and does a lot of the actual work and one who is more showbiz and operates as more of a frontman. Guess which one I was. Early on in the development of the idea I recruited my other best friend, Baccarat, on a wage rather than a contract, putting us in the unusual position of being a trio.

Baccarat is six foot eight, gay, Indian but really *very* Welsh, which when he was growing up in the 1970s in Port Talbot made him an ethnic and sexual minority of one. He also happens to be one of the best people in the world. No question. That's not just my opinion – anyone who has met him agrees. The fact he was a trained dancer and looked great didn't hurt either – we rather cynically needed to try and shake off the rather tired look of a dull pair of white, nerdy, electronic bumpkins – but mostly he was just great to be around. We needed that like air.

We actually formed as a splinter group off the back of a 1990s mega-stadium rave act. At the time we were a collective of sorts, the concept being that this idea that peeled off the main mothership would be more of a commercial venture, slightly prankster in tone. Dare I even say situationist without punching myself in the face? Basically it was designed to try and keep us all afloat financially. You couldn't do it today as everyone in the media had their sense of humour removed a decade ago in a compulsory pogrom.

It was a relief to be away from the freakish isolation of the solo DJ thing and be among friends again. Even if ever so oddball, there's no place like homeboys. Apparently we were all here at the great expense of a record company and were being treated to London's Metropolitan Hotel on Park Lane. Very nice. Only at the slightly preposterous top end of the business will promoters or labels pay for anyone other than you alone. One of the reasons DJs came to prominence is that they are one person. It's so much cheaper than a band with all their gear. So much cheaper and so much more profitable for your handlers. When travelling, hangers-on and sidekicks are rare, so when you get the chance to bring any entourage, you'd better damn well do it properly.

Now I'd hooked up with my UK crew, things were going to get weird, fast. Tour Manager always distinguished himself at totally failing to manage *any* kind of normal. Indeed, he was raised in the Scottish aristocracy, so he'd never even seen any. We learned the hard way that he had to be hidden from the world of normals, like a malformed sibling heir bricked up in the attic. He had probably been that very thing until his escape. Tour Manager wasn't very good with his co-ordination and was absolutely incapable of any kind of verbal restraint. Or diplomacy. Or things like electrical goods or any other fancy human gadgets. He's a grade-A freak from another time and place, and I love him for it.

They pulled up in Tour Manager's swanky car, an event that was made more vivid by Tour Manager owning a *ridiculous* car. All cars should be stupid if you really mean it. On seeing the hotel entrance he wound down the window and immediately barked, 'Revolving door alert! Tradesman's entrance only!'

Outsiders are often baffled by His Tourmanagerness's exclamations. His massive use of high-powered stimulants means his brain operates so quickly that he rarely takes the time to put together understandable sentences. Rather, he tends to issue proclamations or ejaculate aphorisms. I'm often called on to translate. In this instance it was regarding his fear of revolving doors, coupled with a traditional sexual double entendre. Neither of those usually went very well for him.

Outside was a squadron of pissed-up paparazzi, looming and gurning, drooling for the smell of 'slebs.

'Oh my God! Are those paparazzi?' said the elongated figure unwinding itself from the back seat onto the tarmac. It was a rare exclamation from the usually silent Baccarat, who was the gay of the outfit and rather keen on showbiz things.

'Paparazzi!? Bloody *Italians*!' roared Tour Manager, as the paparazzi stood down in the face of our very obvious non-'slebrity and wound back into their savage little boxes, ready to spring again. As our party trooped in I dealt with the very camp European receptionist. He asked if we were all present. All except one, I replied, and I turned to look for Tour Manager, who'd gone off to park his car. Up he bounded to the hotel from the street, all hermit beard and hair, looking to all intents and purposes like a demented Gandalf in a tracksuit, minus any and all magic. He promptly ran at full tilt – WHHAAAAANGGG! – into the invisible sci-fi barrier that was the revolving doors going in the wrong direction. The entire foyer hummed with the reverberation as this grizzled, mad-looking Garfield was almost glued to the window like a bug on a windscreen. With the impact his baseball hat flew off back into the street and was immediately run over by a taxi. In true T-Man style he had a huge panic attack and for no apparent reason turned and ran. Maybe it was the inexplicable tracksuit.

'Is your "friend" going to sign the register or would he just prefer to leave another massive smear?' said our arch new friend behind the desk.

Brass neck gets you in anywhere, but much like an actor, it has to be a self-belief so rigid and deep that it borders on genuine stupidity. Drugs and/or exhaustion can make you shake like a shitting dog or as confident as a king. Try to make it the latter when approaching doors, Pilgrim, if only for a moment. Try to make an entrance, not a scene.

Tour Manager peeked around the corner, gingerly managed the side door correctly and sidled up.

'Never mind your nonsense, missy,' barked T-Man to the receptionist, apropos of nothing at all. 'Red-light district, *immediately*!'

Having checked in at this hotel we knew we had *arrived*.

In fact, Arrived with a capital 'A'. London's Park Lane is one of the most prestigious addresses in the world. Our arrival-in-style was one of many signatures of the Metropolitan Hotel, which during much of the heyday of Britpop and global 1990s exuberance was equal parts legit disco venue (its famous Met Bar) and upscale hotel. We decided not to check out the rooms as we were late for our meeting. We were waiting for our manager in the extremely minimal foyer when Tour Manager and I, looking like nothing more than a couple of bearded, big-haired, deranged vagrants, were approached by hotel security.

'Any chance of you cunts fucking off?' the bald giant said in a cheery voice. 'You're making my nice foyer *very* untidy.'

Which, to be fair, was absolutely true. The trouble with bleak minimalism and sterile environments is they *really* show up the germs. Not having anywhere proper to sit or indeed to attain a repose of anything below mild panic is one of the intended architectural functions. Someone born into this knows. Their purpose is to weed out those too stupid to wait elsewhere and too poor to be in the bar. If the subjects (like us) were too dense to realise they were the stain on the slide, then there was always the gentleman-shaped house brick that was security to educate us further. Tour Manager is a self-confessed expert coward and craven fool, but sometimes his breeding just kicks in. You have to understand that despite being from the top of the British class system, like a lot of his type he could simultaneously not just be eccentric to the point of disbelief but genuinely warm and humble. A sort of Schrödinger's buffoon. However, being talked down to was something he could deal with on an almost genetic level.

'If you'd like to check the register via your dainty colleague, you will find that my companion and I are not merely guests but those of the most *honoured* variety,' replied His Royal Tourmanagerness.

He wasn't wrong. The record company spared no expense when it came to spending our money, and on top of that I was due to DJ later in the hotel's famous bar too. The security guy looked confused and started to turn towards the desk.

Tour Manager then reached into his pocket. 'My good man, please accept this form of identification.'

He handed security his driving licence, which immediately started me chuckling. Tour Manager was both painfully self-deprecating as well as appearing totally insane. He carried nothing at all that gave away his real name. Indeed, few outside his family and me even knew it. Like many of his species he used a Christian name, but people confused his title with his surname. And it was a real title – he was a legit aristocrat, if merely a very minor one. Only his driving licence held a clue. It also carried hidden instructions in the form of a special code for any police who might read it. Suffice to say, it is a long and ancient title and nearly impossible to fake on an official form. Apart from this instance and once when stopped by police for speeding (resulting in a clumsy salute and an escort for the remainder of the journey), Tour Manager never played this card in my view over many years. The security guy went several shades of white and practically pulled his forelock like an embarrassed peasant as he retreated backwards. I was still fumbling with key cards and trying to write with double vision. All this was seen by my manager, as he'd arrived through the doors behind us.

Chib. A deranged relic from a bygone age. Resembles to a tee a Northern Irish Joe Pesci – small, loud and quite deadly. Chib was a manager from a time when the music industry had money and acted like it. I actually heard him bellow into a phone once, 'PUT ANOTHER FUCKING ZERO ON THE END AND WE'LL TALK!' which is about as cartoon rock manager as it gets. He was from the Peter Grant school of management. Everyone, especially his clients, was an idiot. The only way to get anything done was to bully and swear at top volume. When I was told many years later that one of the reasons he robbed all his clients blind was a humongous cocaine habit, I was about as surprised as when I heard George Michael had come out of the closet. The fact he annoyed so many people he eventually had to leave the country was no shock either. I once followed him out of a five-storey venue I was working at and saw him insult every single person on the way down ten flights of stairs. He must have shouted random bespoke abuse at about two hundred people individually. 'All right, wanker? Your hair is *shite*, love. *Lose some weight.* FUCKING UGLY CUNT! Them shoes are fucking *prehistoric*, man. JESUS, IS THAT A WOMAN!? Fuck me, *tall* cunt. MOVE, YOU DAFT SHITE!' etc., etc., etc.

I sort of admired him in a way. He didn't care at all if no one liked him, and it wasn't a pose. There was a sort of purity to it, almost an aesthetic. He wasn't one of those very funny angry Ulstermen with creative, televisually crafted swearing. To be on the end of it was brutal and shocking. Quite funny to watch, though.

'You! Fatty. I need a word with you!'

He never addressed anyone by name when an insult would do. In fact, if he actually liked you it was even worse. We went to one side for one of his famous 'meetings', while Tour Manager got deeply confused by his luggage.

'Sign the deal. Get this fucking pantomime over with. They're all a bunch of cunts at this record company anyway. If you ask me, all this is a joke. You need to get out there and earn. Fuck being "a band". This isn't the cunting '60s. What are you, a bunch of fucking *girls*? Get out there and DJ. Piece of piss and half the aggro. Ditch them other simpletons too . . . and what the fuck is the Marquis de Sad doing here? Fucking lunatic is a natural disaster,' he grumbled, pointing at Tour Manager.

'If I'm doing a DJ tour, he's the tour manager for it,' I said petulantly. It was ridiculous and I knew it, but I had to kick back a bit.

Chib's face exploded into joy. He only smiled when things were preposterous. 'Lord Haw-Haw!? Ye wouldn't get ten miles with that simple cunt. Two minutes ago he lost a fight with a fucking *door*!'

Nothing frightened me. Not at this point in my life. I had the ease and swagger of the truly stupid. Youth will do that to you. I thought I knew it all, and it showed. I found everything funny, especially Chib and Tour Manager in the same room. A rare opportunity. Together at last. Like shit 'n' chips.

'TAXMAN,' shouted Chib. I looked around for the person he was addressing, but for once it wasn't a nickname, he was starting a sentence. 'It's none of my business, but I could do with a client who isn't in fucking jail. You're no rapper despite this *band's* stupid fucking name. Your FUCKING accountant has been giving me ear cancer lately about the money. Get it fucking over with. Go see the cunts. It's not rocket science . . . and here . . . *listen.*'

He gestured for me to move closer. I was expecting something profoundly rude, illegal or sage. Maybe all three.

'I've always wanted to ask, how come you've got an actual fucking aristocrat driving you around?' he said, slightly appalled at the words coming out of him.

'Didn't you bring yours?' I replied.

♁

We had arrived to sign to the major record company parent of the dance label that was taking us on as a 'band'. We were mob-handed as only a crew of hillbillies from the backwoods could be. The fact only two of us were signatories didn't stop us from having a small team of best friends, relatives, dancers and chancers with us. A completely unnecessary aristocrat thrown in for good measure didn't hurt.

Once we'd made our presence felt at the hotel it was time for us all to shimmy over to the Knightsbridge offices of the label to actually do the dirty deed. One thing that always stands out when it comes to legendary things like signing record deals is the sheer underwhelming banality. These occasions are very rarely held in a suitably pun-filled location, surrounded by press. Most of them take place quietly in the label's offices, like a dull civil wedding. As the bride, you dreamed of a cathedral and flowers, but the cheap groom insisted a council office and clerk was better. If you are important somehow, an effort might be made, but usually there's a desultory bottle of fizzy and a grey administrator or company director to bleat out some platitudes about welcoming you to 'our little family' and it being 'a *music* company, not a record company'. These are the guys who share stories about your failings and fuck-ups and laugh. These are the guys who keep the machine ticking over and enjoy stable salaries from your earnings. These are the guys whose taxis and lunches you pay for directly. This is the team behind you that is the first to jump ship when the buzz fades. These are the clicking, calculating cogs behind the smile. It's not that I have a simmering hate for the industry, it's just my life improves immensely whenever I'm away from it. On the other side of the coin, they're the ones that take you from nothing to something. It's a diabolical pact of poorly concealed mutual loathing.

Once the actual signing formalities were over we could ditch the squares and go pro. We were so overjoyed and blindly flattered we couldn't pass a pub or bar between record company office and taxi without a celebratory drink, sniff or general hurrah. In fact, we were all piled into two taxis when we decided we liked the look of one particular 'ye olde London pub' and started waving frantically out of the window to the rest of our crew in the second taxi behind to stop. It had been a very long thirty seconds cooped up in there and we needed refreshment. Leaving the taxis to run up huge bills while waiting outside and successfully convincing one of the drivers to come in 'for one', we hammered through the door looking like a gang of mental patients on day release. The whole place went silent to accentuate our racket. Everyone crowded round the bar, while I quietly slipped off to have a genuine piss and a less genuine refresher. I emerged moments later in the quieter end of the bar, almost opening the door in the face of an old lady. And what a face! She had the appearance of crafted bohemia that you sometimes get in London, but was very faded – part 1930s diva, part bag lady. I was extra shocked as she filled the small passageway and the ladies toilet was nowhere near by.

'This is the gents, love!' I said instinctively, the gak forcing my words out unbidden. She didn't reply. Instead she grasped my wrists hard and glared at me madly. I'm sure I gave back as good as I got – two pro loons locking horns like charging rams. I've always got on bizarrely well with dogs, kids and old ladies. No idea why. They just gravitate towards me. Always have done. This was different, though. My powers were useless here.

'YOU PUT WOMEN ON A PEDESTAL! IT'S NOT GOOD FOR YOU. LEO THE LION YOU ARE.'

Her voice was intense and piercing. Loud but not shouting, like she spoke in capital letters. She had my attention because I absolutely always did lose out to women. Without fail. I thought astrology was ridiculous. I still do. She was spot-on, though.

'IT WILL END YOU, ALL THIS. LISTEN TO ME, LISTEN TO ME. YOU THINK IT'S EASY. YOU'LL LEARN TOO LATE. NO ONE LISTENS.'

Her eyes were clear and piercing, but the words seemed drunken. I was transfixed. Luckily a regular came up behind her, gently pulled her hands from my wrists and shepherded her back to the bar, all while she looked back at me intently. It freaked me out quite a bit. She really pooped my party. Definitely time to leave. All the normal in here was way too weird.

It was decided we'd go back to the hotel to freshen up and then get serious. As it turned out, we wouldn't leave the dangerously expensive Park Lane hotel for a further three days and four nights solid.

After the signing at the record company offices we approached the Met in tight formation, a bunch of loons, hideously outré bumpkins and freaks. Baccarat, Tour Manager, Xenon, Bananahands and myself were the core miscreants, with a couple of extras tagged on. When it came to hotels, we might stick out like a robot frog in your soup, but when it came to bum-rushing the show, as a group we were unstoppable. How were we to know none of this stuff was free? What do you mean, when the record company say they are paying, it really means that *you* are? Read the contract? What am I, a fucking *lawyer*?

You have to understand that we're a different generation. A new thing. There have been many labels, but we're ravers to the core. We were forged in the raging fires of the disco, always one foot on the dance floor in our hearts. We definitely aren't hippies, even though many of us splintered off to become travellers and techno crusties. We aren't punks but we certainly share the sense of anarchy and anti-Establishment feeling, as well as a deep belief in doing it all yourself. We aren't strictly speaking even a proper tribe or urban gang as acid house brought together and mixed so many different types. We are the biggest youth movement in human history and we don't even have a name. We just know who *we* are and that everybody else isn't it. And that includes no-hoper, famous for nothing 'slebs, shit pop stars, crap derivative rock bands and 'artists' who couldn't draw or paint. Essentially the entire clientele of the Met Bar. It was where the famous Brits went to pretend they weren't all Thatcher's children.

I should also point out that being a guest at the Met hotel didn't mean you automatically got into the fabled bar at night. No, sir. You see, it was celebrity central, and as we all know, despite being all kinds of pointless and stupid, celebrity can change the laws of physics if it wants to. My own theory is it's less troublesome to let *some* freaks in the door and be diluted by a crowd than it is to have them making a large scene at the entrance. Depends on how weird you are, though. Weird helps. Weird is a magic cloak that makes all kinds of things happen. We were pretty weird. I don't mean 'wacky' or 'eccentric'. I mean the sort of weird you get when you take smart, curious bumpkins and drop them straight into something urbane and sophisticated. With added MDMA, amphetamines and cocaine. In short, we breezed through the lobby utilising applied fear and gland-exuded oddness. It helps if you look the part, and we did. If you let your mere surroundings intimidate you, then you've already lost.

The Met was at that time by far the most fashionable place to be in London by several factors of posh, so different rules applied. One of them was that the clientele, who ordinarily would not put up with the discomfort of a pea under ten mattresses, were happy to be packed in there like sardines, sweating their mascara right off their faces and looking like well-dressed cattle in a death truck. It was modernist sterile too. People often think that when your brain is folded in six dimensions on gear the weirder places get amplified, but often it's the very plain, blank-canvas surroundings that are the freaky ones. A simple, elegant, minimalist flower arrangement can turn into a triffid. It forces you to concentrate on the faces. If you are at Burning Man or Glastonbury, you are just a freaky drop in the oddball ocean. In these sparse Bauhaus dental-waiting-room places you are truly the turd in the aquarium.

Although I am using thinly veiled pseudonyms, Bananahands actually went by that name. A hearty, rambunctious character, skilled in all forms of construction and decoration, both interior and exterior, with a ruddy complexion and hands like a bunch of concrete bananas. Bananahands had a pint glass from the weird pub in his massive hand, as well as his best anorak on. The Met's gatekeepers were swept aside as we entered the hallowed, sweaty, minimalist haven and were hit by a wall of scent – the smell of people who got others to choose it for them. Some even had their *own* perfume lines. The maître d' scurried over like a weasel on roller skates in a vain attempt to run interference and steer us somewhere we couldn't do any damage, but he was too late. Bananahands had already sat himself down with his empty imported pub pint glass at the only free booth in the entire joint. The table clearly labelled 'Reserved for Mr Hucknall'. Just to be clear, this had to be Simply Red singer Mick Hucknall, a recently slimmed-down fatty who had inexplicably become very attractive to women after becoming a millionaire. We knew this was his table not merely because of the convenient placard on the table with 'Reserved for Mr Hucknall' on it; it was because Hucknall had just walked in with what can only be described as a 'bevy' of models. (I've never heard the word 'bevy' used for anything else, but here it is, doing its thing in its natural environment.) The maître d' went at the jolly Bananahands like a camp spider monkey trying to fuss something to death.

'No, no, no! Come *away* from there, sir, *please*!' He gestured to the placard. 'You can *plainly* see this is for Mr Hucknall and his party!'

As if to emphasise this, Mr Hucknall was stood by his shoulder, appearing mildly annoyed. Bananahands had his anorak off and was sitting expansively, with both arms raised on the seat backs and feet on the table. He looked both very at home and merry, like a friendly cowboy in his favourite saloon, a saloon that happened to be filled with effete, delicate bastards.

'It's all right!' boomed Bananahands in his regional brogue. 'There's plenty of room! I don't mind. The more the merrier!'

The maître d' was about to whelp puppies on the spot out of panic and frustration.

'No, no!' he squeaked. 'There is no room here!'

Bananahands just beamed beatifically. '*Loads* of room! Really, I don't mind. Come on. Get involved.'

By this point the maître d' had squeezed over and was frantically squawking into Bananahands' ear. Bananahands' happy smile was slowly fading to a scowl. Meanwhile, I was frantically signalling for him to stop messing about and get over here with the rest of us before we were ejected on the grounds of significantly lowering the tone. He gathered up his guilty pint glass and anorak and lumbered over.

As Hucknall and his party passed me and Bananahands joined us, there was the briefest of handovers, a Checkpoint Charlie of neutrality as they crossed paths, and I was honoured to overhear Bananahands stage-whisper to Hucknall: 'I hope you choke on your supermodels, mate.'

Tour Manager came stumbling over at this point. He always stumbled – it was his default gait. After so many years of drug abuse he was essentially a collection of tics held together with eccentricity. If he wasn't falling over an inanimate object, he was jerking to avoid something invisible or quite naturally adopting the pose of a villain in a nineteenth-century melodrama, surprised at having seen his own reflection. Base amphetamine is a hell of a drug, and after so many years of use the amount Tour Manager needed to get an effect was prodigious. A single one of his hourly doses would have killed me – indeed, it nearly did once. The effects meant he could never stay in one place for more than a few moments or participate in a conversation.

He tended to disappear and return constantly, like a really shit falcon. As well as his repertoire of physical spasms, Tour Manager had a full suite of accompanying verbal barks, yelps and general ejaculations that made him appear quite web-footed barking bonkers.

'Fuck me, have you seen the size of Famous Lady Singer's tits!' he blurted as he fell into us, returning from one of his constant mystery forays.

'Yes. Yes, I have,' I replied, holding Famous Lady Singer's gaze very deliberately as she turned around from her place right next to me to glare at him. Tour Manager didn't even see her as he grinned and lurched off again, leaving me holding the metaphorical baby. A hideous baby.

Tour Manager was psychotically generous, as only someone naturally so – amplified by obscene amounts of drugs and no concept of money – can be. At this point he was going through his cocaine honeymoon. Unlike most of us, Tour Manager hadn't so much as sipped a drop of alcohol until his forties, coming as he did from a deeply eccentric background and teetotal family. He'd not even knowingly been in the same room as drugs by the time his forty-second birthday came around. When he did get involved, it was with a vengeance. In the same way that people from some South American cocaine-producing countries get taking the drug out of their system by their teens, Tour Manager came upon the pharmacopoeia as a fully formed adult and as such made some pretty wise decisions about drugs relatively quickly. As well as some truly terrible ones later. So at this point he still regarded cocaine as A Good Idea and a great social lubricant. He was extremely free with it. It was only later (although, as I have said, quicker than most) that he ditched everything for unadulterated base amphetamine paste, which these days may as well be described as meth. It has to be said that in all my life and my very wide experience of freaks, Tour Manager is the only man I've ever met who was made a better person by cocaine. Some people genuinely have great trouble coming forth from their shell, and sometimes the mollusc within is very special.

Tour Manager's generous streak with cocaine meant it didn't take us long to make friends with many similarly inclined rock stars. After publicly humiliating us all with Famous Lady Singer's chesty areas, T-Man was straight into the toilets with me and a new friend, a working-class hero who was currently riding high in the UK and American charts. It seemed it didn't take much of an invitation to get rock singers involved in drugs. The cubicles at the Met were, at the time, accidentally famous for one thing: if you touched gently near the flush handle, a handy shelf emerged as if on silent greased rubber runners – access to the cistern. These days any decent kitchen drawer or car glovebox has this action, but to see it in a bathroom was quite a thing, a temporary aberration of over-engineered plumbing, long since welded shut.

'That is properly amazing. Is this cubicle German or something?' I said.

'WHAT! *Germans!?* Where?' barked His Tourmanager-ness in reply. He still held onto a slightly old-fashioned view of the world and its peoples: they were all idiots, unless they were Scottish and well bred, and most of *those* were spectacular idiots too. He also didn't think much of himself either, which strangely enough sort of balances it out. He had a unilaterally poor opinion of humanity, mainly based, quite correctly, on having met some of it.

'Get your gear out then,' ordered our guest. Tour Manager duly complied. 'Don't be tight with it,' he added.

Tour Manager was never mean with anything, least of all drugs. He put out some massive slugs.

'More,' prodded the superstar, a famously rude and gruff man.

I turned to him. I'm pretty tall.

'Look, lad, you might be mistaking this gentleman here for some sort of idiotic star-struck toff. Only some of that applies.'

Tour Manager turned around from his labours. He's not a short man either. Together we towered over the superstar in a very, very tiny space.

'I will fight the two of you cunts to the death, right here, in *this* shitter.'

'I like him more now,' I said.

'Just wasn't rude enough before,' Tour Manager concluded.

☊

I'm quite well behaved for a DJ. Well, it's all relative, right? A few people reading this will think I am Satan personified. Others that I am a wallflower. DJs *do* lose their minds on the road, but I don't think it is restricted to us exclusively.

'I can't stay here! The wallpaper is too weird.'

No, someone really said this. I've not just spent a fair bit of time on the decks, I know a lot of people and have heard a *lot* of DJ bad behaviour stories. We collect them. Well, I say 'we' . . .

With my own abused ears I have heard 'These ice cubes are too cloudy,' 'The thermostat is too complicated,' 'There's not enough magazines in English' (in Malaysia) and someone needing an entirely new luxury room because 'the potpourri smells funny'. 'The toilet is in a stupid place' is another, and one of my faves, as is the nameless superstar who insists on a heated floor wherever they go, and yet somehow refuses to consider shoes.

There are major American DJs who feign injury when things aren't to their liking and try to get people fired. With one or two you will be *truly* lucky if they bother to turn up, after they've insisted you pay in advance. You may never see them or your money again. And yet they are not in jail, they are very much in demand. There are more than a few promoters like that too.

I know DJs who are perfectly nice to your face but who will instruct their management to charge a venue their *colossal* wage *twice* because they missed a flight, saying they would get on a plane home if they weren't paid again for the inconvenience of not being able to catch a plane properly. I've seen DJs who are working half as often start to charge twice as much to make up for it – which is about as concise a description as you can get of the insane thinking of our agents and managers, who are pricing DJs right out of the game.

Top of my list for sheer waste is the EDM giant whose

team spent *months* with boffins making a system that controlled the entire (stadium) show's lights from a tablet – 'cos a professional lighting guy knows nothing at all about lights – all at a cost of just under *$1 million*. And when the mega-doofus got there and couldn't immediately understand how it all worked, he just threw the tablet away over his shoulder.

It cost. One. Million. Dollars.

I'm no saint. Although in my defence, my hissy fit was a scam to get a hotel upgrade. My issue was with a massive horrible sofa. It was bright purple and over eight feet tall at the backrest. No, that isn't a cartoon *'eight feet tall'*! It actually was an eight-foot-high bright purple sofa. It looked like Barney the fucking Dinosaur was lurking in the corner silently watching you have a piss. As the words 'can't possibly co-exist with furniture that hideous' came out of me, I experienced something alcoholics call 'a moment of clarity': that I was truly lost and had passed a point of no return.

Eventually you start to see just plain ignorance too. Like the DJ who sent wine back that was 'bad' even though the cork was plastic. The same one threw a fit once because his carpaccio was 'raw meat', then spent twenty minutes patiently explaining to the Italian waiter what carpaccio 'actually means'. In Italy. It was like watching a baby tell off its dad's forehead with a spoon and some of it's soup.

In the end it all boils down, like a bad distillery, to plain *rotten* behaviour. I could do this one all day, but the sun would go in too early. Suffice to say, once you start abusing women or kicking people out of cars in the middle of the Ibicenco heat or, the most heinous sin of all, wearing sunglasses while you play . . . well, you've gone over to the dark side, Pilgrim, never to return. It is a small business, the business of show, and everyone knows about you. Of course, this doesn't prevent bookings. No one ever stops booking someone who sells tickets, no matter what they've done. But I'll tell you this: it's all waiting for you when you start to fade . . .

Why the bad behaviour? Well, there's isolation and there are drugs. There's massive ego too. But it's also about being in a bubble. Even I've done things that I look back on and wonder who the fuck it was walking and talking and doing all that silly nonsense. It's easy to laugh at DJs complaining, but the life can be genuinely stressful and exhausting. Which adds mental croutons to the demented soup. I don't think it can be excused, however. It's not right being a dickhead, even if there are reasons.

The isolation of living in hotels is another aspect. Hotels are microcosms of the world, and you get what you pay for. Hotel staff will literally deal with anything if it's worth their while. Riding an incontinent goat down to reception is kind of uncool and inappropriate in a Travelodge in Swansea. No one is paid enough – and certainly not enough by *you* – to deal with a wobbly wanker and goat shit when they arrive at work first thing. Some places offer complementary shitty indoor goat rides 'cos not only are the staff all paid *very* well, more than likely it will be *you* paying them very well both before and after, whether you intend to or not. Listen up, Pilgrim: the difference between being a cunt and a rogue is simply that rogues tip well.

Decompressing after touring is weird. Picking up the phone in your own house for room service is a sign you are definitely losing it. And it's not like a band, where you do a long stint away with a gang and then come home (although we do those sometimes). It's a mini-tour. Every weekend. Forever.

One of the reasons DJs (and other public figures) lose the plot is that it begins to become less a job of work and more an extended celebration of themselves. You start to party to the sound of your own fabulousness. You see each J.O.B. as a daily birthday party. It's weird and lonely and unnatural, so what the hell? May as well go cloven-hooved, great steaming googly-moogly on it all. Then one day it's a job again and not a party. And people need you to do things that frankly aren't nearly as awesome as making little food friends out of room-service leftovers and are SO BORING, and that is it then – you've forgotten what it is that you do.

You are supposed to make other people happy. Not yourself. *That* is what you do.

As Oscar Wilde said on his death bed, 'Either the wallpaper goes or I do.' That nasty paisley is still there to this day in a Paris hotel. A lesson to every insane DJ, forever.

⌒

Back in London, after generally failing to merge with the shiterati downstairs in the Met Bar, it was time to form our own clique, so we moved the show up to the suite.

It is fair to say that Xenon was certainly 'the quiet one'. For the duration of our working together he never once offered his opinion on anything at all unless specifically asked. Even then it wasn't easy to get. His large skunk habit from waking until sleeping, every single day, didn't help either of us. Nor my joining in with it. You had to work out from oblique references what he wanted 'cos he'd never pitch in directly. Sometimes it was easy, though:

'I'm hungry,' Xenon observed, when we'd settled into the suite.

'Xenon, man!' I howled. 'This is one of the world's top hotels, fella! You just pick up the phone and tell them that, not me. Not only is it high quality and impeccable service, the record company are paying!'

'Will you do it?' he countered – thus, in one exchange, encapsulating our entire friendship.

I decided at this point that enough was enough and it was, on this momentous evening, time to stop fucking about and to celebrate our existence riotously. This involved (in no particular order) getting far, *far* drunker, bombing base 'phet, dabbing MDMA, shovelling pills wildly into our fun holes and inhaling maximum amounts of cocaine. It still being a civilised time in history and with smoking rooms being available, we also filled the place up with ill vapours like an old *Doctor Who* episode, replete with cheap-looking monsters bumping into everything in the haze to an analogue electronic soundtrack.

At the point of maximum paranoia there was a knock on the door that sounded like the boom of distant cannon fire. Baccarat actually screamed like a girl-child. Xenon adopted the pose of a meerkat. I hiccupped with fear. Tour Manager disappeared so fast it was as if he was a Victorian magician throwing down a smoke bomb and dropping down through a trap door. Which is quite an achievement in a crowded room. The room's volume went from welding level to guilty silence. The usual gesticulated panic ensued as to whether we should open the door. If so, *who* would open the door and, more importantly, *why* would any sane person want to be knocking on our door anyway? In these situations I always find that a large element of anger and additional volume in your voice helps the case along nicely. I should also note we'd used every bit of toilet roll to turn me into The Mummy, for reasons that escape me now but which I am absolutely certain were both essential and well thought out at the time.

'WHAT THE HELL DO YOU WANT?!' I bellowed like a man-goat, pressing my bandaged face against the wardrobe door.

'Room service,' was the small reply. I went over to the right door this time.

'THAT IS WHAT THEY ALL SAY IN FILMS! EVERY SANE PERSON KNOWS THEY MEAN TO MURDER EVERY SOUL IN THE ROOM. PROBABLY WITH A SILENCED PISTOL . . . DO YOU HAVE A SILENCED PISTOL?'

'No.'

'WHAT DO YOU HAVE THEN, *YOU BASTARD*?!' I screeched, wondering what could possibly be worse, or more efficient, for a close-quarters assassination.

'A small pizza, a coke and thirty-two beers.'

'I'M OPENING THE DOOR. LEAVE IT ON THE FLOOR AND STAND WITH YOUR BACK TO ME AT ALL TIMES.'

I opened the door on a young African man, impeccably turned out in Donna Karan, who was busy being somewhat startled by my own outfit. You know you are staying somewhere posh when the guy delivering your pizza at 3 a.m. is *way* better dressed than you are.

'WHAT? WHAT ARE YOU GAWKING AT? HAVEN'T YOU GOT A MOTHER? CAN'T YOU SEE WE'RE TRYING TO HAVE A LOUD PARTY?' I lowed at the same inappropriate volume I had utilised when the door was between us.

'I do have a mother, sir, yes. I am sorry, I can't turn around, the corridor is too small and I have to get your signature.'

I pulled the bandages down from my face and leaned in conspiratorially. 'I can't do autographs at this time of night, man! Where's your professionalism!?'

I grabbed the trolley and slammed the door. As I turned to face the room I could see very clearly what we had all become, and why no one should ever have to see it.

'Xenon, don't do that again, man! Who needs food from *outside*? Who needs *food* for that matter?! I told you that it is perfectly possible, *in extremis*, to cook using the trouser press. It's safer to keep it in house. Once you involve civilians it can all go *very* wrong.'

I was approaching the point that Tour Manager always called 'demonic'. In my mind I was some sort of a cross between a Rolling Stone and an astronaut, but to those around me I probably appeared like some sort of quacking idiot with a Napoleon complex.

'You're entering your demonic phase,' quipped Tour Manager, quite unnecessarily and cheerfully.

'Thank you *so* much, your royal highness, with added emphasis on "highness".'

I get stressed out when things get messy. We desperately needed to tidy up. I'm not very rock 'n' roll at heart. I just don't have that rotten core where I can leave others to pick up the pieces. Don't get me wrong, it happens all the time, but rarely deliberately. You must always at least wipe down surfaces you've been sniffing from. However, don't stress about how much 'cos the hotel *totally* knows what you've been up to. It's a courtesy to the cleaner. I know if I saw evidence of debauch it would make me jealous, and it might make them jealous too. Leave a tip even if it looks a bunch of forgotten loose change. It's a properly shitty job, cleaning up after you.

'I need a wee,' said Xenon.

'FUCKING HELL, XENON MAN! THE TOILET IS RIGHT THERE!'

Tour Manager was right, I was boiling over. As Xenon went into the sterile, minimalist bathroom, I suddenly had the most juvenile and petty thought of my life:

'Quick!' I whispered. '*Everybody hide!*'

It seemed ridiculously appropriate, and unusually every weirdo in the room complied immediately and with gusto. The fact we were only capable of hiding in a sort of 1950s cartoon sense made it all the better. Baccarat hid his lanky frame behind the curtains, with his giant feet sticking out the bottom, a few dived tittering under the bed, and someone even tried to imitate a lamp by putting the shade on their head. It was that unoriginal and poorly executed. It was also perfectly marvellous.

To a muted chorus of chuckles and whispers we heard the toilet being flushed, the universal sign (whether you used the toilet or not) you were done, and I shushed the remaining hiders as the bathroom door opened and Xenon came back into an apparently empty room.

'Oh!'

. . . we heard, followed by footsteps and the sound of the main door to the suite opening and closing. As we peeked out sniggering it was clear he'd left the place entirely.

'Someone get him back quick! There are innocent civilians out there!' barked Tour Manager.

'*Extraction!*'

I grabbed the key and looked out to see Xenon disappearing slowly into the distance of the long hallway, looking left and right like a wee lost soul.

'I can't go E.V.A. without a tether! I might never find the way home!' I squawked.

Moments later I emerged slowly from the room, still mummified and with a sheet tied around my waist. More fabric followed – towels, pillows and even jackets and coats. Luckily he'd not got far, or else was on his way back. He was peering into the spy holes in the doors, presumably looking for us. I came to a gentle halt behind him and steered him gently back to the room. He was visibly relieved, as indeed we all were, that he'd survived his spacewalk into the vacuum of normality and was back in the bosom of our unusualness.

'Xenon lad, what happened, man? Why did you leave us?'

'I don't know. You'd all *gone*.'

I had to think about this. It wasn't easy. I had to inhabit the role of Xenon's brain. Some time passed.

'Hang on. When you came *out* of the bathroom, out of the *only* door in and out of there, did you think you'd come out into another room?'

'Yes.'

'Xenon lad! That would mean a *revolving bathroom*, fella . . .'

'Yes.'

Chapter 3

'Cos She's the Taxman

'YOU CUNTS ARE A LIABILITY!'

Chib was at full force. I was stood in his office, a sparse affair in a huge Victorian pile that seemed to house the entire music industry: hundreds of doors behind which were PRs, studios, labels, stylists, grasping proto-hipsters, accountants, lawyers and furious managers. I was trying futilely to explain to him that prior to this peak in my career I was a zero. Less than nobody. Someone who didn't even have a proper birth certificate, never mind an official persona on the files of any government. It's a long story for another time, but a combination of events, accidents of birth and a long, *long* stint as a complete waste of flesh meant I was about as legit as a baboon made out of balloons.

Chib hated our accountant, and I understand the feeling was fully mutual, I imagine mainly on the grounds that our accountant saw right through Chib as someone who was as bent as a jelly boomerang. I'd only just engaged an accountant, for the first time in my life. In fact, I was fairly sure he was the first one I'd even met. Xenon and I were furiously trying to get to grips with being grown-ups in a crash course of slow panic. We'd been instructed to do all sorts of sensible and prudent measures a few months previously, up to and including putting half of everything away for tax. It was like telling a Labrador to eat half a sausage. Don't get me wrong, we didn't spunk the lot on sweeties, spats and pet cheetahs. We were, in our own fashion, listening and trying. We figured (correctly, eventually) that the days of large studios and records costing millions to make were over. We could do everything ourselves. So we bought equipment for both live gigs and a home studio, and we did. We reinvested.

'You gargantuan wobbling *tits*, the fucking RECORD COMPANY budgets for all that shite,' roared Chib.

I was beginning to reflect that maybe some of the problem was Chib not having access to all the money. The set-up was that the money came to him via the accountant, and we got a small wage after expenses. There were a lot of expenses. We had no idea that to live in one of the world's major capital cities meant it cost the entire GDP of a small country just to walk out of your door in the morning, out of your rabbit hutch that cost more to rent than a mansion would back home. *Everything* was at least 400 per cent more expensive, and often even more. The entire music business is based on the premise that kids are so overjoyed to get paid a pittance out of their own earnings and to be in the big city that they don't ask any questions. They're too busy. We never asked any questions. However, someone very scary was now asking a lot of questions, and it wasn't Chib.

'You're being audited by the Inland Revenue. Fuck knows how they came down on this so quick, but you'd better jump to it. Get El Bastardo to do some fucking work for once.'

I assumed he meant our accountant. Knowing who Chib was referring to at any given time was a sweary lottery. Did I mention Chib was my manager? Managers are not to be confused with agents. Regardless of orientation there is a sexual/power element to a lot of representation. Managers of good-looking boys are often gay, while women are very under-represented as clients but are pulling strings everywhere backstage. Sexual scores are settled in the form of power plays. Agents will pick up the phone when it rings but never to make a call on your behalf. They field interest, manage enquiries, book the diary. A manager oversees your whole career. Some people, particularly in dance music, do both roles combined for a higher cut of your income. A manager takes 10 or even 15 per cent of every penny you earn, although, to be fair, a good manager is usually the main reason any money is coming in at all. An agent can take a similar amount or charge a booking fee; some even do both. Combination managing agents can take as much as 20 per cent of everything, some even more.

Let me spell it out for you. If you get paid 1,000 in your local currency, you immediately give away 200 of it. But the next person in the queue doesn't take another 10 per cent of what remains, they take it from the gross. So you have just 700 left before you even get to see it. Then you pay tax, but you don't pay it on what is left, you pay it on the original amount. So if we imagine you live in a nice country with easy tax laws, let's imagine they want only another 20 per cent of your money (it is half in many countries). That's 500 left. So you only see half of what you are paid, and that, of course, is before other more subtle deductions. And bear in mind this is an ideal scenario based on trust and logic. *Neither* are your friends in the music biz. You may also be paying back a record company that has only loaned you money you think is yours. Or a bank. Or you may have a manager that doesn't even tell you what you are earning. Or a record company that presents the figures for your extremely successful record showing that in fact you owe *them*, despite it being at Number One. If this makes you feel queasy and irate, it only means you're perfectly normal. And I've not even talked about the seedy underbelly yet – these are just the standard accepted practices. Smells a bit whiffy, doesn't it?

You understand then that when you are gawping at your favourite DJ, you are actually looking at a team of people. Sorry if this bursts any bubbles, but this goes for your 'underground' stars too. You're looking at a manager and his team of at least two others, although big management companies can employ a dozen or more. Your agent doesn't work alone either: they have people whose sole job is to book the travel and do the logistics. There are interns and runners and IT people and tour managers. There's always a driver. There's usually a dealer and definitely some sort of spouse/groupie/sex monkey. There's sometimes a stylist and hairdresser – no, *really*. A PR company rep for sure for the big dogs. Press too. These are the people your money pays for. These are just the legitimate shadows in the booth, never mind all the completely spurious hangers-on and droogs. Do you see why there is so much at stake yet? Why the fees can be so stupidly high? Why allegedly sane adults can take something as ridiculous as playing other people's records so very, *very* seriously?

Couple of weeks later and we were nervously huddled in a corridor so beige and sickly it was exactly the colour of a dying man. Hospitals and school corridors have nothing on Taxman's. It is entirely deliberate, of course. Experts spend years finding these depressing shades of corpse. The entire psychology of Taxman the world over is one of fear and absolute totalitarian authority. I suspect even the myths and tropes of 'Death and Taxes' and the undertaker-like image all originated from central office or after a brainstorm at their Christmas party. Like the police they play a role and play it well, backed up by absolute power and no accountability – pun intended.

I think I was too stupid to be truly scared. Xenon and I were a business of sorts. Partners. We were joined by our accountant, Tommy Smiles, his cute name matched by his delightful manner and approachability. Looking back, some part of me wonders if maybe it would have been better had Chib been the accountant and Tommy the manager, 'cos when faced with the Bitchfinder General you really need a hard bastard in your corner.

Tommy made soothing noises, interspersed with slightly bewildered interjections about how odd it was to be at this stage so soon. By this point we'd been in existence as a small venture for only about six months. True, we were peaking, doing well, but we sure didn't feel wealthy or successful in material terms. The day-to-day was still a fairly mundane struggle. We had Tommy, who to give him his due wasn't just any old accountant but an insanely expensive music-biz specialist, with a client list that was a who's who of hit-makers and cool artists. We didn't feel dodgy, we felt legit. A little out of our depth maybe, but 'in good hands'. Even Chib, for all his faults, was a player, a serious dude.

Like all authority pantomimes, they made us wait a very long time in a very cold and boring place. Then we were ushered in to face a panel not unlike a savage modern talent show, with us the desperate auditionees, they the powerful judges. I was like a cocky kid pulled over by the cops thinking he was clean but forgetting he had a knife in his jacket. My instincts are always right about things in a way that even my stupidity can't fuck up. I nearly always see right through things for what they are. The trouble with this gift is, if you side-step the showbiz and address the undertone directly, you are breaking the fourth wall. You look like a lunatic if you sweep away convention, swerve the small talk, ignore the meta-language and address the brass tacks. The truth is never popular. It's why we do everything we can to avoid it and string up anyone who speaks it. In short? I was faintly amused at all the posturing. This was, I later discovered, The Wrong Thing to Do.

What could they do? In my innocence I thought that if you'd done nothing wrong, there was nothing to fear. I had no idea back then that right and wrong have nothing to do with justice. It's something you *buy*. The poor are eternally overwhelmed and exist at the whim of the law, while the rich simply ignore it by paying others to engage. It's as old as time. If anything, your quaint notions of natural law are perfect for keeping you oppressed. The 1 per cent have no such restraints. Did I point out we'd already paid a shitload of tax on the large advance sums from the record company and the publishing? This is how naive I was: I actually said to Xenon that they may be calling us in to give us a rebate. What an idiot.

As with any harsh panel, there were four, which I'm convinced is entirely for show. One of them does all the talking, while the rest make up the numbers and scowl. The four hearsemen of the apocryphal glared at us with withering scorn. I'm also certain they intentionally chose a lady who was actually very attractive and young in a hideously severe way to lead the inquisition. After a chilly greeting, the first thing Morticia did was lay down a weight of documentation that made the Magna Carta look like a takeaway menu. Binders, boxes and Bible-thick bundles where dumped with dramatic gravitas on the judicial bench separating us. 'THONK' was the sound it made. In large type. It sounded like the trapdoor opening under the noose.

I don't think it helped that Xenon was into his skunk. He loved his weed. If you spent time with Xenon (and back then I spent nearly all my time with him when not travelling solo), you smoked it too. Even if you didn't want to. Our studio was at his place, and his house was constantly under a pall of blueish-tinged vapour that hung in the air and around him like a nimbus. He smoked it from the moment he got up until he went to bed. He smoked it to come down and smoked to perk himself up. He smoked it when there was bad news and smoked it when there was good news. Suffice to say, he smoked. But the prospect of this 'meeting' meant an extra-large calming dose was required. Which I'm sure I helped him with.

You fall into a trap when faced with authority. It's a simple game, and to them that's exactly what it is. It's like a toddler playing cards with a croupier. They simply tell you they know everything and ask you to tell them what that might be. Then they wait for you to answer. The entire room is set up for interrogation. You talk, they listen. If you are a good inmate, they might reward you with a word or two if they like what you are spilling. In essence, you're guilty until you prove you're not. Which is in fact the complete opposite of what we sweetly imagine justice to be. The onus is entirely on *you* to prove your innocence, without preparation, in a case they've gathered with no disclosure on their part. They hold all the cards in a game played in a blacked-out room, where only they know the rules, and they've handcuffed your arms behind your back so you can play only with your chin. In Chinese.

Xenon had turned into a meerkat. He just sat in rigid, stoned silence, wide-eyed and in a state of high panic. I started off calm, which for me meant loud, cocky and loquacious. Then, as it became clear we weren't getting a lovely present of a cheque and a cheerful apology from them, that in fact we were before a kangaroo court, I did what I always do when I get nervous, which is talk even more. This, of course, is exactly what they'd hoped for.

The fact I genuinely had no idea what it was they wanted me to guess was not helping. It also got progressively worse as it started to dawn on me that this was an audit not only into our small business, it was into *me*. My entire life. If they were expert, patient anglers, then they'd surely discovered the perfect fish: an ancient fat pike in a small decorative lake that had never experienced a lure and line before. Ironically, Xenon was a citizen. He was a homeowner and a taxpayer, and it was very clear, very quickly, that they weren't here for him. They were here for me.

After a mild preamble they gave up all pretence of addressing the other two and swivelled their four lizard heads entirely in my direction for the rest of the dissection.

'Do you have any records for your earnings in the period between 1984 and 1989?' the chief foxy Gila monster enquired.

'You mean when I was sixteen years old?!' I squeaked in indignation.

'How much were your total earnings at the radio station you were head of?' came next.

'What do you mean, "head of"? I got paid a pittance at that place. Everyone was odiously exploited there.'

'It says here in this interview from three years ago that you launched it,' she countered, reaching for the gigantic box file in front of her. As she leafed through it you could see that every single piece of press we or I had ever had was in there. Someone cleverer than me once told me that you don't read your press, you weigh it, darling. Even at this early stage there was a lot of paper. Until fairly recently every university and college in the world had its own radio station and magazine or paper. Whole departments in the music biz were dedicated to 'regional press'. What I didn't know is that even back then companies existed that specialised in collecting every mention of you anywhere in existence, companies engaged by everyone from your own record company to the taxman.

'You are quite high-profile now, aren't you?' piped up one of the previously silent lizards on the left. I should note that Xenon's very powerful crops were giving them a very reptilian tinge, which really wasn't helping. Don't get me wrong, I wasn't sat there hallucinating. Christ almighty, what do you take me for? Some sort of blithering amateur? No, it was a subtle suggestion, a flicker that can be either amusing or borderline psychotic depending on the environment, I guess. There was absolutely nothing funny about this situation, so why did I have to stop myself giggling like an idiot?

'Do you have shares in the radio company? Are you an investor?' came from lizard stage right.

I just gawped. Anyone who knows me today, never mind in my youth, knows I am about as corporate as a small fruit tree and about as financially motivated as a hippy jellyfish. I'd literally met the first professional, other than my dad, a couple of weeks ago, and now he was sat next to me. I'd never even met my bank manager, never mind spoken to him about anything. I began protesting to them because that is what you are supposed to do when you're in the hot seat. You don't know that it's a game of poker and they are starting high, stupidly high, stacking the whole game in the big numbers. And in the pre-internet days, to be sat in a room with someone who had the equivalent of a Google's worth of your life on the desk in front of them, neatly printed out and filed in chronological order – well, it's quite intimidating, to say the very least.

You see, the powers of Taxman are absolute. There's no law to protect your privacy if they want to investigate. Indeed, there's no recourse to anything. The relationship of the tax-paying serf to barons, kings and queens is as old as time. They've had a lot of practice hammering us and letting their peers off scot-free.

You're sitting there a squirming, perspiring car crash, your voice rising an octave sentence by sentence as you hopelessly try to explain that you aren't some sort of corporate fat cat but a thin cat of pathetic proportions. You don't understand that the whole game plays this way. They start so high it's ridiculous, and by the end of it you end up paying them four times more than is entirely fair. That is how the game is played. You understand me, Pilgrim? I'm not relating this possibly on the surface quite boring tale of taxation to you for anything other than educational purposes. Can I be concise? The first thing that will happen to you if you do well at anything – never mind playing records – is the taxman will come a-knocking, and the volume of that knock is a thing to be feared. You thought it was all limos, ladies and cocaine? Sorry, kid. It's mostly paperwork, admin and lobbies.

In our favour, Tommy had told us that pretty much anything we used for work could be written off. Your clothes are 'stage wear'. Your car gets you to gigs. Most electrical goods can be tied in to what you do in the studio. We were ready on that front. Or so we thought . . .

'Let's talk about your working expenses,' she hissed, reaching for a relatively small file from the towering stack before her. 'Silver chain – Mexican. Sunglasses – Gucci. Italian shoes. Rings by Vivienne Westwood. All very nice items . . .'

The fact I was wearing some of these items – and more – right in front of her seemed, on the surface, to be lost on her. I started to writhe and contort myself, attempting to hide each item I was wearing as it appeared on the list. She was, right now, reading out a list of items I was currently wearing! Don't get me wrong, I'm no show pony. Never been much of a fashionista. I do like to accessorise well, though.

'Are these things entirely *valid* as a performer's *costume*?' she enquired.

By this point I couldn't even speak. I was a ham, hung out to cure. A hog on a spit, rotating over the flames with a grenade in my mouth instead of an apple.

'Is there anything you want to explain to us? I will be clear here: we have certain information and it would behove you to reveal it voluntarily. Or we will consider it withholding.'

Behove! *Behove?* Does anyone even use language like that in the real world? The whole thing seemed to be spinning out of control now. I was barely aware of anyone else in the room. The head inquisitor had just turned up the flames, cranked up the bastardo, closed the deadly door of the iron maiden.

'Look, there's nothing. I am a *no one*. I was on welfare a couple of years ago! This is the first time in my life anything proper has happened, and you are making out like I'm some sort of evil genius!'

'We know everything, all we are asking is that you tell us. To *not* tell us is tax avoidance. You don't want to be a tax avoider. Tax avoidance carries heavy penalties.'

'For GOD'S SAKE, how many times does it need saying? There's no secret pot or chorus of leprechauns!

There's nothing in the mattress 'cos even the mattress is rented!'

These semi-amphibious creatures have remarkable powers, and I do not doubt for one minute that they possess the abilities of the greatest lie-detecting equipment science can muster. They could tell by my squeaks, sweats and pupils like saucers that I was completely ignorant of whatever they were fishing for.

'You want to tell us about your property?'

'*Property!?*' I bleated, so high-pitched a bat could navigate with it. 'I've never owned anything more than a few books and records in my life!'

She read out one of my previous addresses from years ago, a hovel I had shared with a mate. Not even a whole house but the upper floor of one, for which I had needed state assistance just to meet the rent and pay the elderly rich landlord.

'How can you possibly accuse me of *secretly* owning something as big as a house? There has to be no end of records and evidence to show who owns it, and that I do not.'

'Certainly. Do you have any of that evidence here?'

'Of course I don't!'

'It's not our job to look for proof. It's yours.'

From her face I could see we had lost. She was patiently explaining to us we were fucked. She also knew we were far too disorganised to rally any sort of appeal or round two. Most of the stuff she referred to was from so long ago I couldn't even remember what they were talking about, let alone have paperwork for it. Some people keep receipts, appointments diaries, cheque-book stubs and taxi dockets. People like me have never done that. Not once in our lives. Our minds are simply elsewhere. Permanently.

Tommy was no use. He was mortified and baffled by what had happened. 'Never seen anything like it,' he said. Absolutely shocking it was, apparently. He'd barely said a word in there but, to be fair, he hadn't been engaged to manufacture a past for me. I could barely hear him as we staggered out. Xenon's face was as haunted and bloodless as mine. We knew we were in trouble, but what would transpire was not one but two *huge* bills: a collective one for us that would lose him everything, as he was daft enough to pay his half, and a freshly minted individual one for me on top of my half that would dangle overhead forever. It drove a wedge between us that would never heal as far as Xenon was concerned.

Listen, I'm not the fucking Beatles here, man. You may find it ridiculous that someone successful complains about paying their dues, but let me be crystal clear here: I was not successful then, and I'm certainly not successful any more. There was a brief blip in the middle when my record company, agents and managers did very well out of me, but I was too busy and fucked-up to notice only *they* were getting paid. I wasn't rich at this point either, I was poor. Just starting out really. And I never, *ever* recovered from it financially. Twenty years later I am still suffering from this brutalisation. Don't let it happen to you.

And how do you think I feel when the über-rich corporations and stars of stage and screen waft about like tax-dodging butterflies, sipping on life's nectar while I'm stuck in a dusty drawer impaled on a giant pin? Furious? Apoplectic? Cheated? Abused? Definitely. Offshore? Fuck yeah. Gone. The fact I never earned a large sum again after those golden years is neither here nor there. Even if I had, I would die rather than give it up to a system that fucks the poor and parties with the rich. Seriously. Come and get me. When you do, there's nothing for you to take any more. My ultimate victory.

Understand this in simple language, all humour aside: in the end they decided that I owed them a sum that was dreamed up based on the fictions they had created. I was handed a tax bill commensurate with a property- and radio-station-owning mogul because I could not *prove* to them that I was not, in *that* room, during *that* hour. Unlike the rest of Western civilisation I was guilty until I proved myself innocent. This is the madness you enter into in the tax system. I was given a lifetime burden and, Pilgrim, this hangs over me to this day like the sword of Damocles. It was something I was expected to pay out of my enormous fictional future earnings from a fanciful career only they had imagined. The fact I lived on a weekly allowance lower than the average working-class wage and had zero assets and savings was utterly irrelevant. Reality has no place in the system. The system is a virtual reality more reminiscent of *Tron* or the inside of Donald Trump's head. If you enter the system without the proper guidance or knowledge, you're a goner. You're food.

There is a solution, of course: it's not real, none of it, so treat it accordingly.

In the music business it is entirely feasible to be at

Number One and have *nothing*. I remember reading the biography of Adam Ant in the 1980s and being completely shattered that someone could be a 'star' and yet not be rich. It's all a myth. The history of the industry is paved with the corpses of the 99 per cent who were one-hit wonders. You aspire to a shadow, a twisted cabaret. The perception of it is completely fantastical.

Not even your representatives are on your side. Oh, they *say* they are, but really they're not. You think my issues with the industry are old-school? It's a very modern thing to write off veterans as irrelevant. Pilgrim, I am still waaaay ahead of you. Always have been. The game may change, the pieces on the board may shift, but the rules are always the same. The biz makes the money. The source isn't important – that's you and me, by the way. *We're* the source of the money, treated like royalty while actually completely powerless.

Take streaming, for example. I've been making records with wildly varying degrees of success since the 1980s. When I get asked what I think of Spotify I immediately go into a bit of a twitching, foaming paroxysm. You may have heard in the past that some major names have pulled out of the 'service'. It's no coincidence that these names have enough clout to counter the wishes of the major labels they're on. What follows is the view of a much, *much* lesser client.

I first heard of Spotify some years ago from a friend of mine – it transpired later that these chats were in fact with one of the authors of the international legal deal for Spotify – who was a proper mate despite being a fairly powerful music-industry lawyer. He explained it to me at great length at a party at his palatial gaff. Being a bit dim, this took me something in the region of eight hours to absorb. Credit to his powers, though, as the next day I remembered it all. However, I had difficulty actually believing what he was saying, so the following year every discussion we had was essentially about the future of earning revenue from music via the internet, which he has since become something of a go-to guy for, and I definitely have *not*. I should say at this point that fifteen years ago nothing was being earned from the internet – an alarming state of affairs for the fat cats. This was something us thin cats were OK about because we still sold music and made a living amid all the free downloading, which, at that time, was mainly the domain of a handful of nerds instead of absolutely flippin' everyone.

Every discussion with him went something like this:

Me: 'So you're basically saying us artists will earn significantly less, but more often?'

Him: 'Exactly! *Brilliant*, isn't it?'

Me: 'So we're basically saying to the entire world, "What used to cost £10, then £1 now costs nothing"?'

Him: 'Not *nothing*! You still get publishing for the playing of your song, of course!'

Me: 'How much?'

Him: 'Not much, but . . . [*jazz hands*] *more often*!' (It's more like nearly nothing and hardly ever.)

Me: 'But why would anyone use this and not just the usual free internet methods?'

Him: 'Aha! Because it's *legal*!'

Me: 'What does "legal" mean? Wait, does it basically mean the record labels get paid?'

Him: 'Yes! *Brilliant*, isn't it?'

Me: 'No, not really. The labels have never liked us much. They think we're idiots.'

And then, wait for it . . .

Him: *'Surely it's better for the artist to get something rather than nothing at all?'*

Me: (in perpetuity, in all regions) 'AAAAARRRR-GGGHH!'

And here is the crux of not only the pro-streaming argument, but the argument for all internet media revenue collection: *'Surely it's better for the artist to get something rather than nothing at all?'* After many years of consideration my crafted rebuttal to that is always: 'Please will you fuck right off.'

Like a lot of sinister get-out clauses, *'Surely it's better for the artist to get something rather than nothing at all?'* bears little scrutiny. All you have to do to see through it is apply it to your own income. Would anyone be happy working the same hours in the same job for practically nothing? Yes, it really is that simple. I can only give you a figure based on my own income from publishing, but it is now basically 10 per cent of what it was just a few years ago. Yes, I've taken a 90 per cent cut. If you think it's just because I'm old and a bit shit, then bear in mind it was a steady figure for over twenty years, before dropping by 90 per cent over the last four years – almost overnight in economic terms.

Did I say I only have my own figures to go on? Spotify themselves say they 'only take 30 per cent', with '70 per cent going to the rights holder'. The artist is not 'the rights holder'. You've never owned your rights unless you're unusually well managed, possibly by Jesus. It's the record/ publishing company owning the rights and getting 70 per cent of not very much. In essence, what has happened is the oldest story in our business. The tragic tale of the bizarre contractual deal between artist and company has carried on as normal in the digital age . . . only worse. The artist not only gets a very small percentage of a much smaller amount, but most contracts view online revenue as different to record sales and – *surprise* – this means the artist gets even *less* where streaming is concerned. Most contracts covering digital rights were written well over a decade ago and they reflect that. The digital part of the deal is even worse than the already laughable deal you get from records. You understand that the person who made the thing gets nearly nothing, right? A report from the BBC puts the figure earned per stream at 0.007 US cents.

Note that Spotify say they 'only take 30 per cent'. '*Only*'! It's a *third*, for chuff's sake. A whole third before anyone else – the record and publishing companies – gets anything. I'm not a scientist but even I can work out that 0.1 cents is fuck all but 0.007 cents is *microscopic*. You'd have to be played a thousand times to make 7 cents, which is about four shiny English pence. Bear in mind also that these figures are highly debatable. Many people, if they bother to break it down, report getting far less than 0.007, and that is a big factor in this: some artists aren't really bothered, nor do they even understand how it all works.

No wonder the majors speak so highly of Spotify – they

own 18 per cent of the shares in the company and taking equity in new services is becoming commonplace. So how on earth can you fight something if your 'representatives' are in on it?

I think the real issue here is empathy. It's almost impossible to empathise with 'artists'. Bloody great flouncy, boozy, lavender-smelling fops. How can you feel anything for us in our ivory towers with our beautiful toothy faces and plastic-surgery issues? It's impossible for you to picture any of us with kids and bills and wolves sticking their weird doggy cocks through the letterbox and laughing at us. That our idols might be just like us – or maybe even worse off – bursts too many cultural bubbles. I mean, if the average DJ or singer earns less than most people in full-time work, what the hell does that say about something like *X Factor*? Who are we applauding, and why? How crazy do you have to be to try and find the end of the rainbow, even when you've been told no pot of gold exists? How dim does that make us as a species? How doomed?

There is another issue: the tyranny of the big name. Lately, society as a whole has become far more geared towards the top end. *Everyone* thinks they are some sort of star in the world's worst show. These arbitrary but plausible figures I am making up show that really only something like the top 10 per cent in my profession make a living, and roughly only the top 0.1 per cent are wealthy. Like actors, 90 per cent of us are out of work, as are many in other jobs. You might think getting played a thousand times is easy for Rihanna, and it is. But a thousand plays is a dream figure for home-based underground dance boffins. You lucky, *lucky* bleeder. We *dream* of getting 4 cents. Some will say, 'Oh yes, but you still make silly money in a live situation.' The simple answer to that is: 'Yeah, but what if we *don't*?' Or, even simpler, apply it yet again to your own job: 'Sorry, no one pays for what you do any more. My solution is you work every night and at weekends as well, and still make very little.' If at this point you feel untrammelled rage and confusion, don't worry! It just means you either work in the business or are still a human being. And then a phalanx of mega-cashed fame-droids march across our faces with something like TIDAL and you forget everything in a vortex of righteous hate and envy.

We have to puncture this myth that being a pro in the music business is some kind of sex holiday. It's not. It's a type of office job during daylight hours, doesn't stop in the twilight and goes through into the next morning. Every night and every day of the year, if you are up and coming. Add non-stop travel to that if you have any degree of success.

So I guess the crux of it all is this: are we able to empathise with those who don't deserve it?

Of course, the reason this will not bring about some sort of industrial action or have any kind of effect on the constant stream of newbies and wannabes is that no, nobody is able to empathise with what this job actually entails. Because if anyone could actually put themselves right in it, they'd realise that 90 per cent of participants will never make a living; that while the other 10 per cent *may* do, it's only for a short time and even at its peak it's ridiculously harsh . . . then, seriously, no one would do it. And we don't want that, so we pretend *everything is fine.* Which is what the industry has relied on since the 1930s.

All this is exacerbated wildly by Gentleman Amateurs. By this I mean hobbyists who have well-paid, full-time jobs but who in their spare time make and play music, possibly on shiny gear and with well-funded record collections many pros would kill for. Over the last fifteen years, DJs and producers have gone from literally a handful of professionals to being so widespread it can hardly be called a profession any more. I will never forget doing a demo for Pioneer in around 1997 for their CDJs and one of the execs telling me that the very idea of a huge corporation like Pioneer making a piece of kit for a couple of hundred pro DJs and clubs was laughable. How on earth would you recoup the billions of yen spent on R&D, manufacture and marketing? No, they were *always* designed with the home market in mind. They knew thirty years ago we'd *all* be at it. Which is why they are a global giant robo-business and I'm not.

And hey, listen! There's nothing wrong with being a hobbyist! Some might call it healthy competition. And, yes, ladies can be amateurs too. I don't care if you hate me, it's waaay too late. The major labels fought over my soul many years ago, and the only loser was me.

I always liken it to sport. What's the difference between a wildly talented amateur and a shit-awful professional? Is it showbiz? I think the distinction now is that everyone is a portly forty-year-old huffing and puffing in the park, with jumpers for goalposts, and a lot of them genuinely think they are Pelé. And I've heard responses to this along the lines of: 'But, Secret DJ, you made some *awful* pop records in the '90s, and I made some coma-inducing bedroom analogue yesterday, so therefore you can't tell me what to do because I played in a dumpster once in Williamsburg! Yes, a *real* dumpster. It was *very* authentic.'

Fair enough. But it's not a question of *taste*, it's a question of a functioning business that benefits the people who make the product, instead of only a handful of fat cats – a story so widespread in society now it's not funny any more. I'm not here to tell you that you're rubbish and a bad person because you don't get paid; I'm telling you that by doing it for free you're really messing it up for the ones you *do* think are good. You are crushing your idols. In all kinds of global business it suits the super-rich just fine 'n' dandy if there is a vast base of 'product' that is completely unregulated and made for fun by people who don't really care if they get paid properly.

A cynic might say that a tame paddock full of amateur product in an unprotected field could not be a better situation for a predator, and is to be very much encouraged. The media, arts and fashion worlds *absolutely* rely on it. So if you don't care about anything else, at least *charge* the bastards properly.

And what are the effects of no one giving a shit? Well, for a start you will see an awful lot more music from people who do it part-time, and a lot less from people who are genuinely good at it but are forced to stack shelves or are shut indoors because they can't afford childcare. And if you think that music is fundamentally a 'fun' thing and very much suited to hobbyists, you really don't know much about how all the records you've ever loved were slowly, professionally crafted and sold to you over the last sixty years.

☊

The industry argues that these are the complaints of the old and irrelevant, that the young have nothing to fear. This has always been its stance. It's always been about the young and frankly not very experienced being told everything is fine, so shut up and take what you're given. Don't listen to those bitter old guys. They don't know anything. They're just jealous. They're yesterday's men with saggy bits and no serotonin left. Old moaners don't understand about '360' deals and 'alternative revenue streams'. Thing is, we actually do understand. Indeed, many of us participated in the embryonic versions, back when they were seeing how high they could pee and being frightened by their first fizzy willy. These arguments always, without exception, come from those who *gain*, never from young artists themselves. And why should young artists complain? The same people who told you in great detail that everything is fine have just introduced you to cocaine and a taxi account. They never tell you that every single lunch, gram, cab, brass, bumhole and brunch they enjoy on the clock comes out of *your* money. You're too busy being too awesome for buses.

Listen, I get it. Things have changed. There is no going back, blah blah blah. But a culture of silence only suits the rich. We have to stand up and take ownership. From politics to disco, from work to warfare we're being shafted daily. It has to stop. For that we need to start being *bothered*. And for that to happen we need to discuss how things really are, instead of just passing memes around on social media. In their arsenal against us, the powers-that-be rely on no one reading the small print and everyone accepting the status quo more than anything else. And no one likes Status Quo really, do they?

So here it is, the final stage of the long battle between the idle, drug-addled idiot and the canny business heads behind the curtain. I say 'battle', it's more of a massacre really. And why isn't there more talk about this if it really is so dire? Quite simply, our Americanised culture has demonised any discussion of loss as for and about 'losers'. We no longer talk about anything except in deeply right-wing hyperbole, in capitalist and dehumanised terms. Our *artists* don't do *business*, horrid filthy stuff. That's what those awful managers and agents are for, and surely *this* is their final victory. This business we call show is all about face. Surely only an idiot and loser would talk loudly about such issues?

Hang on!

Of course, these days it doesn't matter what I say. What do I know? All that matters is *your* opinion. There are a few terms that have been knocking about lately to explain the vast wave of stupid washing thickly across the globe: 'post-factual', 'post-knowledge' – basically, fancy terms for idiots taking over, usually coined by clever dicks who think they are exempt and above it all. Anyway, it all seems to boil down to one thing: our slow Americanisation has sent the cult of the individual spinning into a dense singularity that has killed consensus. It doesn't exist any more in a time when everyone thinks they are The Balls. Only individual opinion matters, from the bottom to the top, from clever to stupid. All that matters is *you*, and what you think. Everyone else is wrong. Especially those manifestly more right than you will ever be. Me included.

Could society be any more suited to people deluded into thinking they're a star? Could it be any more ideal for the very powerful white men who milk this giant mad cow? Is there a better totem of all this insanity than the DJ, standing in a spotlight with their arms out like a bad Jesus, ostensibly doing nothing while in the background the tills are ringing like the bells of Notre-Dame?

I sometimes get asked about how to become involved in or excel at the business of DJing. It is a business, sadly and ultimately. I'm often at a loss simply because I've been doing it so long that I can barely remember, and things were very different when I started: for example, it was new. What I can do is tell you what *not* to do. Luck and timing are such big parts of it there really isn't much I can say about those two, other than make your own luck and put yourself in the middle of things. Chance encounters happen all the time, but you won't be able to take advantage of them if you aren't physically close to the biz. So don't think you can pull it off from your bedroom in the sticks. If you are serious about it – and you have to be – you need to move to Berlin, Vegas, Ibiza or London, like *yesterday*.

Don't rely on anyone, 'cos you'll get ripped off. It's merely a matter of time. This pool is full of happy, clappy little otters, and the sharks think they're hilarious. There are people in the biz who have literally never paid anyone, and the reason they are *still* not paying anyone is there are always fresh otters throwing themselves happily into the pool every five minutes. The otter bones, skulls and burping sharks don't seem to put the newbie otters off at all because each otter thinks they are particularly clever and special. Even the dead ones. Especially the dead ones.

Always in writing, *everything*. Don't do business on social media; use it and then steer the words onto your email. The rip-off merchants don't expect otters to keep records, pay tax and retain correspondence. They think we're too busy opening clams with pebbles and rubbing our tummies with our wee hands. If you aren't sure who's a shark and who's an otter, just show them a contract, and if they go white as a sheet and start stammering, you can bet they won't sign it, and you have a shark on your hands. For chuff's sake, don't leave everything to agents and managers. They're often sharks too. They tell you it's all about you but, believe me, to them you are totally disposable. One of the worst things you can do is merrily go off on the road and leave the biz in the hands of someone else.

Learn the tech, Pilgrim. And no, I don't mean sync and laptops. If you can't set up the whole sound system yourself, don't know what a crossover or a limiter does and don't own a soldering iron . . . well, let's just say you've got a lot to learn. Carry spares, carry tools. Be a pro.

Nice people do well, bad people do better, but there is nothing wrong at all with 'merely' doing well. Trying too hard to get to the top usually involves clambering over the corpses of your peers. However, if you concentrate on being a pro and doing the job well, you will advance regardless. If you only focus on the magnitude of your career rather than the quality of it, you will only ever be somebody people want to avoid.

Don't overvalue what you do. People who get stressed and are too up themselves become deeply unhappy, and their heads resemble an overtightened wingnut. If you are pompous, you will explode when asked to do the boring simple things like speak to people, take requests or deal with tech issues. These things *always* happen, so why expect them not to? You will die early of a heart attack if you stress about billing and your place in the game. People *know*. If the small-town promoter who puts the gig on just to be on the bill himself puts you lower down the poster than him, don't make a scene. Everyone in that town already knows he's a dickhead. A reputation for humility and kindness is like gold. A reputation as a bit of a knob might as well be a countdown to no gigs.

Don't live in fear. If you are scared of a bad mix, you will be a timid selector. The 1 per cent of the crowd who are taking notes will find fault with you regardless. Understand there will always be hate. In fact, hate is far more of a driver in the biz than love. If you engage with the haters, it won't be long before they contaminate you with their negativity. Be Zen. Ignore them. They really, *really* hate being ignored. If you do actually train-wreck a mix, there's no reason why the rest of the set can't be awesome. A DJ performing live has more in common with radio than a recording. It's a stream that only moves forward, and mistakes and blips are lost in time. Leave it, move on. No one will remember but the haters. Leave it to them like a gift.

Mistakes are fine. In fact, you need to be very suspicious if there aren't any. You see all those bangers, glitter bombs, videos and confetti cannons? It's a sure sign of cheating when flawless mixes mesh with spectacle. Mistakes are a sign of reality. Do not fear them. Fear is the mind killer. I've had the most awful things happen in my time. I have even left the decks to another DJ and gone home early in shame, only to find that I was literally the only one who thought there was a problem. People like Jimi Hendrix made a career out of 'mistakes'. Indeed, much like his use of distortion, the entire dance music culture is based on the crimes of slowing down and speeding up records and touching the vinyl – something hi-fi buffs and engineers would have a heart attack about. Lifting up the needle that is actually playing by mistake is the first trick you learn to style out. Indeed, some wily veterans deliberately create an imagined crisis. A certain legendary DJ used to pull all the plugs when there was no vibe and create a 'power cut', standing there making 'I dunno' faces while people groaned and mumbled. The roof-loosening cheer when the 'power came back on' was something you could suddenly build a great party with. Cunning.

Don't get me wrong. I can't help but notice a lot of 'mixing not important' articles lately, mainly written by and for newbie DJs, Gentleman Amateurs and Balearic Silverbacks who can't mix well. A proper DJ selects well *and* mixes. Making it a polarised argument about one or the other is ridiculous. It's nearly as bad as when minimal nearly killed everything stone dead – empty music made by empty people, all about bringing the bar down so they could join in. Don't be fooled. Be highly dubious about anything that tries to sell you quick fixes. It's hardly rocket science already, so asking to make it even easier is bordering on criminal. Liken it to a language: try as you might, *nothing* can replace going to the country of choice and speaking it daily.

You know how you *know* you're a DJ? You dream about it, as I mentioned at the beginning of the book. Everyone has 'anxiety dreams'. Mine are about things going wrong. I'm at a gig and I can't find the tune I'm looking for as the one playing is running out, or someone accidentally disconnects a cable and the crowd think it was me. They are a combo of things that have actually happened, amplified a thousandfold by fear. A psychologist might add more, but you get the gist. Fear is normal when dealing with crowds. Fear of mistakes is pointless. They'll happen regardless. I'll never forget once when a famous lady DJ was playing and I saw with my own eyes a shambling munter trip over the main power cable in the Space car park and the entire thing went dark. A couple of days later a music publication printed letters from angry, spotty herberts about the 'mistake' by the lady DJ and how women shouldn't be allowed near switches, dials and microchips lest their vaginas break everything. To survive such levels of pure stupid you have to be prepared to accept responsibility for others' mistakes, whether it's just or unjust, 'cos when things go wrong, they really go *boing*.

Don't make the following schoolboy errors, Pilgrim:

Monitors and settings: how many times have I arrived to a set of monitors even louder than the main system and every dial at ridiculous o'clock? Answer: a lot. Reds flashing, sound guys sweating and basically the DJ and their mates having their own private booth-party while the people who pay them get to watch through a little rectangle. When your monitoring is too loud, then your headphones are maxed out, your mixing suffers and, most of all, you put a sonic wall between you and the people you should be at one with. I'd say of all the schoolboy errors this is the most common.

Closely followed by 'too loud'. The sort of people who think volume is better than clarity are the same people who think one car is faster than another because it is red. When everything front of house is maxed out, you've nowhere to go. You're beating people over the head, not massaging them. And this isn't just a beginners' issue. The amount of times I've warmed up for a mega-bot and they have their contract demand that the system has to be turned down until they come on is, frankly, an embarrassment to our scene. The fact people mistakenly cheer a few decibels more volume instead of the quality of the DJ's first tune is truly saddening.

Schoolboy error number three? A fixed set. Again, not restricted to the inexperienced. If anything, touring DJs are the *worst* culprits for this. In the age of the internet there is no excuse for not having everything at your fingertips. Arriving like a rigid plank, doing your tired turn and never looking up are signs of someone who really isn't there.

Might as well put a mix on. A pre-recorded mix is about as likely to change what the next tune is, according to what the crowd is into, as this type of DJ is.

Banging warm-ups? So obvious but so commonplace. I don't just mean the first set either. Egos parachuting in and ignoring the night as a whole, seeing everything in terms of themselves . . . yeah, say no more. Forgotten your records? You had *one* job! Christ Almighty and His Mambo Band, how hard is it to arrive with the tools of your trade? Most things are forgivable, some aren't.

Sure, read this, sneer, leave your nasty comment online. You *never* make mistakes. Oh, this is all *soooo* obvious. Well, not everyone is as awesome as you think you are. Some are even humble enough to want to learn. I've never been accused of humility, but I'm not so stupid that I think I know everything. Even after so long I still fuck up. I still go to school. I still listen to my peers. Once you stop being fluid, once the cement dries, you become forever stationary. A statue. A waxwork that looks like a DJ but is simply a monolith with your likeness, wheeled on and wheeled off stage like a giant limestone dildo. Keep moving, Pilgrim, keep learning. I still try. I know I'll sometimes fail. Knowing failure cannot harm you is the key to staying alive and being a happy little otter. Instead of shark bait.

♫

I know it's not easy to be entertaining and literate about business or riveting topics like tech or tax. But it is a major part of this tale. Listen, and listen good: you *cannot* win.

You have to open the brown envelope. Stop sneering at people who keep receipts. Don't wash your hands of the boring stuff and hand it over to a shark. You will not escape the inevitability of responsibility. Only a sociopath thinks they are smarter than the law. Only a drug-addled nitwit thinks they are special. Oh, wait . . .

'WAKE UP, YOU FUCKING SHAKESPEAREAN TRAGEDY!' Chib was shouting at me. As usual. 'You need to make some fucking *money*, son. That or go to jail. It's time you and that weirdo you hang about with got on the road.'

Chapter 4

Von Ryan's Express!

Tour Manager is very similar to Mr T from *The A-Team* in lots of ways. Actually, not lots of ways, one way: he just ain't getting on no plane. Which is ridiculous for anyone, never mind a tour manager. He doesn't like flying and he doesn't like travel and he doesn't like foreigners – things you would say are the core of the job. Unlike Mr T, however, it's *way* too late to try and drug him in advance.

The plan was to start the tour in Europe and do a couple of gigs at the end of the winter skiing season, and then fly to America, doing a couple of gigs as a prelude to our industry's yearly conference there (yeah, I know, there really is one), before going on to Ibiza, early in its season, to see out the rest of the dates there. A short tour comprising three major locations and seasons, a Bermuda triangle of lost ambition. We were leaving London. Again.

Arriving at the airport in the traditional mode of me as Sherpa and Tour Manager as great white hunter involved the usual tumble of bags, barking waffle and claptrap.

'I can't possibly be seen with you in a departures lounge!' honked Tour Manager. 'You look like a dealer and reek of cheap drugs. And your shoes are *grotesque*.'

His Tourmanagerness didn't approve of cheap drugs, despite the fact his favourite was the cheapest of all. He was entirely teetotal and thought weed and hash were strictly for idiots. He was a fast man. It was all about tempo with him. He staggered instead of walked. He leapt instead of stepped. He wittered instead of chatted and rarely constructed an ending for a sentence for fear of not starting the next one. His tall, thin frame topped by a huge bush of hair and beard made him resemble almost exactly a germinating dandelion, a bit Basil Fawlty spliced perhaps with a triffid. A mental triffid. Maybe a bit of raccoon thrown in. A haunted raccoon.

Whenever he was involved we would be perpetually late for everything, despite being constantly on drugs that make you go faster. It was as if he emitted some sort of temporal warp, a black hole of entropy where the laws of physics were bent. Consequently, my hiring a tour manager meant that my taking care of myself and being *slightly* overworked but reliable had turned into me being *very* overworked and *totally* unreliable, totally reversing the laws of cause and effect. In short, we arrived thirty minutes before the flight was due to leave. I was about to miss my second flight ever.

'I'm sorry, but if you only had hand luggage I could bend the rules a bit and you'd just make it, but we simply can't take all this overweight luggage and get it on the plane.'

'Don't call him that!' quipped T-Man, never one to let a gag pass. It was a compulsion like a Tourette's tic. Long ago he'd decided that anyone not as thin as him was fat. He'd peaked with his obsession a couple of months previously, when a kid came running up to him in his club intent on pressing the flesh. With him was his girlfriend, who was, not in any way unusually, slightly on the heavier side.

'Your Tourmanagerness! Your Tourmanagerness! It's

great to finally meet you. Love your place. This is my girlfriend.'

To which our hero turned, scoped her and simply declared, 'Stop eating!' before promptly walking off.

☊

We'd missed this flight. The gig was in Austria the following evening, and like all cheap tourist flights, we were supposed to be flying late the previous night with a view to landing early the following morning. The only redeeming quality of the cheap-flight phenomenon is the cheap part, so, rather grudgingly, I went to buy us two more tickets for the next flight, which was the following day at stupid o'clock in the morning.

'Now I know why they have hotels in airports. Best get us some rooms then,' I pondered aloud.

'I know! Let's get a hotel in the airport!' T-Man had an annoying habit of not listening to a word anyone said and mistaking the actual surrounding audio for his own inner thought process. I will spare you the usual check-in performance. For the purposes of this book simply imagine that every time we try to check in anywhere it's a colossal spastic jazz solo of embarrassment, bags and mishap. Fast-forward an hour (it takes at least an hour for us to do anything grown-ups do in minutes) and we have acquired a room. Tour Manager refuses to share a twin. As well as being the worst tour manager ever, he is also too posh for things most people take for granted.

Now comes the famous Freak's Dilemma. Do you push

through or go to sleep? One of the many, many reasons drugs fuck you up is because sleep becomes the enemy. And you really don't want to get into a fight with your own body, on the grounds that both of you will *definitely* lose. Part of this job is being awake almost perpetually, if not for totally legitimate reasons, then for many, many completely spurious ones. Sleeping now was a particularly bad decision as I was perfectly capable of going without, but I rashly assumed that as Tour Manager never slept, with only about a four-hour window to try it in, he wouldn't.

I woke up about forty minutes before the flight was due to leave. The second flight. Hammering on his room next door did nothing for a further heart-attack-inducing ten minutes. When Tour Manager sleeps, it is as biblical as his face. And to witness a woken T-Man is to witness Tour Manager of the Old Testament. If funny, fast and jolly T-Man is the positive gospel of the disciples, a recently woken from a death-like drug comedown T-Man is the smite-y, scowling T-Man of plagues and rage.

'FUCK OFF!' was about all he could say, and he did so with great vigour and sincerity. He didn't have time to put more drugs into himself.

'We have to go right now!'

'FUCK OFF!'

'I have all the bags. STOP, PUT THAT AWAY!' I yelled, as he tried to get his drug paraphernalia out.

'FUCK OFF!' came the inevitable reply.

'Look, we have to move, the gate is only a few yards away!'

'FUCK OFF!'

We crashed into the check-in desk almost exactly as late as we were five hours ago. We were similarly refused – by, it transpired, exactly the same person who had refused us previously, now at the end of her shift and looking like it. I turned to the sweary apparition beside me.

'I've never missed a gig apart from the last one you made me miss. I'm not missing another. There's flights to Zurich and Geneva. We can get a train from there. In fact, we may even be able to get a train from here to the Channel tunnel. It's completely feasible.'

'Fuck off,' sighed Tour Manager, already completely exhausted after being awake for nearly forty-five minutes without any substances.

We managed to find a cheap flight to Zurich. Tour Manager's medicine was locked away in the hold, so I did my best to avoid him for the whole flight as he wasn't a lot of fun on a comedown. No one is fun on a meth comedown. Especially if it's one you've been avoiding for ten years by taking it every single day on an hourly basis.

On the plus side we managed to avoid France. Tour Manager was very much opposed to France in general, mainly on the grounds that he went there once. He asked a Frenchman for directions, who upon turning around appeared to be a urinating tramp. A French tramp who then gleefully pissed all over Tour Manager for the crime of speaking French badly. After being micturated upon, the decision to leave immediately was quick, and the judgement on France final and unwavering: a bad place, not to be trusted.

'If you look out of the windows on the left, you will see the majesty of the Massif Central of France,' announced the pilot over the tannoy.

'FUCK OFF, FRANCE,' bellowed Tour Manager with the last drop of energy he had.

☊

Arriving in Zurich was painful, 'cos an untreated T-Man is merely an extra item of baggage that swears and complains, like a trolley with a squeaky wheel that goes only in wide circles. We dragged through passport control, crawled through baggage reclaim and oozed through customs. The cheery efficiency of the Swiss staff is rendered obsolete when confronted with someone for whom the act of reaching for their documents is a death sentence and speaking to anyone an inhuman torture. Thankfully, unlike most major cities there was no hours of journeying from the airport outskirts to the city centre. Being Switzerland, Zurich airport had a perfectly good international train station attached right to it. After what seemed like hours of trudging around I found the departure board showing trains to Austria. There was one leaving soon and we had to rush. Getting Tour Manager to rush was not going to happen.

'Fuck off!' he explained when I suggested we had to hurry. I already had two trollies full of bags and record boxes in a very ungainly convoy. T-Man wasn't even prepared to carry his own passport. He was, without doubt, the worst tour manager ever conceived of. My concept. My execution. My funeral.

It can't be disputed we were quite a sight as we barrelled through the pristine modern corridors and esplanades of Zurich, me wrestling wildly with two piled-high buggies that were hard enough to control one at a time, accompanied sporadically by a lanky wizard who was as reluctant to keep up as a grumpy toddler.

'COME ON, MAN, WE'RE GOING TO MISS THIS ONE TOO!'

'FUCK OFF!'

Et cetera, ad nauseam.

The train was as futuristic and precise as you'd expect from a forward-thinking nation. We'd arrived from England, so we were used to trains being a method for billionaires to amuse themselves and thoroughly abuse the despicable peasants. A form of national torture-as-pastime, much like British food. The idea that a train would be affordable, clean and efficient was as alien to us as rents commensurate with your income. This Swiss carriage was so serene and welcoming after so many hours and miles of hell even T-Man couldn't complain. As the train set off he immediately went about tearing the luggage apart looking for his gear.

I love trains. I don't care if planes are faster, they are horrifically uncivilised things. The fact that a slave, doomed to die while serving on a Roman galley, officially had more room than the average passenger on a modern plane is something I can never forget, especially when I'm crammed into a torturous economy seat. Even cheap trains are majestic and enjoyable, but go to Europe or Canada and they're a new level of fabulous. The Swiss have it down to a fine art. Not only are their trains beautiful, modern and timely, they sweep through some of the planet's most staggering landscapes and we raced smoothly across some of the most awe-inspiring vistas known to our species. Totally lost on us, of course – we were arguing.

'Look, we're about to cross a border. This part of the world is nothing but borders. About five different countries all meet here. We're not on a plane, man. You can't just unpack a chemistry lab and get busy. You have to hold out for a bit longer.'

'FUCK OFF!' replied Tour Manager over his shoulder, as he presided over several square metres of unpacked baggage like the world's messiest pathologist, a bad Quincy who hated his autopsy subjects, socks and cables draped over his shoulders. We'd only been on the train for what seemed like minutes when we started to slow and an announcer said fluently in four languages that we were now about to stop for border control and to have your passports ready. I knew immediately that if Tour Manager was so drained he couldn't find his drugs, he definitely wouldn't find his passport.

'Have you got your passport ready?' I chimed helpfully.

'FUCK O— AHA!!' he trumpeted, holding aloft a large packet of base amphetamine sulphate, a vile, powerful substance best avoided by everyone except some soldiers, pilots and long-distance lorry drivers. He completely ignored the busy train full of civilians and openly tore at the bag, then commenced the hilarious pantomime of trying to get a hit. Tour Manager loved his whizz, but anyone who has ever tasted it knows it's the most unpleasant thing you can possibly put into your mouth. And that is a decision reached by experts who've put all the nasty things on the planet into their fun holes. He hated the taste of it and was dramatically against anything he didn't like. Taking it usually involved gloves, tools, several sugary drinks and the substance being wrapped in layers of paper like a Christmas parcel. Watching him forced to take it raw was like watching a bulldog chew a porcupine. Before he'd even opened the bag he'd pulled more comical faces than ten 1970s impressionists. His mug contorted involuntarily in anticipation of what he knew was about to happen, a facial shivering akin to a swimmer about to leap into freezing water. He squeezed his eyes shut and went for it.

'EYAG! HURP! GUUU! FUGGID!' he said loudly, while hopping up and down and gurning. The civilians had given us a fairly wide berth a while ago, but they couldn't escape the spectacle. It made me gag just thinking about what he was ingesting.

'Feeling better now?' I ventured.

'Fuck off!' he replied happily. Even the taste of a thousand heinous chemical processes couldn't detract from the relief he felt. As the train slowed and came to a halt and the medicine coursed through him, he started to come around.

'Which FUCKER *ruined* our luggage?!' he roared, glaring up and down the rows of innocent bysitters.

'That would be *you*, dude. Don't bother tidying it up, as if that was ever likely. You need to find your passport.'

'Passport? What for?'

It was pointless explaining. Time did not pass normally

for him. During periods when he was 'sober' his mind was on a kind of standby mode, engaged only with the autonomic system, trying to get drugs inside him, thinking about getting drugs inside him, and with a sort of 'out of the office' auto-reply that simply read 'Fuck off'. He may as well have been unconscious with a sign around his neck that read 'FUCK OFF' in capitals. Possibly in red ink.

'I don't need a passport in bloody Europe! The whole thing is a morass. All joined up. Anyway, I feel better now . . .'

'Congratulations. But you really need your passport.'

'Pish-posh, twaddle and nonsense!'

'No, you *need* your passport. The Swiss aren't in the European Union. This is a border. The train won't move till we've all been seen.'

'Nonsense! It's only fucking Switzerland! It doesn't matter!' Bear in mind the train is packed with mostly Swiss, and he says everything at the top of his voice.

'It does matter, mate.'

'Bollocks! Chocolate! *Cuckoo clocks!* Banks! Not even a proper country.'

The Swiss border guards got on. These lads had Heckler and Koch semi-automatics and they knew how to use them. They were nice and polite going through the carriage. Finally they got to us and went, '*Passkontrolle!*'

I obliged. By now His Tourmanagerness was frantically rummaging as he was faced with guns and his own folly.

'*Reisepass bitte?*' they asked Tour Manager, who duly answered, 'I can't bloody find it!'

The guard spotted he was obviously English, so nice as

pie he switched to fluent English. 'Your passport please, sir.'

T-Man went over his shoulder, 'JUST GIVE ME FIVE FUCKING MINUTES, YOU MASSIVE FUCKING SNOW NAZI.'

The guy went white and turned to his mate, who just looked really sad. They turned around, saying to each other, 'When will they ever forget?' or something similar. They didn't even come back, they were so mortified.

I was very annoyed, and I said so, whispering, 'Pssst . . . you dickhead! We're guests! Don't ever do that again if I'm around! These people on the train are all Swiss!'

'WHAT? THE FUCKING SNOW NAZIS? NEUTRAL CUNTS. AND THEY'VE STILL GOT THE JEWISH GOLD.'

The rest of the passengers started moving away to find another carriage, ideally on another train.

I was mortified. I pulled him over physically and hissed in his ear, 'Listen, you fucking freak. I'm not travelling across all of the fucking Alps and half of Europe just to hear you insult every nation that exists en route. If you are going to travel with me, you have to fucking STOP with the insanity. Just for once. PLEASE.'

'You're entering your demonic phase again. You should have some durgs!' he said cheerfully. When he was high he was as cheerful and immune to criticism as he was surly and minimal when dry. That wasn't a typo by the way: Tour Manager also had a habit of making up words or sharing a joke that you'd never shared with him. Over the years I could tell the difference when not many others could. 'Let's get some durgs in!' he'd shout, assuming people could not instantly do anagrams. Really very simple, obvious anagrams. He'd constantly refer to drugs as 'durgs', which actually baffled an awful lot of dealers. The fact someone hadn't met him before never stopped him from using a completely private idiom immediately upon meeting them. Or, in the case of my French friend Guillaume, simply refusing to use his actual name and using one he had come up with. Tour Manager rang me once years ago when I used to live in Paris. Guillaume and I shared a place, and Guillaume answered the phone. Tour Manager immediately misheard Guillaume's name and dutifully called him 'Stuart' for the next five years. Guillaume would answer the door and Tour Manager would cheerfully greet 'Stuart'. The phone would ring and His Tourmanagerness would become annoyed and ask 'Stuart' who this Guillaume was that he was referring to.

'Hello, T-Man,' Guillaume would say when T-Man called.

'Who the hell is this?' His Tourmanagerness would reply, always confused and slightly annoyed that the person he was looking for didn't answer immediately.

'It's Guillaume. How are you?'

'ZEEL-HOME?! WHO THE BLOODY WEEPING ARSEHOLES IS THIS?'

Guillaume would sigh and resign himself to his fate. 'It's Stuart.'

'Ah, hello, Stuart! Why ON EARTH didn't you say it was you?!'

It came to a head of steam when Guillaume got a girlfriend called Elsa from Sweden. She immediately became 'Swedish Stuart', Tour Manager entering our house for evermore with the greeting, 'Hello, Stuart. And Swedish Stuart, of course.'

☊

As the train pootled along amid the divine Alpine panoramas, Tour Manager's constant need for sugar kicked in. Usually his brain was entirely separate from his body, working at hyper-speed while his body dawdled several seconds behind. His body seemed to require vast amounts of sugar, which, being old-fashioned, to him meant actual sugar. He constantly chugged syrupy drinks and in one week would quite easily go through a family-sized one-kilo bag of processed white sugar, in the form of mounds of it heaped upon breakfast cereals (which he ate throughout the day) and ladlefuls in hot beverages. Now it was time for his body to demand that everything stop for sugar.

'Where is the restaurant car?' he demanded.

'You're showing your age if you think things like that still exist, but I saw a trolley dolly coming down the next carriage when I went for a piss.'

'I NEED SOMETHING SWEET AND FIZZY IN ME! IMMEDIATELY!' he yodelled at the cowering passengers. I should also point out that since his drugs had kicked in, he was, as usual, incapable of sitting down.

For the sake of the narrative I will break the fourth wall again and explain that in reality the trolley did not magically appear at that precise moment, but for the sake of a smooth transition let's imagine it did and that several dull minutes of silence did not pass. Completely ignoring the rest of the carriage he gestured grandly over to the approaching refreshments and, as per usual and without preamble, started shouting orders in the comically slow English that country reserves especially for multilingual cosmopolitans.

'YOU! DO. YOU. HAVE. ANY. MOORSEBERRY-SHREWSCAKE?' he lowed, peering down the aisle at the attendant over the half-moon glasses that he kept permanently on a chain round his neck as he lost anything not physically attached to him within minutes, and pointing like a deranged referee. Tour Manager's inability to converse normally was compounded by his constant spoonerisms. His souped-up brain would be some seconds ahead of his mouth. I lived for these moments. Not only would he do them often, he'd do them at length while claiming loudly he wasn't doing it and that you were an idiot for pointing them out so incorrectly. People on fast drugs don't have time to be wrong.

No one but me knew he wanted strawberry cheesecake. We were in Switzerland. Or maybe France or Germany – it was hard to tell in this beautiful and unique part of the world. He was shouting at someone who didn't speak English in a country that had no cheesecake, someone who had never even heard of it in their own language. And it was highly likely that they had their own perfectly good word for it even if it did exist for them. Which it didn't. And when they didn't understand, he'd just say it again far louder, failing to notice he was repeating the spoonerism.

'Moorseberry shrewscake, man! Don't look at me like

I'm an idiot! WHERE. IS. THE. MOORSE. BERRY. SHREWS. CAKE? This child is clearly an imbecile.'

My personal favourite came when he was arguing about drugs with a simpleton and in a fit of pique shouted, 'I would *never* sully myself using a hypodeemic nurdle!' You needed to be on your toes just to understand what he was on about at any given moment. And that was if you knew him as well as I did. To a stranger he was often simply a madman. An ill-mannered one at that.

Slowly but surely the train had steadily emptied during the journey. I couldn't help but notice that this was *not* due to people disembarking, as the carriages on either side were almost entirely full – more than likely filled with escapees from ours. Going by the station names I realised that we were getting close to our destination. This was the tour manager's job, of course, but I'd taken full responsibility for everything pretty much from the moment I rashly appointed His Nibs. The train started to slow for its approach to our destination, a small village in the Austrian Alps.

We disembarked erratically. The station exit opened into a gigantic, snow-covered car park, and T-Man noticed a bus shelter near by. Thinking it was similar to a large airport car park we took a seat alongside some of the others who were waiting. Everyone seemed to be puffing away happily on cigarettes, which T-Man approved of greatly, being a very keen smoker himself. People seemed to have very little patience as they came, waited for about five minutes and then wandered off. After about an hour of mind-numbing boredom and extremity-numbing cold I asked one of the others when the shuttle bus arrived.

'This is . . . how do you say . . . the smoking area?' came the reply.

'It looks just like a bus shelter!' His Tourmanagerness yelped.

'This is your fault, as usual,' I grumped.

Eventually our host tracked us down. Of course, he had been waiting patiently not a hundred metres away. We decanted into some sort of chalet and I finally had some time to myself. Which may even have included sleep.

The next day I was overjoyed to discover how beautiful this place was. I'm a mountain man from mountain lands and this was the Alps. The deal here was unusual: instead of one well-paid gig, I was to play every night for a week for a very low fee, but I also got all-expenses-paid skiing. I love it. Tour Manager had never even been ice skating, of course. In the winter months in Europe many of the same faces you might see working in Ibiza will go to work in the ski resorts. Like Ibiza, every night is party night. So while it wasn't really good business for me to be there, it wouldn't hurt my career *too* much. Well, that is what I told myself. Chib would disagree at a length and volume totally illegal under the Geneva Convention.

We got to the fitting rooms for the ski gear. Before anything could happen you had to fill in a questionnaire about various health issues, etc. In the section for your age, it had a list of fairly standard options: five to ten, ten to fifteen, fifteen to twenty years old. Then it stopped and merely said, '*Über* 50'.

'Hey, T-Man! That's you, that is! Herr Über Fifty!'

'Shut up! I am forty-nine! *Unter* fifty!'

'*Über* fifty!'
'*Unter* fifty!'
'*Über* fifty!'
'*Unter* fifty!'
'FIRE!'

The assistant looked at us like we were from Mars, far too young and sophisticated to know the Bugs and Daffy reference.

🎧

The small club was ideal. It was rough and ready, but it was full to bursting every night with heinously drunk kids from all over the world. Drinking was a big thing there. You started après-ski in earnest at around 4 p.m., and it was some serious Viking shit. You were generally still doing shots fourteen hours later at 6 a.m. Then start over the next day, and the next, and the next . . .

Don't tell me you're a DJ if you only play to people just like you. A real DJ plays in every situation imaginable, and not only that, does it willingly and does it *well*. Rooms like this are full of people who are mainly drunk – drugs are almost unheard of. Therefore, they have absolutely no problem telling you what you should be playing. People on drugs are able to 'be', to exist within a moment. People on booze are a riot in syrup. If you can make a room full of kids from all corners of the globe dance to underground techno, some of whom have never heard anything like it, *and* they have fun, then, Pilgrim, you might be suitable for the job. If you can keep your cool when twenty Scandinavian death metal fans surround you and threaten to kill you and drink your remains unless you play something they like, then, my child, you may have the right stuff. If you actually make them all jump up and down and shake their hairy bits as they stomp to house music, you can even call yourself a DJ.

It's a piece of piss to make fans dance. It's a walk in the park making people in Ibiza or Las Vegas dance. It's what they came for. It's being out of your comfort zone that makes a pro. Pros don't cry about someone having the temerity to make a request. All I ever see on the internet concerning DJs are precious, passive/aggressive memes about 'NO REQUESTS' and 'RESPECTING THE DJ' and, more regularly, huffing and puffing about the tech and format. And I can guarantee all of these are from, and for, amateurs. A pro gets the job done and doesn't cry about it. Make people dance. Shut up. Go home. Sleep. Repeat. Minus the sleep part.

Seven days of this sort of winter-season grind is enough to end most people's life. For me it was a holiday. Anyway, enough fun. Time to go pro.

Time for New York City.

Chapter 5

O.P.U.L.E.N.C.E. – How to Survive in NYC

We'd met Bobbie Baluga a couple of seasons ago in Ibiza. He was a deeply religious American DJ who'd lost his life-long partner and was emerging from years of grief. And, boy, did he ever emerge!

In the film of this book, a vintage plane takes off from Europe and a red line follows it as it crosses the Atlantic. We'd done the torturous arrival and ride from JFK into town, which is not too dissimilar from the Zombie Taxi into London. It was Bobbie's birthday and his manager had insisted we come over as a surprise. Bobbie was kind of in love with all of us. I'd given him his first ecstasy pill in Ibiza a year previously, and Baccarat was kind of in love with Bobbie right back, being the gay of our outfit. Tour Manager was pretty much the funniest person Bobbie had ever met, so he was definitely part of the gang. Us three were the surprise. All pretence of business was thrown out of the window, along with a tightly scrunched up little ball that was all the adult responsibility.

New York. You can't arrive and not want to taste it. It's a myth, mainly self-perpetuating, that America is the crazy fun-times land of the free. It's not. People aren't robot-toothed, beautiful, funny and living in lofts. They're often ugly, humourless and living in caravans. It's extremely repressed and conservative, as shown by its punitive laws on how and where to party and its frankly paramilitary police. Even its version of hedonists are often teetotal. One of its dance music heroes is fucking Moby, for Christ's sake. But you still can't help but feel the buzz as you get into New York properly. I'm no tourist, I travel for a living, but this didn't feel like work at all. For once I was off duty in a major city, even if it was technically within the Venn diagram of my work world. There was a smell of promise in the air. Pure vibes.

I don't like stark, modern hotels. I like slightly fading, grand old ones. I like everything about them. I like the bars, I like the decor. I like the cranky, creaky old elevators, the even crankier and creakier old staff. I like the big rooms and their shoddy interiors. I like the dull views out of the back onto fire escapes and Hitchcockian rear windows. I even like the constant honking of a thousand lunatics on their car horns – well, if the room is high enough above them all.

We'd checked in and dropped the bags in the hallway of the sprawling but shoddy apartment-esque rooms. The phone rang.

'You fucking useless shitehouses best be doing some fucking work over there,' said a familiar shouty Ulsterman.

'I just had an argument with an American about calling a full stop a "period" and then called him a semi-colon, if that counts?' I had a thing with Chib where even if I was in the midst of something actually resembling work, I'd wind him up and pretend to be doing something extremely pointless.

'Earlier we went to Central Park and made gigantic lines out of the snow that is left over, and then took photos of ourselves pretending to sniff them.' Wherever we were in the world we also used to pose for photos of us doing something bone idle, which we'd then send to him, often having to do so at breakneck speed on the way to and from airports. This would include stopping en route at a shop, buying inflatables and swimming gear, finding a pool and staging a photo shoot of us 'relaxing' during the ten seconds it took to arrange, and then sending the photos to Chib knowing full well it would bring on a small coronary episode. Chib worked his clients ridiculously hard, so we returned the favour by pretending that his brutal schedule was a total cakewalk.

'Ayie getcher FUCK,' is an approximation of what Chib said before slamming the phone down. I can never be sure of exactly what it is he says when he is angry, as he descends into some sort of Iron Age Celtic dialect. Ironically, I work really hard and rarely have a moment even to see a city in daylight, never mind have any downtime there. But this was different – we were going to have four whole days in New York. I've been to many capital cities for less than four hours.

Bobbie Baluga was entirely nocturnal. Many of us full-time DJs are. It makes a sort of sense. You are awake nearly all weekend and always all night, so why punish yourself by going to a diurnal phase and then back again twice a week, every week for years, when you can just shift entirely to the night? This doesn't go down well with your 'team', however, so it tends to be the upper strata of DJs, such as Bobbie, that can get away with it. We lost day one waiting for Bobbie to wake up, and wrestled with jet lag into day two. We were given directions to a restaurant to surprise him and luckily arrived mere moments before he did. We got to hide behind some parked cars and stage a mock mugging. He may have enjoyed it more than we intended.

'Aayyyiiiiiiii,' he screamed at impossible volume. Bobbie was very camp. As camp as only a true-born New York queen can be, one who'd earned his stripes at the Paradise Garage and more. This was *his* town and he would be as gay as he wanted to be on his birthday. We leapt out with our faces covered and asked for money with menaces. This was a town that took mugging very seriously, but we were obviously a joke. We weren't even armed.

'A mugging!? Why, I'd give you fellas my money in *advance.*'

Bobbie was a very funny guy and we brought out the worst in him. He loved the worst as only someone brought up so religiously could. We were ostensibly there for dinner, but really we were his surprise gift: the 'hot boys' from Ibiza he'd fallen in love with. We didn't mind at all. What could be better than seeing New York, with one of its very own legends as a host? We were from Europe. Being gay wasn't a crime with us. It was quite flattering considering some of us were older than he was and yet inexplicably somehow considered eye candy. We were about as hot as a tepid cup of weak English milky tea. If our scene ever had a version of Liberace, it was Bobbie – slightly repressed, camp as Christmas and genuinely, effortlessly arch and funny, universally loved as a showman and artist.

Dinner was over with quickly. We weren't here to eat. We were professional international idiots and we had come to freak out. Bobbie was, on the surface, teetotal and uptight, but give him the slightest nudge and he'd roll his eyes and profess how *naughty* it all was and then join in like a real trouper. I suspect he wasn't being entirely truthful when we first met and he told me he'd never done any MDMA. But this was America, and no one was very open about that sort of thing. You'd think that wouldn't be the case in the home of rock 'n' roll, but it really is very uptight there. Most of the hype is false. I'm speaking very generally, of course. If you seek, ye shall find . . .

Bear in mind this was slightly before the EDM explosion that turned Las Vegas into a giant clockwork rave theme park. America didn't invent electronic music, despite loudly claiming it did. I myself grew up on Krautrock (itself a derisory label dreamed up by history's 'victors') and a deeply European sensibility of electronic instruments used in a very musical sense. I owe far more to Vangelis, Kraftwerk and Giorgio Moroder than I do to anyone from Chicago. I was very happy to dance to house music, but for me it arrived late. For much of the past thirty years America hasn't been particularly keen on much of its own dance music, perhaps due to the people who made and enjoyed it. Indeed, it would be fair to say that America's mainstream has pretty much only just 'got it', three decades late. The rest of the world has been raving non-stop since the 1980s, when the golden era of hip hop merged into the acid house phenomenon. Recently America got on board, declared it owned everything, as usual, and then decided to call it all electronic dance music, or EDM – as far as I can tell, mainly because they got confused by how big, complex, subtle and beautiful it all is, and decided it needed to be stupid, obvious and simple.

In fact, one of the US's finest, Derrick May, has said, 'EDM is "Disco Sucks" waiting to happen,' which won't make any sense at all if you're under forty, but in 1979, in a typically vast American enormodrome, many thousands of disco records were ritually torched as part of the 'Disco Sucks' movement. Ostensibly Americans woke up to the fact that disco wasn't just very, *very* gay, it had been doing a very gay dance right in their faces and they had been too dense or aroused to notice. Yes, they really didn't know that the Village People were gay. They really didn't. Many actually thought they were a bunch of like-minded tradesmen and municipal workers who'd formed a cross-disciplinary choir.

In shock and possible closet-based guilt for actually enjoying it all, Middle America launched into an all-out assault on the fact that disco had dry-entered the mainstream. In the ritual burning, the pitch was so damaged the game was actually called off. There is a deep irony there, though it didn't harm the push to kill disco one bit. In fact, it was their brightest, hottest and most insane hour, a shitty lighthouse winking hate on a cliff-top of intolerance.

An even bigger factor than any musical considerations was, of course, simple everyday bigotry. Disco was not just gay, but black and Latino. In a standard racist tactic, ancient boiling hate was dressed up merely as a matter of taste. To racists, disco was simply bad music and had to be stopped for everyone's own good. The fact that stopping things for the greater good is textbook fascism also seemed to be lost on them; that the last time public burnings had happened at this level was at Nazi rallies seemed to be equally ignored.

The angry mob's desire to stem an imaginary tide was compounded by disco's total dominance. By 1978 *very* mainstream names were 'going disco', and to all intents and purposes it was *everywhere*. All hate needs is a plausible reason to hang its hat on and it can get away with anything, up to and including 50,000 people rioting at a stadium over something as innocuous as oom-tish-oom-tish. You don't have to be a genius to see that you don't get that degree of hysteria over simply a matter of taste. If you did, there would be a Burning Bieber-Man festival every week by now. On that day in 1979, in that very stadium, if they could have got away with ritually burning something else black, shiny and sexy instead of just vinyl they would have leapt at it. Repeatedly. Until it was dead.

And it absolutely and efficiently *worked*. Once the word had got out, 'disco' became an expletive. Under the guise of 'taste' everyone from the platinum-selling producer to the kid on the street put disco at arm's length, some because they do whatever they are told by fads and fashions, many because they always properly hated black people, gay men and Latinos. But Europe continued to love and nurture disco. Don't worry! It only sounds like I'm saying Europe is better than America because I am. In the intervening time Europe built dance music into a towering global empire and sold it right back to the US in massive spadefuls.

Which brings us to today. In true commercial US style, America tardily took it all on board and completely removed any and all of the redeeming features from the dance culture it helped to found. Then it totally ignored thirty years of European dance music and claimed complete authorship of the parody that is left over. We know this rebranding as EDM – electronic dance music. During this process America continued to outright refuse any proper acknowledgement of the pioneers of house music in its own backyard, replacing them with manufactured pretty-boy stadium versions. And they're *white*, always so white – maybe because despite waiting patiently for thirty years for them to change, those heroes of house music resolutely continued to be black, gay and Latino. Some of our biggest legends are all three. This EDM johnny-come-lately attitude is never writ more large than in the hysterical way they trumpet a photo of Daft Punk without their helmets. Previous magazine covers with their exposed faces on the front and an open and transparent twenty-year career in Europe may as well have never happened. If America doesn't know about it, then it simply does not exist. God knows what will happen when it's 'revealed' that Daft Punk are, in fact, French. It was enough of a blow to many Americans that they weren't actual robots.

My sincere hope is that in-bred bigots and murderous armed lunatics don't use EDM as a cipher for their insanities and project onto it. America has always had a vibrant and globally competitive dance scene. At its best it can't be beaten. It has always been very much for the minority, however. You had to find it, it didn't find you. Disco was the same. It was not for everyone, until suddenly one day it was. Now EDM is treading the same path, dancing the same steps across a very dangerous dance floor. And there is love at the centre of all this. The best parts of disco and EDM are about unity, tolerance and happiness. Which, let's be frank, annoys the tits right off some people who can never stop being furious at everything.

Middle America and its almost-medieval religions has neither diminished nor mellowed. It's a sleeping dragon of biblical proportions – pun intended. There's a very real possibility of a repeat of 'Disco Sucks'. Derrick May said all this far more concisely than me in one killer sentence. There could feasibly be a clash between Middle America's self-appointed moral guardians and their own children. The trick here is to learn from recent history and prevent this from ever happening again. EDM is everything disco was. It too started out black, Latino and gay, and now it's as white and straight as an accountant's hard-on. It's large, brash and it came from the drug- and sex-crazed ghetto and is currently literally *everywhere*. Crucially, just like disco, at its most ubiquitous and commercial it's truly terrible music. This is the dangerous truth at the heart of it, one we should start admitting.

Just like disco, EDM now informs the sound of many a mainstream hit record. One day that 'many' will reach a tipping point and become 'too many'. Just like disco, there is a very real danger that as the bandwagon rumbles ever onward, the backlash will throw the baby out with the bathwater. Intolerance doesn't do nuance. When the hate tsunami hits, it will try to take everything down with it, top to bottom. All it takes is one look at global neoconservatism and the politics of fear to see how easily the masters of hate can hijack anything and turn it to their own purposes. In America it can be a stadium seat at a ritual burning or the murder by police of one of its innocent citizens.

In the UK in the late 1980s the Conservatives used dance music as a smokescreen to introduce a sweeping set of draconian laws banning all manner of public gatherings and lawful protests, and even socially cleansing the 'traveller' subculture almost out of existence. The threat is not just very real, it's happened in our lifetime already. Is there a connection between increased police brutality and youth subcultures? I am putting it to you, Pilgrim, that sometimes there is, and we need to be extremely mindful of it. America doesn't care so much when everyone is in their place racially and sexually. When there's a crossover and a previously marginalised culture goes mainstream and 'infects' their precious white youth, it can wake the dragon and the effects can be widespread and sometimes horrific. At times of economic hardship and political conservatism, scapegoats are needed. Let's not be one. Not again.

If these questions are about what we can do to prevent a repeat of some truly awful mistakes, then surely music is the answer and, as ever, love is the message. We need to ensure we're all working to get that message across and make that music work for us rather than against. I predict a riot, sure . . . but wish upon a star.

☊

Bobbie Baluga lived through all of the above and so much more. At this point in time in the US, and for the purposes of our tale, house music was still very much for the faithful and converted, not at all for the public at large. And here we were in the home of disco, hanging out with one of its bona fide legends. We were at his house, which was special. I always say you are eternally a tourist until you step into the house of a local. Everything else is just commerce. We got to see the studio and vast walls of records, and some original memorabilia that would easily make at least one franchise of a house music version of a Hard Rock Cafe.

We cruised around town in Bobbie's huge truck as he proudly showed us the sights of *his* city. It was an education. As the sun set we went back to the hotel and started to get ready to get serious. This was New York, and it was *night-time*.

Now I'm not one to preach. Sorry, scratch that – I am *totally* one to preach. But when the ketamine comes out, I tend to go home. It's just not for me. They use the stuff to knock *horses* out, man. HORSES. When you end up taking some in the innocent belief that it is perfectly wholesome cocaine . . . well, it's not very nice, to say the least. You are expecting a delightful lift and you get something akin to some sort of psychological witch's ducking stool. What was supposed to be sharp and witty becomes dull and moronic. Instead of flying you are wading. You get my drift.

You'll be disappointed to discover that my own drug use was fairly tame. Well, relatively speaking. There are people who can be creative and functional on drugs. True, they're mainly dead, but they did exist. I understand that to some people reading this I will come across as some sort of deranged beast, but the fact is that to many I will seem pretty tame. We're talking day-to-day use here. The week has always been about getting shit done for me, and only a madman takes drugs in recording studios. *Everything* sounds good to you when you're on drugs, but that doesn't mean that it sounds good to everyone else. For me the drugs were about making it through the weekend's work and travel. It wasn't recreational. Now, however, I was on holiday in New York, so it was time to be *highly* recreational.

I was clear to indulge, and I'd already done the wrong thing immediately by ingesting Ket. I wish I could say I was spiked, but in my long experience no one ever spikes anyone. They're too mean. People spend a lot on drugs and tend not to give them away. Which I think is very bad form. There are exceptions to this, and a major one is to be a DJ. Then you tend to walk around like some sort of chemical dartboard, with people throwing sharp arrows of lunacy at you. All day and all night.

We'll talk in depth about drugs another time, but suffice to say, on Bobbie's birthday we were all very merry. Bobbie himself was not partaking as he had his big birthday gig the following night, and Bobbie Baluga took DJing *very* seriously. In fact, I've often said that, rather unsurprisingly, how good you are at something is directly proportional to how much work you put into it, and Bobbie worked *all the time* at being a DJ. Every single waking hour was about the weekend. Even on his birthday weekend there was no way he was going to get fucked up if it might possibly affect his work. Yeah, Americans, you see. Not as crazy as advertised.

We were in New York, fucked-up and wanting to get right into it. Baccarat was so excited he was practically vibrating.

Maybe he was actually vibrating – it was hard to tell by this point. Tour Manager was strangely quiet. What usually happened when we went abroad for more than twenty-four hours was his drugs would wear off and/or get used, he'd have no idea where to get any more and so he'd promptly go to bed 'with flu' for the entire duration of the stay. The usually quiet Baccarat, like many gay men, has an inner diva that will come out *screaming* in the right circumstances. And these were definitely the right circumstances.

I had to ask a question, which took a lot of effort 'cos I could barely talk.

'Bobbie! Where . . . shall we go now? The night is young . . . and we're *not*.'

I had to find a place for freaks to see out their high. We weren't fit for human consumption in any normal sense. I was having a lot of trouble forming sentences. People can experience drugs in completely differently ways, but ketamine is always universally hardcore. Very few people can avoid its syrupy pull into the dark. It disassociates you entirely. It's as if the steering wheel is taken out of the vehicle. Your windscreen wipers have also been snapped off and your lights stolen. And your wheels. Things are happening around you, only not *to* you. You're watching from a remove – that is, if you can see anything at all. I was certain I was swaying, nodding, and my eyes were probably rotating independently like some sort of chameleon. A very drunk chameleon.

'*Yeah, Bobbie, we want to PAAARRTAAAY!*' screeched Baccarat, piercing my reverie and, judging by the look on his face, nearly giving Tour Manager a heart attack.

'You'll have to forgive my colleague, Bobbie. I think he might be one of those gays I've read about.'

'No shit? Never had any of those round these here parts!' replied Bobbie, with a sly wink and a comedy hick accent.

Time. Time also. Ketamine fucks with time. And it's not just the drug, it's the drink too. Most idiots like us drink constantly before, during and after our drugs and take other drugs along the way, until you're sloshing about the streets like a naughty jug. I didn't know where we were, but we were definitely in New York somewhere. People kept approaching us on the street, which felt odd. They continually asked me things. I had to be very careful not to reply as I was convinced I would simply quack like a duck. Tour Manager kept appearing and disappearing, while Baccarat was sashaying everywhere, which *always* meant trouble.

Then we were in a bar. I love New York bars. Everything about them is right, above all that the proper ones are *entirely* about drinking. The staff actually know their job, which includes making you feel welcome, as well as spectacularly drunk. As usual, if we stopped anywhere for long we were surrounded. We were a fair old spectacle really. Baccarat is six foot eight, Tour Manager is very striking and I'm very noisy, and we all had weird accents. Most of all, we really, *really* didn't give a shit about anything, which, I've discovered, is quite unusual in America. I think I was having a good time. I was laughing a lot. Then Tour Manager leaned over.

'There's no women in here. None. Zero. Fanny-free. Devoid of the snatch. Empty. A bird-free bird sanctuary.'

'Well, it's early for New York, isn't it?'

'It's 2 a.m.'

'See! Early.'

'This is a gay bar. The gays have taken us to a gay bar for more gayness.'

'Nah! You're being paranoid, man.'

'What's teabagging?' queried His Tourmanagerness. When confused he very much resembled Sam, the blue eagle from the Muppets.

'What? I have abslo . . . absalts . . . absolut . . . no idea. For making tea?'

I was confused by the conversation's turn, and that's saying something considering the general tone of our discourse over the past few hours. Tour Manager simply pointed to a sign over the bar that cheerfully said 'STRICTLY NO TEABAGGING' in large, friendly letters. I pondered this.

'I imagine the constrains of the licence prohibits the manufacture and consumption of your own refreshments on the premises . . . much like a cinema!' I countered with mild pride at achieving a long sentence. (I've since learned that there's a similar situation in a later John Waters film. I don't think he was there too. It's just a coincidence.)

'It's a gay bar,' T-Man repeated solemnly. 'I went to the lavatory and every bit of scrawl was about cocks.'

'It's *always* about cocks. Look! Bobbie's here! I thought he went home?' I slurred.

'Of course he is, 'cos it's a gay bar. Look up.'

I looked up. As happens so often when you're mortally hammered, you experience everything through tunnel vision, so I was completely unaware that there was a mezzanine level above us with male go-go dancers lining the walls. I'd definitely lost the argument.

'ALL RIGHT! ALL RIGHT! IT'S A FUCKING GAY BAR!' I honked like a goose god.

Everyone immediately went quiet and all eyes turned towards me.

'HE DID IT!' I squeaked, pointing at T-Man.

'It's a late drink,' shrugged Tour Manager, nonplussed and, for once, the most sober.

Baccarat started laughing heartily. Then Bobbie joined in, as did the rest of the bar. Bobbie shepherded us over to a corner. All the time Baccarat was getting into his stride and doing some of his party tricks, which involved stretching.

'Bobbie, I think this might be a premises . . . for gay men to . . . socialise in . . .' I wittered.

'Help! Call the police!' said Bobbie, archly.

'Will they be real police or pretend burly-stripper police?' I asked.

'I can arrange for both, if you like,' he said.

'Bobbie, what is "loaf roasting"? I saw it written on a wall in the toilet,' asked Tour Manager, his face quite genuinely puzzled. Tour Manager rarely asked any questions. For us this was a night full of questions.

'LOAF ROASTING?' I blithered at top volume, producing a shush from Bobbie. 'In what sense, man? In a bakery? In what context?'

'Well, specifically it said "Donny Roasts His Loaf" in very large letters,' Tour Manager informed us.

'Ah! Well, you see, that is when bald guys . . . you know, big bald boys . . . they lubricate their heads and . . . you know?' hinted Bobbie.

'WHAT? WHAT ARE YOU SAYING, MAN?!' I shouted, incredulous and, if truth be told, slow and confused too.

Tour Manager intervened. 'I think when one lad loves another lad very much, they wear each other as some sort of sexual hat.' He seemed quite cheerful about it.

Bobbie was deeply amused by my confusion. 'Sometimes they forget and come out of there looking like a very guilty monk,' he chortled.

'I've learned so many new things in such a short space of time,' pondered T-Man, while Baccarat started doing ballet moves on the bar to a chant of 'TEABAG, TEABAG'. (Maybe that bit was from a John Waters film. I'm not to be relied on by this point, mentally speaking.)

'I don't even want to know about that one,' I sighed. 'I'm not high enough for all this.'

There must have been more. More of everything. We were somewhere else and yet no space or time had passed. The streets were a neon blur, future canyons of noise. There were more in our party. Well, there was Tour Manager and myself, and then Baccarat and his entourage. Baccarat was very good at the whole gay thing. I pulled him to one side.

'This is New York, man. *New. York*. We can't just sashay about being . . . well, *gay* all the time. We need to go to a club. Like, something we can't get anywhere but here.'

'How about a hip hop club?' chimed Bobbie, who

always seemed to appear like an elf from nowhere, if he was there at all.

'Yeah! I hate hip hop. It's perfect. Yeah, let's do it!'

☊

There was a queue around the block. Maybe a hundred people. Not a white face to be seen. The fact we went straight to the front and in the door was shocking in itself. Easy to forget your friend is seriously famous in his home town. I can only describe the atmosphere in there as uniquely 'heavy'. Everything about it oozed danger. There was a sea of stares, a wall of silence to greet our almost constant apologising. We apologised for approaching someone, we apologised for passing them, we apologised if we brushed against anyone or looked at anyone. We were sorry for existing in every way. Listen, Pilgrim, I know clubs. I've worked in every kind of environment where people dance to music that's possible. I've played jump-up dance hall to tribesmen in Tibet. I've played soca on an island in the Caribbean so small and isolated you have to charter a seaplane to get there. I've played the coolest afterhours in Indonesia and idyllic beaches in Brazil. I've done stadiums, radio and TV. I've been to the 'darkrooms' of Berlin. But I've never been anywhere as scary as this, and I've worked in Bosnia during a ceasefire's end.

It wasn't the music, which was moody, slow and aggressive. I've been to techno clubs that were far, *far* less fun. It wasn't the fact it was, like all the best clubs, almost pitch black. It wasn't really a race thing, 'cos we're kind of ignorant of it all, coming from multiracial Europe. It was just pure aggression, not only towards us but towards each other. Everyone in the place was hostile to everyone else.

'I love it here,' said Baccarat, eyes shining.

'But you hate hip hop!' I replied to an empty space. He'd already disappeared into the throng.

'There's no women here either,' noted Tour Manager. He was constantly on the lookout for women, so it wasn't uncommon for him to say this. But something chimed . . .

'Bobbie, is this another gay club?' I sighed. If it was, it was a good trick 'cos it really didn't seem very gay. Quite the contrary.

'Wellll . . . technically it's not *gay* at all. A lot of these boys have done hard time. *Hard* time. The rest of the week these boys love their girls and wives. For them, after prison, there's nothing homosexual about fucking a man. Fucking is fucking . . .'

'I want to go home now,' I whined. 'This country is *very* weird.'

'Me too,' agreed Tour Manager.

🎧

The following night was Bobbie's birthday party gig. We'd hung out a lot but I'd never heard him DJ properly. That is to say, I was never off duty and in the crowd for the duration, on the dance floor. Unlike a lot of my peers, I spent a lot of time in the crowd. Whenever I could. I didn't have any other life outside of house music. I existed almost entirely nocturnally, so the only way I got to see other humans was late at night. If I was driving to and from gigs, which was frequently, and I was within a hundred miles of it, I'd call in to Tour Manager's club. If I had a rare Saturday off, I'd go straight to the nearest friend's venue. Indeed, I've spent so long at one major venue there's a me-shaped hole in the upstairs bar and a wee dent in their famous dance floor exactly the same size as my feet. If you're reading this to learn something, Pilgrim, learn *this*: you will not progress in this game if you live in the DJ bubble. If you don't hang out, *dance* and participate in all aspects of the scene, you will forever be on the outside looking in.

Bobbie was busy tonight, so we all piled into a yellow New York cab and raced across the city to support him. To be in this city on such an auspicious day as Bobbie's birthday, and as his special guests, was enough to bring the giddy levels way, *way* up. It's easy to feel jaded when you're deep inside the business, but at times like this you're transported back to when it was fresh and you were just a kid. I was out with my buds in the town that helped start it all, off to see the master at work. The taxi practically flew through the steel and concrete geometry.

At this time a lot of New York venues were dry. Meaning no alcohol. This was partly due to the repressive conservatism of the country, and partly down to simple licensing. It's a hell of a lot easier to open a dry venue than get a licence to sell booze. Another aspect was the asceticism of parts of the scene. The 'real' heads, those who considered themselves superior to everyone else, took it so seriously they considered booze to be both unnecessary and something of an evil, something that hampered the vibe rather than added to it. They may be on to something there, if a little overly puritanical about it.

We decanted at the venue, a small gang of professional fools, international-level idiots. The queue was *huge*. The queue is something of a ritual to the initiated. It's hard to describe the feeling to the current me–me–me generation and equally self-absorbed veterans who think queuing is for other people and would never countenance going anywhere where they weren't on the VIP list. Large venue or small, the queue used to be *everything*. The guest list was very short and usually for people working on the night, their friends and maybe one or two low-level people you needed to keep happy for business purposes. The queue was where you made friends. The queue was where you got *hyped*. The queue was where the party started. If it rained, you huddled. Nothing was going to stop the vibe. Then it was all about being picked. The door whore, the person holding power over the portal, ruled with an iron sausage. When clubs got popular, they attracted 'tourists'. These had to be weeded out. You want participants, not gawkers. You want to be free to be freakish, not in a zoo for normals to stare at you.

On special nights like this, however, everyone was one of the faithful. Bobbie was a bona fide American hero, and tonight it showed. We were hustled past the queue and straight through, Baccarat loving it as he swished and flounced past the unlucky. We were first in, the place still bright with working lights. There was a small backstage, where we immediately went to work on the only booze in the whole place, specifically there for us Euro monsters.

The locals were faintly amused at our antics, slightly aloof from our silly foreign habits.

Within what seemed like minutes the place was transformed. People literally ran into the main room to secure their spot, a place many wouldn't leave for the next sixteen hours. Indeed, the same went for us. We formed a gang – right at the front, of course – and cheer-led Bobbie and the crowd near us without pause. It was the best kind of venue: basic, a large box, ceiling low so the sound wasn't lost, dark, no frills and all about the sound system. If EDM is the Vatican, a proper house music club is a small wooden chapel, puritan and deeply devout. There was no showbiz. Very few lights, in fact, just a dark room filled with beautiful music and a communal feeling of mutual worship.

There were moments of connection: people hearing our accents and asking where we were from; remarks on my T-shirt, which coincidentally had the name of the club on it, though the club sold no merchandise, so it was a talking point (OK, it wasn't a coincidence).

People were actually *dancing* instead of standing around photographing themselves. No one was drunk except us, so no one was behaving badly. Except us. The variety of sounds was staggering, a million miles away from the current vogue for the same dishwater-dull drone that never ends, a baroque cathedral of sound instead of a minimalist corridor to nowhere. Now and then we'd pop round the backstage bit to use the toilet or take a break. At one point a queue had formed inside the venue for people to give Bobbie birthday presents. Offerings for the high priest.

Time moves strangely. Sometimes it feels like you've

been in a club forever, sometimes like you arrived ten minutes ago. The end is never in sight. And then suddenly there it is. Chants for more. More happens. Again you are lost, until it's clear it has finally come to a halt. You were the first in and you're the last there. The lights come on. Bobbie makes his escape. You now have to deal with the aching loss, coupled with the euphoria that refuses to wane. You remember . . . *this* is what it's like. *This* is why you do it – to help make people feel this way. At times like this, there are no questions.

☊

The next day was more America. There's a lot of it. We did the usual colossal spastic jazz mess at check-in and waved goodbye to Baccarat, who was allegedly going back home, but we were certain that as soon as our backs were turned he'd be in a pink limo right back to gay New York. We were bound for our industry's annual conference in Miami. A week-long sprawling debauch for the Brits, an opportunity to network for the more serious Americans.

The Winter Music Conference, or WMC, had set itself up in the 1980s as the go-to conference for the industry. Naturally, being American, the organisers really believed that. We normally had all our business done for the year by the time it came around, but it didn't hurt to be seen there. Our hosts usually locked up all the booze, drugs and women when the Brits were due to arrive. We were still labouring under England's bizarre Victorian licensing laws, which meant we tended to go at things like Vikings

in a blind panic that everyone would stop serving us at
11 p.m., and God forbid the Queen might see us being
badly behaved. The change in the UK laws didn't undo
this conditioning. The Brits drink hard, fast and noisy. I'm
not proud of it. It's embarrassing.

I often have to check my luggage for drugs. Usually a nice
airport security staff member will do this for me, but I like
to do it myself first. Don't get me wrong, I'm no idiot. It's
futile and stressful to transport anything under prohibition,
but people genuinely do throw drugs at you. Sometimes
literally. With the best intentions in the world, they can put
a 'gift' of drugs in your bags at the club. It doesn't occur to
them that in a few hours those same bags will go through
X-ray scanners and past dogs and machine-gun-wielding
hormonal steroid-beasts. Also there's every chance someone
like Tour Manager will put some in there completely
innocently 'for safe keeping' and then immediately forget
they are there. So it's always best to check.

As we were due to board I went to the toilet and had
a rummage. In a rarely used crevice I discovered a bag of
dried nonsense. I couldn't quite work out what it was at
first. I had a sniff and a feel. Looked like leaves or herbs,
but not marijuana. Possibly the remains of mummification
or a satanic ritual. I went back out to the departures lounge.

'I think I've got a large bag of magic mushrooms. I'm
fairly sure they've been there since last summer and have
since been through every airport in the world, utterly
undetected. They must be worthless now.'

'Mmm.' Tour Manager was rarely interested in any drug
other than the fast stuff. He had a sort of tangential, angular

wisdom in his dealings with drugs. He'd tried them all in fairly quick succession during the first couple of years and had ditched them all for meth. He had a strange logic: to him all the stimulants were fairly similar, so he settled for the most powerful, cheap and readily available. He hated alcohol so he never showed much interest in depressants. There was only a small window of interest in MDMA and hallucinogens. He was known to have a wee dabble in the name of science.

I went over to the bar and ordered tea for two. With extra hot water. I ditched the teapot and put the contents of the bag in the pot of hot water. I figured the mushrooms had been there so long they had to have lost most of their potency. Plus, we didn't have time for any sort of brewing process – wheels would be off the tarmac in twenty.

'URG!' Tour Manager had a habit of saying words from 1950s children's comics that were only ever written down, never spoken. 'PPPFFFT! This tea is *vile!*'

'Shut up and drink it.' I felt bad-but-not-bad. You should never spike a friend, no matter how much it needs doing. 'It's psychedelic tea. It will open your mind.'

'Oh, righto.'

He had this weird thing of being incredibly difficult one minute and completely amenable the next. Sometimes he just wasn't paying any attention at all. We both drank the tea.

I woke up feeling most peculiar.

I was on the plane but not actually on the plane. It looked like a plane's interior but it was like a cartoon of a plane. Or rather a line drawing of one, a good draughtsman's job of work. I was experiencing a strange sensation, as if I was floating. I turned to Tour Manager, who for once looked fairly beatific and serene.

'I feel floaty.'

'You're flying.'

'Am I flying? That is *amazing*.'

'If you press that magic button up there, a sexy woman appears.'

'*Really?* Wow, that is also amazing. Can I try?'

'Please. Go crazy.'

'Hahahaha.' I pressed some buttons and a lovely lady appeared. I gestured to my tour manager.

'He says I'm flying!'

'He's quite correct, sir. You are flying.'

'That is just . . . *amazing*.'

'It's fairly commonplace, sir.'

'Oh no. That is *very* cynical, madam. It's a beautiful thing. You should try it.' I turned to the seat next to me.

'*Aaaeeii!* He's vanished! *Completely disappeared!*'

'I think he went to the lavatory, sir. Is there anything I can get for you?'

'Please just bring him back! He's not a bad person at all, just a bit different.'

'I'm right here, you idiot,' said a voice next to me.

'*Aaaah!* How on *earth* do you do that?!'

'Well, what happens is, you take loads of antique hallucinogens and I don't.'

'What? Where is the angel lady?'

'She's a boiler. You did a load of mushrooms before we took off.'

145

'Of course I did, you old fool! I know that! So did you.'

'You're being an idiot, and no, I didn't.'

'Am I? Tsssst, hehehe . . . oooo. Watch! Watch! Watch this.' I pressed the 'call' button again. The attendant appeared once more.

'Yes, sir?'

'Ppppffffft . . . hhhhhhf . . . Excuse me . . . tssssfff pppffft hehehehe . . . HOW HIGH ARE WE? Hahahahaha! HAHAHAHAHA!'

'About thirty thousand feet usually, sir.'

'Aaaah . . . hahahahahahahahaha! Hehehehe ffffft!'

Tour Manager intervened. 'I'm terribly sorry, but he's a bit simple.'

'Pfffffft hahahahaa!'

She looked at me like I was something on the bottom of her shoe and left. I could barely contain myself as I manfully tried to wait more than a few seconds before pressing the 'call' button again.

'Can I get you anything, gentlemen?' she enquired.

'Ppppfffft . . . hfhfhfhffff. HOW HIGH ARE WE NOW!? Ahahahahaha.'

'He's a type of high-functioning savant. I'm his doctor, pleased to meet you.' Tour Manager was doing his best to shine and was waggling his ridiculous eyebrows at her and doing his best impression of a civilian. Normality was not his strongest attribute, but coming from the aristocracy had its advantages.

'Doctor!? Hahahahaha! Excuse me! EXCUSE ME! How high are we now? Pfffftttttt. *Doctor!*'

'Yes, it's quite sad really. I may need some help with him

at the other end. I have to say, you seem like a very *capable* young lady. Perhaps you could assist me? Have you ever considered the nursing profession . . .?' he warbled on in his best version of normal, but looking to me exactly like a humongous freak pretending to be something else *really* badly. The stewardess seemed to see through it too, as she was backing away as professionally as she could without actually bolting and causing a massive panic and possible explosive decompression.

'Bit stuffy in here, needs a door opening,' said Tour Manager, as he twisted both nozzles above me and sent a jet of Arctic air into my dry eyeballs, producing a reaction akin to being maced.

I don't remember anything else.

♁

Next we were striding across boiling hot tarmac, a haze in the air. Well, T-Man was striding. I was rolling. He was pushing me along in an airport wheelchair.

'You see, this . . . *this* right here is how the whole "tour manager/artist" thing should be,' I told him. 'This is deeply appropriate. I knew you'd get there in the end if you persevered.'

'It was this or get carried off strung up like a pheasant by the paramilitary police,' replied Tour Manager.

'What? Why? You wouldn't sell me out to them, would you? I'm as innocent as a lamb here!'

'You emptied nearly a whole plane. No idea where they put the other passengers. The noises coming out of you were like something out of *The Exorcist*. And the vomit was of a greenish hue too.'

'Those mushrooms must have been even more ancient than you, T-Man. Can you go a bit faster?'

'Please fuck off. And have a nice day,' he countered.

This chapter has been removed on the advice of our legal department.

B-SIDE

We Are Not Your Friends

There is something slightly fevered and off-kilter about the music business. Other industries tend to have a sort of 'management/worker' polarity that is obvious, but only in the arts do we pretend the workers are of more value than the management. And it is a pretence. It's a bizarre symbiotic embarrassment, with perfectly sane and competent adults pretending to be drooling infants and formerly humane and compassionate grown-ups systematically exploiting this. I've never understood any of it, and I've been, at various points, on all sides of the set-up. Why an artist doesn't even seem to want to grasp how the business works is truly beyond me. And how some of the company men sleep at night considering what they get up to is a genuine shocker. Never is this situation more clear than every March, when we all decamp to America en masse.

Miami. Unlike New York, this should have been *all* about business. The WMC is our yearly conference and we actually have some weight there, a modest amount of pull. The conference itself happens in hotels, venues and clubs across the city. We never bothered with any of that. We always went straight to South Beach and rarely left the strip. We'd go out all night and sleep through 90 per cent of the legit events that were held at sensible hours. The 10 per cent that were left we'd happen upon accidentally, nearly always at night or else stumbled into just after getting up at the crack of 2 p.m. For us, majestically striding up and down the strictly art deco brilliance of Ocean Drive or driving up the bustle of Collins Avenue was the stuff of fantasy. We were in *Miami Vice* or *Scarface*. Being pretty much intoxicated the whole time really added to the surreal 1980s-TV quality of the place.

Around conference time it was generally impossible to get a decent hotel anywhere. Often the WMC coincided with spring break, an American ritual in which young men go around topless throwing liquid at each other (possibly another gay thing, it's hard to tell with Americans – they're a very sexual race). The results are chaotic and the flesh is omnipresent. We were lucky that Bobbie Baluga's people had arranged a small hotel for us as part of his entourage of transvestites and performers. Every American DJ came to the WMC, as did DJs of many other nationalities. Bobby had brought half of New York along with him as cheerleaders. Most of the players in the industry stayed in the luxury beachside hotels where much of the conference itself took place, only having to stagger down from their diamond-encrusted suites into a ballroom to attend something important between cocktails. Legendary hotels such as the Delano, the South Beach and the Ritz-Carlton were at the hub of things, pretty much all in a staggered line up Collins. At this point in the WMC's history people from outside the industry were starting to come simply to be there, attempting to squeeze into the club nights and blagging their way into the poolside daytime events to hobnob with their heroes.

We were miles away from the action in a strange little complex of tiny beige huts that resembled a Japanese prisoner-of-war camp for Oompa-Loompas. We didn't care. It was highly unlikely we'd spend any time in there at all. You'd find us at all hours of the day and night at the beautiful chrome 11th Street Diner, plotting our own downfall.

'We should go see Quag Allurgie,' suggested Tour Manager. 'He's always bang in the middle of everything.'

'I dunno. Isn't it a bit early?'

'No, they'll still be awake from last night.'

'Very true.'

We set off for one of the larger and therefore less cool hotels. At the northernmost end of Ocean Drive were some monsters with thousands of rooms, packed to the rafters with partying 'bros', 'hos' and the lesser but more plentiful elements of the WMC who could not afford the luxury locations. They were still very nice hotels, but nothing like as overpriced or highfalutin as the boutique ones at the centre of the game.

We arrived in a vastly long corridor, and even from a hundred metres away we could tell exactly where Quag Allurgie's room was. In the far distance a THUD THUD THUD could be heard, and as we got closer we could see people spilling out of the room into the corridor amid the general whoop of a party. Everywhere Quag Allurgie went was a party.

We squeezed into the tiny room full of red-eyed zombies and spotted Quag Allurgie's long-suffering wife sat on the floor. Elizabeth was small, pretty, spoke like a docker and was as highly strung and hyper as a rodent. We attempted to sit near by. For some reason everyone was rubbing their eyes and looking extra, *extra* bleary, as if there was some sort of hay fever epidemic going on.

'Hello, Liz, where's your fella?' I asked.

'Fuck knows, mate. He's been in and out of here all night and most of the morning being dead shifty.'

It was very unusual *not* to see Quag Allurgie in the middle of a party. Quag Allurgie needed to be the centre of attention or he'd simply die. He needed to move around like a dolphin in a hammock being sprayed with drugs or he'd just shrivel up like a bad sultana. For some reason he was one of those people who are always referred to by their full name.

'I need to see him,' said Tour Manager. 'He's ordered a load of drugs off me.' Tour Manager was no dealer, but for Quag Allurgie he made an exception. Quag Allurgie was almost supernaturally charismatic, and even someone as weird and potent as Tour Manager was not immune to doing whatever Quag Allurgie wanted him to do.

Suddenly the door to the room was booted in with some force, and someone yelped in alarm. The entire room went silent as a colourful figure raced into the room at a speed that was clearly way too fast for the length of the place. As it approached the window a girl began to scream and people began to stand and put their hands over their mouths as the figure leapt over the balcony rail into space. There was a moment of silence . . . then *uproar.* The room was high in both senses of the word. At least six storeys. Some rushed to the rail. Someone started to cry. Others shouted to call the emergency services. Only Elizabeth seemed nonplussed.

I pushed through the throng of people and looked down. Quag Allurgie was fully clothed in the pool, waving.

'He's been practising for days,' said the long-suffering Liz.

'That is how you do the pool thing, you demon,' Tour Manager told me, gesturing.

Liz, Tour Manager and I went down to the poolside bar to see Quag Allurgie, soaking wet, sat at the bar with a cocktail and looking smug and triumphant. He had one of those metabolisms that meant he had almost zero per cent body fat. His face was the visage of someone who took a lot of drugs every single day of his life. His voice, by far his most distinctive feature, was an incomprehensible low mumble. It was part of his hypnotic power. His voice droned and rumbled nonsensically for hours until you did whatever he wanted just to make it stop. But the eyes were sharp. They never dimmed. No matter how many drugs were poured into him, he was always the deadliest fish in the aquarium. He was a sort of reverse Dorian Gray: he appeared utterly wrecked externally, but the eyes were freakishly clear.

Everything was a contest to Quag Allurgie, a game only he knew was being played, to rules only he knew the function of. The short-term fallout of this was that he was a lot of fun to be around, but only in very short doses. A by-product of the perpetual motion machine of his vast ego was constant japery. He couldn't sit still if his life depended on it. He had no friends, only followers. The Cult of Quag was a constant hymn to the glory of himself, but there's no denying it was hugely entertaining to be around. He was the sort of person who if their number came up on your phone it meant only one thing: you had to do something for them.

'Hhzzzunfud a hurr hurr,' mumbled Quag Allurgie to Tour Manager. For some reason both his wife and I understood everything he said. Consequently his hypnotic powers didn't work on either of us. It was something to do with his charisma, coupled with the fact they couldn't understand him, that made people fill in the gaps in their own minds and try to be helpful to him. Don't get me wrong, he wasn't disabled in any way, but he had such a thick accent and had taken so many drugs – possibly amplified by him not really caring if anyone could understand him or not – that the result was this strange mumble. Being hard to understand is a very old gypsy trick. It helps in negotiations if your opponent ends up negotiating *both* sides of the deal for you. It was as if someone had merged an evil Stephen Hawking with Keith Richards and put it all inside a miniature Iggy Pop.

'He wants some of your gear, mate,' I translated to Tour Manager. Quag Allurgie was already climbing up the stool and onto the bar top like a monkey, his wife pulling at him to get down. He always dressed in faintly ridiculous catwalk couture, usually offset with some sort of novelty item like a tiny clown's hat or a plastic nose and glasses. He was the eye of the wacky hurricane, yet he somehow pulled it off. This was the slightly spooky thing about him: he was ridiculous and utterly wasted, but somehow rose above it.

'Yeah, because what he really needs now is something to make him totally deranged and awake for days,' said Liz very sarcastically. She was very good at sarcasm, more a handler than a spouse.

Quag Allurgie leapt off the bar and came at us like a territorial simian brandishing some sort of tiny weapon.

'Arg! What is he doing?!' yelped T-Man. Quag Allurgie was wielding a kind of pipette from a tiny bottle and waving it menacingly at Tour Manager.

'Sz lugwid asud.'

'He wants you to have some liquid acid, mate,' I interjected.

'Keep him away from me!' squeaked the intended victim.

Quag Allurgie started to rummage through Tour Manager's pockets, looking for the drugs he'd commanded be brought to him, while holding the pipette to his face like a tiny pistol. T-Man knew it was futile to resist and duly froze in a comic statue of fear.

'I'll have some acid. Been a while,' said a voice that sounded just like mine.

Without pause, and never taking his eyes of His Tourmanagerness, Quag Allurgie squirted the dropper in my face.

'Aaah, shit!' It felt like most of it missed, but I caught a few droplets.

'Stop whinging, you child. Nothing there! It's not *actual* acid,' barked Tour Manager. I wiped my face. There wasn't much. I was lucky.

'That was close!' I exclaimed, relieved.

☊

An hour or so later, alone on the beach, I was a hideous drooling carcass. The epidermis takes in external substances as much as any orifice. Quag Allurgie knew this, of course, and had been telling people all week they didn't have to have a large dose of acid; he'd just put a drop on their hand and they could suck it later. Thinking they'd had a narrow escape, many ended up awake for days in a psychedelic hole.

Quag Allurgie thought that not only was this hilarious but he was doing everyone a favour. Indeed, we learned that the reason for the outbreak of red, weeping eyes back up in the hotel room was Quag Allurgie had convinced everyone that putting cocaine in your tear duct was a far superior method than sniffing it. He even demonstrated by theatrically putting two fingers into the powder and rubbing it enthusiastically into his own eyes and making huge noises of satisfaction and bliss. Of course, he immediately switched fingers on the way up to his face in one of the oldest sleight-of-hand tricks in the world. The fact everyone else ended up with lava eyeballs was merely apparent evidence of Quag Allurgie's almost supernatural ability to take more drugs than anyone else, and it didn't stop anyone trying to compete with him. If there was ever a moment that described him more succinctly it was this one, with him sat triumphantly in a room full of weeping, gullible child-idiots, the only dry eye in the house.

I could describe the twenty-four-plus hours of acid trip to you – the monumental realisations, the clouds parting at my thoughts, the mystery beams of light in the sky, the colours, the uncanny coincidences and the sheer dazzling beauty of it all – but in reality I probably lay in the shape of a swastika for a day and a night in some dirty sand near the gutter of the strip, being stepped over by tutting, healthy Floridians.

I rose like the world's worst kraken. I'd lost a significant amount of time, some items of clothing and other small possessions and 99 per cent of my dignity as a former human. I shambled off in a reptilian fashion to try and find out where I was in relation to the midget hotel and my esteemed colleagues. Sorry if it seems like I glossed over something monumental there, but I honestly can't remember much. And we're trying to keep it real here. This isn't fiction. It's not big or clever. It's also hard to explain to civilians and amateurs how very mundane it can all be sometimes. I staggered across South Beach for hours, the after-effects blurring my sense of space and time, a lost Pac-Man bleeping across unfamiliar grids, eternally afraid of cartoon ghosts. Many hours later I accidentally stumbled into the crazy-golf hotel, giddy with elation at finally seeing something familiar, however ridiculous. Transvestites dressed as giant showgirls parading and sashaying across the tiny courtyard never seemed so welcoming. I almost collapsed into the room, only to encounter Quag Allurgie, Tour Manager and a few ladies looking like they were having some kind of tea party. It was strangely stilted and posed, with all the qualities of a Victorian sitting room.

'Wuus du fuggayu bin?' enquired Quag Allurgie, casually raising his glass and his eyebrows and looking me up and down like I was an insect.

'I think he said, "Where the fuck have you been?" Hey, I'm getting the hang of this!' piped up Tour Manager, pleased he'd understood.

A sudden racket from the courtyard behind me elicited concerned faces in the room. T-Man got up and looked past me. Quag Allurgie leaned back casually in his chair to look around me and remarked idly, 'Msssuv tunny buddle.'

I turned to see two lanky transvestites going at each other and their friends pulling them apart. Tour Manager pushed past me and announced loudly, 'LADIES! LADIES! *If indeed that is what you are. Please . . . we're trying to be civilised over here!'*

Something about Tour Manager could pour cold water on a situation sometimes, not least of which was his appearance, which itself was shocking enough to silence a room. He returned to Quag Allurgie and the mystery female guests.

Tour Manager loved prostitutes. And I mean 'loved' in every sense of the word. He'd given up on meaningful relationships with women many years ago and now focused entirely on professionals. He hung out with prostitutes and strippers and called some his friends. He wasn't sad, furtive or dirty about it all. Very much like his attitude to drugs, he was quite loud and proud. He had a blasé attitude to many extreme things that almost made them seem normal. I was pretty much the opposite and had never even met any naughty hire ladies until I started hanging out with him. I'd led a sheltered life. He was also quite wealthy in a modest way. It transpired that while I was rolling around in the gutter looking at imaginary stars, he'd called an escort agency, and now there were three small women in the room looking somehow both bored and nervous. They were clearly Latina.

'I got us some prostitutes,' he chimed cheerfully. He had this very Scottish thing of really revelling in the obvious.

'For fuck's sake, man, look at me! I've *literally* been in a ditch for a day . . .

'Doo dzz,' interjected Quag Allurgie.

'TWO DAYS?!' I repeated.

'Mn yd.'

'HE'S BEEN OUT OF HIS MIND IN A DITCH FOR TWO DAYS AND NIGHTS,' howled Tour Manager across the room. He reserved this volume and tone for anyone foreign, especially those in their own land.

'*No lo sé*,' replied one.

'Brilliant. I'm in a room with a man who needs subtitles – a man *with* a title – and no one else can speak English. I need a shower, if there's any chance of you taking your depravity elsewhere?' I whined.

'Hey! No, but listen!' T-Man got up enthusiastically. 'I know you're totally gay about women . . .'

'IT IS NOT HOMOSEXUAL TO OBJECT TO PROSTITUTION, MAN!' I wailed.

'Guhay,' mumbled Quag Allurgie, nodding sagely.

'. . . but I called these ladies to escort us chastely!' continued T-Man. 'Quag's wife is about anyway, and you're a shit wingman, so I got these in for appearances.'

'Wu shd huvvug gumma fdbull.'

'*Football?*'

'Yud.'

'Yes, Quag had this brilliant idea: we don't have to fuck them, we'll have a game of five-a-side!'

'Here? There's only three of them.'

'I can stretch to two more. If I'm going to waste some money, it may as well be a lot of money. YOU. YES, YOU! CALL YOUR SISTER.'

Apparently all this was already partially arranged. One of the girls got a phone out of her purse and moved outside to make a call.

'This is ridiculous. Where will this epic sporting event take place anyway?'

'Hrrr.'

'Right here, of course! Bed is big enough.'

'We haven't even got a ball!' I wailed, clearly losing the argument for sanity. I was still feeling the worse for wear and I wouldn't ordinarily even engage. My soul was a dive bar's brown ceiling and my brain a small half-eaten curry in an airport.

'AHHH.' Quag Allurgie looked impishly triumphant as he produced the biggest orange I had ever seen from somewhere.

'Right. Shirts and skins. We'll be shirts!' crowed His Tourmanagerness. Quag Allurgie cackled constantly. He was never happier than when the going got weird. If he was capable of liking another being, it was T-Man when he was in full flow. Tour Manager began negotiating with the girls to take their tops off, while I retreated into the bathroom to regroup. I looked in the mirror and saw a filthy maniac. I looked closer. One of my pupils looked like it was a different size to the other. I looked even closer and saw it was slightly elliptical, like a goat's.

'I THINK I MIGHT BE BROKEN!' I wailed to the next room. You know you've overdone it when your eyes are different shapes.

'Eeek,' came a small sound from behind. In my state of disrepair I'd not noticed the huge bath was full to the brim and sitting on the edge were two bewildered-looking girls who vaguely resembled the ones in the next room. How the fuck had they got in here?

'THE OTHER TWO HAVE ARRIVED,' I shouted. 'APPARENTLY THEY TELEPORTED.'

'GOOOOOOAAAAALLLLLL,' came the chorus of reply.

The next room was like a scene from a bizarre Renaissance painting. The headboard of the huge bed was acting as a goal. A short topless girl was standing on the pillows in the classic pose of a keeper, looking earnest and on guard. Tour Manager was waving his arms triumphantly in the air, while Quag Allurgie was performing minor skills with the orange and dribbling it around two other topless ladies, who, to give them and their country of origin due, were reasonably skilfully trying to tackle him. Quag Allurgie fell onto the bed dramatically.

'FOUL! OH, DIRTY, DIRTY FOUL!' howled Tour Manager.

'It wasn't a foul, he dived,' I replied instinctively. I wasn't much for sport of any kind, but T-Man had a lifetime obsession with it.

'Call yourself a referee?!' he barked. 'I will appeal. Demand a Stuart's enquiry!'

'It's a steward's enquiry, you tit!' I countered.

'See,' he indicated to Quag Allurgie. 'He's a born ref. Told you.'

'Hzz tudddly grudd ad uhd,' agreed Quag Allurgie.

'The skins should have a free kick really.' I knew I was participating almost automatically but my subconscious screamed that this was beyond ridiculous. You have to understand that when you get into this sort of state you take these things very seriously. Down the alternative way madness lies. I read once that the title of *Naked Lunch* was Burroughs referring to the moment when you actually look at what's on the end of your fork. Sometimes you really don't want to see things for what they are. You just swallow them and soldier on.

'Free kick. No, you need to go further back – your dive started here.' It was too late. I was part of it.

'Wzzzut fug!' complained Quag Allurgie.

'It was! Don't argue with the ref! What's your number?' He turned his back so I could see the imaginary number on his shirt. 'OK, take your free kick!' The girls looked at me blankly. 'Bollocks. OK, you can have it.' At this, Tour Manager excitedly leaped over and chipped the ball in the air.

Another weird aspect of Quag Allurgie was that he was deceptively agile and physical. The entire room seemed to creep through treacle as in slow motion he dipped, turned and somersaulted backwards in a move that would shame a Brazilian professional. He caught the now slightly shaggy yet still freakishly large orange in a stellar overhead kick that shot across the short distance at shocking speed, stopping only to explode in the face of the girl in goal, lifting her into the air as more girls entered the room to add to the general cacophony that seemed to follow Quag Allurgie everywhere he went.

We all rushed to her immediately. Her friend turned to Quag Allurgie, more aghast than angry, and exclaimed for the first time in perfect American English, 'Mu. Tha. Fuckah. Yo' busted her *moneymaker*!'

'Well, at least she won't need an orange at half-time,' quipped Tour Manager. 'Has she got another sister for the substitution? You'll have to add injury time, ref!'

It served to wake me a bit from the delusion. It was time to get out of here. Generally I never minded our antics as we only ever hurt ourselves, but this was a signal for me to move on. I went to find the concierge and try to get another room or a shower. It was pointless. The place was toy town and I was a giant lumbering about it looking for solutions to imagined issues. As I aimlessly crossed the tiny courtyard for the *n*th time, Quag Allurgie rolled over. Literally rolled, as he was on some sort of scooter. Being Quag Allurgie it was no ordinary scooter but a large one about the size of a small snowboard, big enough to easily hold two adults. It even had a small handbrake like a bicycle. Like a magnet, Quag Allurgie had a tendency to pick up odd objects. He didn't even have to steal them; people just gave him things. It was part of his oddly compelling personality.

'Cmun. Dnn bu zuppy. Gd un. Fff tu Dulurnu.'

This was an offer to join him visiting the Delano, an upscale hotel that was the unofficial hub of the WMC. The big dogs stayed there. Quag Allurgie promoted a highly credible club. Our industry has this thing about rock 'n' roll promoters who are far more eccentric than any of the artists. They often seem to be attached to the best clubs. People who are in permanent party mode make for good parties, unsurprisingly. I also have a theory that DJs and producers are so mind-numbingly boring and devoid of personality that the universe creates ridiculous promoters to fill the vacuum. Quag Allurgie had been at it for decades and consequently was very well connected. Not unlike our sister industry of rock music, if you're a player it doesn't matter how eccentric you are, and if you're famous you have carte blanche to do whatever you like. Quag Allurgie was a great example of this.

He was also in possession of a diamond-hard arrogance and a confidence that only the perpetually intoxicated can muster. No doors were closed to Quag Allurgie. Unless, of course, he was silly enough to move outside of our bubble.

We set off scootering across South Beach, Quag Allurgie the pilot and I his enormous pillion. His incomprehensible roaring served as a sort of siren as we weaved and crashed through the handful of pedestrians. Now and then we ended up causing havoc on the roads. As we bobbed and weaved up the wide streets in the dwindling afternoon it became quite clear to me that we were immune to convention. We were God's special mistakes, put here as a warning. It's quite a hefty privilege, I can tell you.

As we approached the Delano we could see there was a scrum at the entrance as the staff wrestled with the many shiny issues of an arriving VIP.

'Jjjjuurrunnnnammmmmer,' hollered Quag Allurgie as we ploughed forward, weaved around everyone, hopped off our board and up the couple of steps and hid behind one of the facade's huge pillars.

'War mdz uv Pd Tung, war avun gogduls un du bitch,' he slurred at me. This was our cover story. It seemed idiotic to me, and I was off my chops and still awake after forty-eight hours of accidental acid. I imagined, therefore, it wouldn't wash with security either. We didn't look like friends of any major player or as if a cocktail had even been *spilled* on us, let alone taken on the beach. Besides, we'd not brought our tuxedos.

'Fuugid!' Quag Allurgie got on the huge scooter and gestured for me to hop on. The hotel from here on in was a huge, long, smooth corridor lined with columns. Damask fluttered from its theatrical wings as we silently sped through the middle of the hubbub of the throng in its large foyer. We actually passed a flunkey with a tray of drinks. Cartoon-like, Quag Allurgie swiped a glass, downing it in one as we passed through.

'Don't throw it over your—' I blurted as he threw the empty glass over his shoulder, narrowly missing my face. The shattering crack caused every glance in the place to be fixed directly upon us like *Invasion of the Body Snatchers*. Eyes stared, mouths opened and fingers began to point as the aliens zeroed in on us, screeching that we were not one of them.

We approached the glass doors at the back of the hotel at a lick of speed. A small phalanx of aliens, staff and security were waiting for us menacingly. Quag Allurgie deftly pushed me off backwards and performed a small stunt leap as the scooter crashed into the men, our trajectory and momentum carrying us through them, the doors and down the short flight of stairs to the extensive garden and pool. The entire hotel was a paean to Roman architecture. A long corridor ran from the street to the sea. The garden stretched out like train tracks to a vanishing point, with a slim, long pool running through it. As we lurched towards it there was security left and right of the pool's leading edge.

'FUUGGIN ZWUM FF ID!' cried Quag Allurgie, as he dived into the ornamental waters. I gave up. I watched as he gamely swam at full pelt for the whole of the pool's mere twenty or thirty metres, doing his best to outpace the security on both sides gently ambling along in pursuit, rolling their eyes and looking at their watches. The world's slowest movie chase scene unfolded. I began to feel rum and uncanny.

I always feel a strange pride on being ejected from the best places, mainly because it rarely happens. It's a badge of honour to be escorted from the top holes. And at the best places they really do *escort* you. After gatecrashing and causing a scene some venues treat you better on the way out than many lesser establishments treat you on the way *in*, even though you are in fact paying them large amounts of money.

We found ourselves on the strip, in one of the bars that overlooked the ocean. A very polished but internally deceased samba band went through the motions. I say 'we' but, with alcohol added to the general mix of exhaustion and drugs, by now things were very much just *Tron* effects and the distorted faces of amphibians. Quag Allurgie was long gone, but I had no idea. The bar staff weren't serving me, so I pulled a banana from a display and pretended I was in a Latino western. I think I was at the point of trying to arrange fruit on my head like a bearded Carmen Miranda when the police crashed in. I was holding two bananas like pistols.

'FAAAACKIN' FREEZE! STOP WHAT YOU ARE DOING. PUT THE FRUIT ON THE FLOOR AND YOUR HANDS IN THE AIR!'

'Uh? But, ossifer, I assure you, they aren't even loaded!'

'You're plenty loaded, buddy,' said one as they proceeded to brutalise me. I'd never been manhandled before. It wasn't pleasant. After handcuffing me with quite ridiculous force they then sat on me as if I was a sofa.

'Is this really necessary?' I gurgled from beneath them. 'I know I'm generously upholstered but this is a bit much. I'm a foreign national, don't you know! I demand to be escorted to my embassy!'

They completely ignored me as the bar emptied, and the staff served them coffee as they waited for their colleagues to arrive and cart me away, resting up after a long day on their plump new lounger.

Chapter 8

From Ibiza to the Norfolk Broads

There's a strange and interesting anthropological element to this culture of hedonism. Narcotics, notoriety, international travel and idle time were, historically speaking, the sole preserve of the very upper echelons of the ruling classes. Indeed, even to have the antique version of an 'online beef', with imagined reputations clashing on digital parchment, was exclusive to educated people of some substance. And yet all these things are now almost par for the course for anyone who wants them. We've become a species of pampered imaginary aristocrats, if only in our heads. Nowhere is this more apparent than Ibiza.

Ibiza is the epicentre of this phenomenon, the eye of the rave hurricane. It has been for thousands of years. I'm not kidding – if you were a particularly good centurion, you could get rewarded with a furlough on Ibiza. The name Ibiza comes from I-Bes-a, the ancient Egyptian god of dance and mischief. No, it really does. I have no doubt you know everything there is to know about Ibiza, Pilgrim. It's highly unlikely you would have bought this book if you didn't, but let me do a brief outline in case your mum or dad has picked this up to check what you are up to with a torch under the bedcovers . . .

Ibiza is a glittering machine designed to separate idiots from their money. It's a tiny island, barely 24 miles long, and is vaguely almond-shaped. It's been attacked and invaded so often over history that its inhabitants are practically hard-wired to receive unwelcome guests. They merrily wave at invaders and take your money while smiling widely. It's been a refuge, a place to escape to for weirdos, freaks, outcasts, artists and convicts for so long it's practically devoid of normality in some parts. It's been a destination for the rich and famous for just as long, now more than ever. Unlike peers such as St Tropez, Key West or Monaco, in Ibiza you'll find people from every stratum of society. The poor and the young on their first adventures in life rub shoulders with elderly hippies and billionaires. (Christ, I've just realised I am old enough to remember when the word 'billionaire' didn't exist.)

The island is run by the 'disco mafia', a handful of powerful families, much like anywhere else in the world. But with so much wealth in such a small space, no criminality is needed in Ibiza. The 'mafia' simply rule through perfectly normal power and influence rather than anything sinister, much like anywhere else in the world. Indeed, despite all the whining from hippies and conspiracy nutters, roads and hospitals don't build themselves. They're built by those in power. Those cheap flights don't happen because the airlines feel sorry for you. The 'mafia' make them happen. Those bargain hotel deals? Yes, you guessed it. The fact they are often elected officials seems all the more sinister to the hippies and stoners, but again, much like anywhere else, they are merely powerful people. But people none the less, people who were born there and love it enough to make it tick.

Yes, they own all the clubs. And everything else for that

matter. Quite right too: it's their island and remains so long after we leave a horrific mess and get to go home.

🎧

Ibiza is a strange and magical place. For years I had no idea that it's beautiful, or that it's 90 per cent uninhabited. I would literally arrive about six hours before I had to leave. Entirely nocturnal. Billboards, fairground rides and English vomit is enough to put anyone off – and that was just Playa d'en Bossa. How can *anywhere* be that hot at night? It made no sense. Why anyone would go during the day was lost on me. I was from somewhere cold and dark. Heat was my enemy. Ibiza wasn't my kind of place at all.

Inevitably, Tour Manager and I arrived a day before our hotel booking and had to murder twenty-four hours. It was way cheaper to rent a car than two hotel rooms. It was still dark as we drove away from the airport car hire. Fuck it. Let's have a look around. Weird place. No tarmac anywhere. Every road like a roller coaster on the moon. No signs. No lights. Pitch black. The acid we'd taken earlier that night taking effect (I say 'we' – he probably hadn't). We were very lost. We'd been told Ibiza was small, but it was clearly large enough to fox us. The surface seemed to flatten out and we'd not seen any buildings for hours. Or maybe five minutes – it's hard to tell on acid. T-Man loved cars so he decided this was an excellent spot to do doughnuts. He proceeded to perform stunts while laughing maniacally, looking at me instead of out the windows and, frankly, putting the fear in me.

After a while we were stationary in a haze of our own making. A dust cloud of some proportion can be whipped up over time if you are especially daft in a very dry place. The haze started to glow. It felt like a scene in *Close Encounters*. It wasn't individual points of light, more a gradual build. T-Man started panicking that the lights might be the police, so I got out to investigate.

I coughed and hacked through the dust storm and immediately got lost. I couldn't see anything. I tried retracing my steps but I'd lost the car too. It felt like being inside a cloudy liquid. Underwater. Or a boiling hot snow storm. I walked forward. Then backward. To the left and right. Nothing. It was eerily silent too, the ground now rough and rocky. I felt like an idiot when I started calling out.

It might have been minutes but it felt like hours. Then streaks of clarity started to appear across the murk and through my brain. The glow was the sun, the streaks the pale-blue dawn sky. I saw the outline of the car start to emerge about two hundred metres away. The idiot was mere feet away from the edge of a cliff! We'd been screeching around out of our minds in the pitch black on an apron of land that was surrounded on all sides by a sheer drop onto rocks and salty doom.

Tour Manager was going ape-shit in the car, gesticulating madly and leaping up and down as if on fire. I know we're mainly nocturnal, but it's not like we combust when the sun comes up. Maybe he was just happy. He kept pointing and gurning like a seated man raving. I should have been able to hear the car's stereo from here, but it was silent. The idiot was just a few feet away from death. Jesus! It dawned on me, if you will excuse the pun, that if he got out quickly without looking, he might fall.

I started screaming for him to stay where he was, not to move. He seemed to be mocking me, making 'don't move' gestures every time I did. I then used sign language for him to come towards me. He began copying me. Silly arse.

We did this for about ten minutes. Or three hours. Hard to tell.

We were only a few hundred metres apart but miming through glass, so I had the bright idea of making hand gestures for him to wind the window down. I made 'wind, wind' gesticulations, and he eventually clocked it.

'DON'T FUCKING MOVE, YOU MORON. YOU ARE INCHES AWAY FROM DEATH!' we both yelled at each other simultaneously, if with slightly different phrasing. I looked round gingerly and saw that my heels were literally on the edge of another cliff. We'd spent the night, or possibly a few minutes, doing car stunts in the pitch black ... Oh, did I mention he'd turned the headlights off for a laugh too? No? Yeah, doing blind doughnuts on a peninsula of land only about two hundred metres wide, with a sheer drop on nearly every side. We'd both stopped our separate flounderings on opposite edges of it.

When the air cleared further we discovered another feature too: a load of houses and a small hotel, with about a hundred people all looking on in disbelief at the two simpletons. The worst Knight Riders in the world with the least well-equipped KITT in existence.

Quick as a flash T-Man strode towards them and did a hugely theatrical bow, and we got a light, nervous round of applause. There's no possible way anyone could do all that accidentally, is there? I mean, who could be that stupid and still manage to be alive?

♁

This wasn't long after the New York/Miami adventure. This time our usual farce upon arrival was due to us not being picked up by a major venue's people. It wasn't just any club I was going to be working at, it was in fact officially (Guinness World Records officially) the world's biggest club. For such a king-sized gig we'd need a regal amount of substances, and Tour Manager was already thinking ahead. He's not merely a person, he's cultural slapstick. He's effortlessly real. Being awesome is his stock-in-trade; organising things like a real tour manager is definitely *not*.

This included organising his own supply of the drug he took in huge amounts nearly every hour. Look at him. He's not happy. It's way too hot and he's crashing. In the car to the hotel he started to steam like a pressure cooker and was unusually silent . . . until the valve burst and he piped:

'We *have to sort out the durgs!*'

'I have literally a hundred other things to do than sort you out! A hundred things *you* are supposed to sort out, I should mention.'

'You're being demonic.'

'IT'S NOT EVIL TO WANT A LITTLE SANITY!'

'See.'

'I don't have time to do something you should have done yourself, you maniac. I don't understand how you can take a load of meth all the way to America, then not have any in the home of debauchery!'

'Quag did them all in.'

'For fuck's sake, man, you mean *you* did!' Then I had a rare brainwave. 'Then get Quag Allurgie to sort you out!'

T-Man's phone rang suddenly and he flicked it open, annoyed, listened for a few seconds and hung up without answering.

'Who was that?'

'Oh, just Chudleigh! Haven't got time to speak to him. Wait! I've had a great idea! Let's find Quag Allurgie and get him to sort it out!'

'Great jumping Jesuses, give me strength!' I muttered.

We were like some sort of addled Laurel and Hardy. I was constantly put upon and exasperated, and truth be told, a trifle pompous sometimes. He was a pure soul only slightly more hapless than I was. Together we were seismically useless. We arrived at the Es Vive hotel as usual. Quag Allurgie was sure to be there too. The Ibiza conference season inevitably follows the WMC in Miami. After asking at reception we were shown to his suite. We entered to find him clawing at the TV, with various bits of the room in disarray.

'Mm gudden du fuggen purnoh tu wg innud.'

T-Man brightened up immediately as he clocked what was in progress.

'Ah, a connoisseur in our midst!'

Quag Allurgie was merrily disconnecting the back of the TV.

'What's he doing?'

'Ah, well, you see, your *pro* traveller . . .' – T-Man waggled his muppet eyebrows at me to emphasise his point that despite travelling the world for a living, it was in fact *me* who was the amateur here – '. . . your pro traveller knows all about the old "kettle-lead free porno" trick, doesn't he?'

'What are you both on about?'

'Du kuddul lurd ugduvutz du juzz.'

'What he said. You take the power lead from the kettle, unplug the pay-TV power lead, replace it with the kettle lead and hey presto! Free jazz!'

'You learn something new every day,' I said.

'Wool. Yu dud,' said Quag Allurgie, knowingly.

'Shall we go purchase some drugs?' chirped Tour Manager, doing his best not to sound insanely desperate.

☊

Some further hotel palaver occurred until eventually we found ourselves in a taxi weaving dangerously around Ibiza's famously evil roads. I say 'roads', they say '*caminos*' – dirt tracks with razor-sharp volcanic rocks and mad canyon-like holes. Personally I love that the place isn't paved over, but sometimes you find yourself praying for tarmac.

We wound up on a tiny track with quite an alarming drop on one side. Suddenly Quag Allurgie mumbled desperately and gestured to the driver to stop. Apparently we weren't allowed to go any further. There was a furious pantomime as the three idiots were disgorged from the air-con'd bliss of the car into the blistering Ibiza heat, halfway up a serious gradient. Tour Manager immediately started to complain – he was not a hot-weather creature. Quag Allurgie in his usual supernatural way simply trudged upwards. We followed. After what seemed like forever in the baking midday furnace we came across a gate. A very substantial wooden gate. As Quag Allurgie lifted his hand to knock, it started to open of its own accord, making our aristocratic friend leap in the air in shock like a cartoon coyote. Quag Allurgie made large gestures for us to wait outside and scuttled in quick while the gate was closing, leaving us standing, slowly boiling in our own juice.

'I don't know about you, but I'm about ready to fucking die,' said a forlorn voice next to me.

The gates began to swing outwards again. We exchanged glances and saw Quag Allurgie pelting down the track, madly gesturing for us to come in. We didn't need telling twice as we gratefully staggered up through the dust to the building ahead. Like most Ibicenco architecture it was squat, white and quaint, and resembled a spaghetti western film set, probably because they were all filmed in rural Spain. Looking around there were brand-new wire fences, cameras and, hammering towards us like racehorses, two giant dogs.

'Shatan! Tanit! Schtop it!'

Their owner appeared behind them. He must have been six foot eight, if not taller. He wore flowing robes that looked a little like women's clothes and was decked out on every extremity with rings, tassels and bells. He looked like a walking minstrel or medieval jester merged with a lady wizard. He was pretty impressive in every way. Well, nearly – it sounded like his false teeth were loose.

'Sho nishe to she you my friendsh! Pleash. Come thish way.'

Ah. He was Dutch. For once Tour Manager didn't say a word. Even his notorious ability for instant xenophobia was blunted by his dire need to be replenished. We climbed up to the large veranda and entered some blessed cool air. Rather unsurprisingly the house looked half Tatooine *Star Wars* hovel, half Arabian souk. Very Ibiza. Our host performed an amazing feat of folding like origami in order to descend to the cushions and low table. Quag Allurgie joined him, and Tour Manager did his best, grunting and muttering at the uncivilised lack of Western furniture. I stood in the shadows, hovering. I've never been very bendy.

Our host was one of the Bongo People. I hate hippies so much I can't even bring myself to say the 'H' word. Besides, Ibiza has a special brand of hippy that is so ultra-horrific it needs a new title. Bongo People inevitably think Ibiza belongs to them, despite none of them being from there. They dress like impoverished tribesmen, yet manage to live on some of the most expensive pieces of real estate in the world. They claim to represent the island, yet many of them can't speak Spanish. They claim to be organic, but take, buy and sell drugs. Say they're vegan but own cats. I could go on. They put the 'hippy' in 'hypocrite'. But worst of all are the bongos, because there's nothing an idyllic paradise needs more than an endless atonal racket. An amateur racket at that. I've seen Bongo People busking.

Busking with a bongo. Please don't get me started on them 'jamming' with DJs 'cos I only have about a million words left and it just isn't enough. I'm a professional musician and when I was playing we needed MIDI clocks and anti-lag devices plugged into our heads and years of classical training just to be able to successfully play along to an electronic metronome for ten minutes.

Suffice to say, the Bongo People, who choose a bongo precisely because they think it requires no training, really aren't very good at keeping time, and keeping time is the *whole point*. But who cares! It's all about *them*, and that's why I hate them more than anyone on the planet. They claim to be about peace and love, but they're no better, and often even worse, than the people they look down upon. And they're very LOUD about it, nothing at all like us quiet, retiring DJs with our building-sized sound systems. No, sir. Sorry, just don't ever mention hippies again, OK?

Silently and surprisingly reverently, our Bongo host used his crane-like spindly arms to reach for a large sealed plastic container and handed it to Quag Allurgie as if it were a benediction. Quag Allurgie's face burst into a beaming grin. Our host nodded sagely as Quag Allurgie peeled away the plastic lid to reveal the biggest amount of MDMA crystals any of us had ever seen. Like a sacrament he passed it to Tour Manager, who, rather uncharacteristically, matched the reverence in the room and upon touching the tub instantly beamed with pleasure. I was perplexed. Was this MDMA so strong the fumes made you happy? It was passed to me. I instantly smiled broadly in recognition. The tub was as warm as a newborn. This batch had literally just come out of the lab. Each cloudy, brassy crystal cluster looked as if brown sugar existed as a jewel.

'Schpecial, no?' our host grinned. I returned the box to Quag Allurgie, who immediately put a clump in his mouth, enough to laminate a hippo for life in one dose. In a few hours you'd probably be hard pushed to tell he'd taken it. His capacity was legendarily prodigious.

'I like your dress,' said Tour Manager, in one of his disastrous attempts at diplomacy.

I quickly interjected, 'Striking outfit, yes! You must be going out somewhere special later?'

'No.'

This wasn't going well. I was getting the fear and I really needed to start thinking about work.

'*Any amphetamines?*' asked Tour Manager, perhaps a little too enthusiastically, and at a far higher pitch than could be considered conversational, or indeed aimed at anything other than dogs or bats.

'Schorry, my friend. No one likesh thish nashty drug here in Ibizsha.'

Tour Manager looked about ready to cry, while I piped up into the gap in the conversation, 'Have you got anything to smoke?' I was thinking about the hideous crash looming on the horizon already.

'Are you sherioush? Of coursh! I got nicesh Lebanese . . . make you schneeze!'

'Great. Any green?'

'Schure! But itsh a liddle fresh. You might want to dry it out a liddle to schavour the flavoursh.'

I had to get out of here. It was too weird. 'I have a great

technique for drying it out where I set fire to it and store it in my lungs,' I replied, and I started to make looking-for-the-exit faces.

T-Man had, unusually, picked up on my vibe and was violently losing a fight with himself to get up from the floor cushions. It was like watching a deckchair trying to be born. He was out of there if there was none of his personal poison to be had. Quag Allurgie was lost in a reverie, holding the hot box of MDMA like an infant. He wasn't going anywhere soon. We made our excuses and left.

'Fucking *hell*!' Tour Manager was not happy.

'I *told* you there isn't any here. It's far too cheap and nasty for the hippies.'

'Dammit!'

His phone rang again.

'Fuck off, will you, Chudleigh. I'm busy!' he barked. The signs of withdrawal were starting to show now.

'Chudleigh again, was it?'

'FUCK OFF!'

🎧

We arrived back in town, after a long and violent argument with Tour Manager of the Old Testament (my name for him when he is in withdrawal) that we needed to go to the supermarket for provisions far more than we needed to roam the back streets of the Old Town looking for gypsies to sell him high-powered stimulants. We arrived at Ibiza's biggest supermarket and, after destroying half the place with our staggering ineptitude, rolled up to the checkout with a mountain of pointless crap, only to discover Quag Allurgie's long-suffering wife patiently waiting there – something she had become very good at over years of marriage to Quag. OK, look, I admit it. This didn't happen after just leaving Quag Allurgie at the Dutch dealer's. It didn't even happen on the same day or, indeed, the same month. I'm trying to tell a story here *and* keep it fluid and funny. Stay with me, Pilgrim!

'All right, Liz, how's it going?'

Some mutual friends had also arrived and were calling to her.

'How's your Quag?' said one. The first thing anyone ever enquired about was her husband, never herself.

'Ooh, you know,' she replied vaguely.

'Is he OK?'

Something inside Liz seemed to give.

'Well, he thinks he can talk to fucking animals now.'

'Like Doctor Dolittle?'

'Doctor Does-Fuck-All more like. There's a terrace out the back of the place we're renting. Looks out over a big valley. Every night he's out there going "Ooo ahhh" like some sort of monkey. He goes, "Oooooo! Aaaaahh." And in the distance there's a quiet "Oooooo! Aaaaahh." I tried to tell him it was an echo, so he goes out and starts yodelling, "Oggy, oggy, oggy." And in the distance you hear, "Oi, oi, oi." He's telling me it's call and response and therefore he can communicate with nature. Basically he thinks he can talk to animals.'

At this point during the appreciative silence with which

Liz's tale was received a Spanish lady leaned over from the next queue.

'Excuse me, my English is bad, but did you jus' say your hoosband can talk to hanimals?'

'God, yeah, I know. Sorry, I must sound mental!'

'No, no! *My* hoosband thinks he can talk to hanimals too!'

Turns out the two idiot spouses had been bellowing at each other across the valley for the last four days.

We made our farewells. Well, I did. T-Man was, as usual, taking hours to perform the simple task of buying something. I waited. Eventually he appeared, wielding bags and surrounded on all sides by staff either trying to help him or politely make him leave – it wasn't clear 'cos it rarely is with him. He was as flustered and deranged as if he'd just tackled an assault course instead of a perfectly simple supermarket. At this point in the scene I turn to you and look pleadingly with my best Oliver Hardy face. We can't even go to the supermarket without incident.

🎧

As the sun set – something of a ritual on the island for people who think something like that is impressive – we almost managed to achieve enough normality for me to prepare for the evening. I've tried everything over the years in terms of preparation. You can frantically flap about what you will play. You can label and make lists, if you are that way inclined. Dinner with the promoter is most common. A few get high or drunk (as if there's a difference), and some lunatics even go to the gym. I switch off my phone and go to bed. I've tried all of the former methods, but when it comes to staying awake there really is no alternative other than foxing your body into thinking it has already been to bed for the night.

A few hours later I woke up, staggered around a bit, then fell out of the room and into the corridor, trying to find my imaginary tour manager. There was zero answer from hammering on his door. Where Tour Manager was concerned it was just as likely that he was dead as merely wearing headphones. Eventually I got the hotel to open it.

'FUCK OFF.'

Ah. The Old Testament sleeps. When the going gets sleepy, the pros go to work.

Tonight's gig was Manumission. The world's biggest venue, Privilege, was holding the world's biggest spectacle. Full disclosure, Pilgrim? Despite working there quite a bit I've never been a fan. With their typical bullshit fakery the UK tabloids had named it 'Public Enemy Number One', and as a consequence the 10,000-strong crowd were mainly repressed Brits thinking they were being terribly European and risqué by milling around its vastness, gawping at people cooler and prettier than they will ever be. Truly there is no such thing as bad publicity. Even totally sober it's quite a sight. Being quite a sight is what they do. Manumission has about as much to do with clubs, music and dancing as a circus has to do with large predators, comedians and athletes. I wasn't totally sober either. After weeks, months, is it years . . . the effects of *decades* of hammering my brain were taking hold. Not just my brain was suffering – the endless travel and sleeplessness were taking their toll on the rest of me too. I was feeling unpleasant more and more often. I was getting fat and weak, and my eyes looked milky and odd. My speech was affecting an odd slur that I only noticed when people seemed to stop understanding me. Which was more and more often. My hands shook a little like palsy sometimes. On the way in someone stopped me and asked me to sign a flyer. This very rarely happens, so I was happy to do so. I could see the disappointment on their face as I looked and saw my signature was a child's scrawl. It had been degrading quite dramatically over the last year, until I had to get a new bank account as it had become completely unrecognisable. I was convinced it was due to rushing things. I'm so busy, so very important.

☊

I should have been over the moon. Earlier I'd seen a low-flying plane with a banner streaming behind it with my name on. Apart from your name actually being spelled out in lights, it doesn't really get much better, so perhaps you can gather how low my ebb was from the fact that such a thing had no meaning. If you're thinking 'ungrateful bastard', then that merely means you might be correct, Pilgrim. None of this, or much of *anything*, crossed my mind as we approached the place. The world's biggest club is not all that impressive from the outside, but once you clear the vast domed foyer and look into its hangar-like interior it becomes clear. It's a sea of writhing people, not unlike how Hollywood depicts Hell. When I feel like this

I always find the crush of people too much and physically crave strong drink, at the very least. You *have* to get into what's going on somehow. I love what I do; you can't really do the job effectively if you don't. But the really big ones are not for me. They're spectacle. Event. Showbiz.

Respected DJs are queuing up to have a pop at 'push-button DJs'. Plastic DJs, I call them. The established DJs say that the EDM explosion favours spectacle and obvious playlists over skills like mixing and crate-digging. But it's not EDM or America that's to blame, it's *fear*. I'll try to explain.

Shazam–Beatport–Sync . . . Go! It sounds like something you'd shout as you emerge from a telephone box while ripping your shirt open, but it's the unconscious mantra of today's wannabe Plastic DJ. Know nothing at all or just not enough? Then point your phone and we'll tell you what the music is, find it, mix together the day's catch using sync, add some ridiculous novelty headphones and – bosh! – instant Plastic DJ. Just add drugs, cash and booze.

It's waaaay too easy to couch it in terms of tech and blame it on the sync function. A cynical person might say that it's not exactly bad for business if you're the manufacturer of said tech and everyone is twittering and yapping about your company's name. These companies don't merely profit from the reduction of the gap between professional and rank amateur, they encourage it under the guise of entry-level and 'learner' products. They're in the business of 'enabling' as many of the annoying chavalanche of nitwits as they can. The danger is not in the Fisher-Price DJ toys being made for the learner, it's the entire absence of schooling of the beginners. We were the first generation to be allowed calculators in our teen maths exams. The thinking was that maths was too hard and calculators were a tool that kept us in the game. No one ever said we were lazy and stupid, which we were. No, the fault was Casio's, for making evil handheld fun devices like the logarithmic calculator. Silly to blame the machine, isn't it? Getting angry at the sync button is like throat-punching a Teletubby for not speaking properly. No, it's much deeper and, sadly, more worrying.

If I have to endure a horrific EDM reality-show-bothering lump in the DJ booth, it's not the few seconds that constitute the crossover point of two tracks that bother me, like an awful audio Switzerland (Christ, if I see a laptop up there my expectations are already at suicide levels), it's the two hours of unmitigated endless horror either side. The mixing together of tunes is the smallest part of a larger process that is being bypassed almost completely by labour-saving devices. We should be worried about the whole process, not the moments or details.

The sense of obscene entitlement that our reality-TV-bred generation wields is truly astounding. The disease is the idea that we can all be stars and are all special. Not merely unique, mould-breaking genetic miracles, but deeply talented ones to boot. To these deluded fools the idea of just standing around doing as little as possible is not just an option, it's their God-given *right*.

It's a given that an amateur in a bar/bedroom using sync and their laptop is not only commonplace, it's inevitable. However, that's not the problem. It's kids seeing people being paid stupid money, and those overpaid icons not seeming to possess the skills you'd think were commensurate with a position of such wealth and attention – or indeed *any* overt skills at all.

We're talking about people being paid many thousands who've been caught by the omnipresent camera-phone eye with unplugged mixers, faders on zero, headphones nowhere to be seen and one finger on a laptop playing other people's music. It's not really the tech details we should argue about; tech is just the language nerds use to express more complex emotions, like anger, confusion, envy and hunger. So let's talk about the real trouble with DJing rather than just the buttons pushed.

I know when I stopped being a bad DJ: it was when I learned the value of ignorance. Ignorance isn't the enemy. Only laziness is. A lack of awe is also bad. It's all very well shopping for music in the genre *du jour* online. Being out in the world digging in crates in crusty New York second-hand shops and standing in a warehouse full of vinyl can instil a genuinely humbling sense of wonder at the stuff that has gone before, and at how little you know. You need that. To know your place in the universe it's important to be made to feel small, not to be 'in control'. There's a danger in sitting at home with everything at your fingertips, enjoying the epitome of consumerist 'choice'. Sometimes you just have to accidentally buy that dodgy Belgian new beat 1980s compilation or endure the rest of the job lot you bought from a mobile wedding DJ to see the vast scope of what it is you're involved in. Those DJs you worship didn't get there overnight via nicking other people's sets and copying them. They are the sum total of decades of being fully involved.

There's nothing more irritating to a young fool than explaining to them slowly the process of dues paid . . . 'So fuck off, Grandad, and Shazam it!' Not only does Shazam take all the intelligence and invaluable research out of the process, it really is quite spectacularly dangerous because a thicko might pull out their phone not merely to find a record they like the sound of, but because of a cheer or indeed just at random, in effect sourcing a track for its effect in that moment, with no musical or brain processes involved at all. When you Shazam something, in those seconds you are truly losing out. Every time you do it you literally pour lost knowledge out of your head onto the ground in a sad wee think-puddle. Again, like sync, it's a tool, and a tool in the hands of a master makes beauty and truth. When you rely on a tool without thinking, the hand that wields it is just a hand. How can you possibly love and grow with anything if you avoid all contact with it? You can't become a DJ by plucking tunes out of the air, like naming a Womble. Indeed, you can't really do justice to the music if it comes too easy. Being a DJ is about being an *authority*, which comes through contact and immersion, not mental tourism. In a nutshell, in this information age the true hazard is that information gets confused with knowledge. Just 'cos you have something doesn't mean you *own* it. It's no surprise at all that in the age of the liar and the professional amateur, with our leaders winging it and making everything up as they go along, so do our entertainers.

Spectacle has replaced music as the most important thing in a DJ's performance. When confronted with the accusation that he'd used a pre-mixed CD *sans* headphones at a major gig, Steve Angello happily confessed. Not only to being guilty, but that it was necessary as part of his incredibly complex job of playing someone else's record at the right moment to go with some bangers and glitter.

Later he compounded this by claiming you don't need headphones to mix anyway. 'Yeah, right,' groaned a planet. It's nothing new. A decade ago at Fabric I saw one of clubland's most revered figures getting caught red-handed by the owner, leaping, gurning and fist-pumping like a chimp while frantically twisting at the mixer like he was delivering a difficult robot baby with two jelly spanners. Unfortunately the actual channels being throttled were not, in fact, in use – a mix CD was merrily working away. Is there any excuse at all for cheaters? Are we talking about the spectacle overtaking the craft? Certainly, more than ever, people describe going to *see* a DJ. They have *seen* their spinner of choice, not *heard*.

Fear is at the centre of it all. For sure, there's always, *always* fear at the upper levels of anything. No one does live mixes, radio scares DJs to death, and some at the top have people that do everything from mixing to selecting to even buying their tunes for them. The latter are petrified of losing. Fear kills everything it touches. The conservative impulse is to preserve your hard-earned, to live in a constant state of mild fear that you will diminish. Fear makes good, rational people do crazy things, and even crazier things to justify the first part. They're stuck forever in a loop of lunacy. The spectacle and the showbiz have overtaken everything, even notions of honesty. *Everywhere.*

French philosopher Guy Debord described this in the 1950s in his ace manifesto and accidental instruction manual for current politicians, *The Society of the Spectacle*. In it he spoke of a day when nothing at all would matter; only impressions were important. If you like: the gig is meaningless compared to the press review of it. He also predicted that the art of the future will be to overthrow all previous art or nothing. So who cares what we have, as long as it's not the last load of old rubbish! It really doesn't matter if the mixer isn't plugged in, as long as everyone is talking about it. It doesn't matter if you can't DJ, as long as thousands are stood *watching* and none are listening or dancing. Indeed, this is the crux of the argument for modern art. If I sign this book and you pay me a million for it, then it becomes a work of art worth a million, because a million of our currency has said so.

In essence the final triumph of the professional amateur is to replace skill and knowledge with spectacle and showbiz. Why worry too much about labour-saving devices making us pointless and stupid when the real problem is that everyone is convinced they're a genius with a never-before-thunk-of get-rich-quick scheme? This begs the question, what is the difference between a shiny outstanding amateur talent and a shit-awful professional? Sport is a handy analogy. Tell me the difference between a terrible professional and a truly gifted amateur? What's the answer? Is it showbiz? Maybe it's just biz.

Yes, of course there's always a punkier, looser attitude among the Young Turks turning up late on any scene. It's healthy to burst bubbles and prick egos. However, there's a fine line between being fresh and irreverent and just being lazy. You know where the pearl in the turd is in all this? The fact that you, dear reader, will ultimately decide.

Imagine a world where everyone has got the bug out of their system thanks to early exposure. Imagine a crowd that truly respects the professional because they themselves have tried and failed or seen one too many awful laptop sync-ers and found them wanting. We know rubbish when we see it. When you stop and listen even more is revealed. Strain your ears, not your eyes, and you'll hear the small mixing imperfections that show a DJ isn't cheating. You'll hear the very real difference between an MP3 and vinyl, and your ears will thank you for evermore when you treat them to something proper rather than the tossed-off amateurism of the Plastic DJ cheaters.

I have hope because I've also been writing for a long time, and writers were the first against the wall when the internet came along. After something like fifteen years of an ocean of amateur words in an aquatic planet of damp nonsense, businesses are once again actually paying people who can really write. We've seen the alternative – a world of professional amateurs winging it – and it isn't pretty. If the written word can recover from the internet, so can music. So can politics. People will pay for quality. They will demand truth. Trust me.

Perhaps the last word should go to the man who invented house music, God rest his soul. Frankie Knuckles may have been responding to a spoof piece, but his words still carry weight:

> I've spent forty years at this craft of DJing. Every time I step up to play, to this day I'm scared beyond imagination. But I never let it get to the stage where I perpetrate a fraud on the public . . . Not every mix is perfect. Nothing in life is perfect.

I'll take real over perfect any time, Frankie. Yes, sir.

🎧

Have I wandered too far off-piste? I say all this because I was standing in the biggest venue in the world, possibly the place where EDM started, Ground Zero for spectacle. I was working there that night, but I like the small venues. Always have. It's *really* not false modesty. I mean, come on, Pilgrim! Have I even been *remotely* modest so far? But the big ones are tiring. Maybe I'm suffering from exhaustion – it's hard to tell. My entire generation is a medical test case, an entire stratum of humanity for whom drugs and flexitime are the norm and staying awake for three or four days solid is a weekly rather than once-in-a-lifetime experience. Who knows what will become of us?

There's a kind of vibe and tempo to a proper club that's absent in these mega-discos. People aren't really engaged and dancing here, they're more shuffling about and mooning at things. Consequently it's hellish to try and get past them with a purpose. Usually I go in the artist's entrance, but on this occasion my driver was leading me through the front for some reason. Dancers at least leave space when they move around, whether they mean to or not. A packed, gawping throng is almost stationary. As we pushed and heaved through Dante's second level we heard odd snippets of peculiar conversations left and right.

'Man who can fellate himself . . .'

'Dwarves!'

'Tits . . .'

'Elvis . . .'

'Topless trapeze . . .'

It was all very standard for Manumission. The music was definitely not important. If anything, it was a form of audio smoke, an effect designed to enhance the night rather than the reason for being there itself. The entire extravaganza was centred on what the organisers called 'The Show'. Manumission had a new theme every year that was utterly pretentious, totally lost on everyone, including those performing it, and, worst of all, usually quite cheaply and quickly put together. There was one constant, however, which also made it hard to see any difference each year: lots of naked girls. True, sometimes there were naked men, although it often seemed a little cursory. I never said much about it to anyone, but it made me feel quite uncomfortable.

Meaningless spectacle given enforced meaning is more puerile than anything, to my mind. The gigantic attempt at 'sexy' ends up feeling slightly strained, like the air before a riot. A few performers with genuine talent lost amid the vast nothing. My thoughts equally adrift in the yawning sarchasm. My vision blurs too. Something about the sensory overload in these places leads to a kind of shutdown.

In Ibiza, sex sells, but what if you aren't buying? The legendary Manumission girls would parade around proudly, and yet I felt sorry for every one of them. In there, of course, it was *your* problem. Clearly you're repressed and incorrect. I worry that I may have been chemically sterilised by my lifestyle.

I really needed a drink. Whatever was still sloshing around in me in terms of intoxicants badly needed topping up. I feared very much that there may have been some blood in my system's alcohol.

The venue was so vast it had its own microclimate. Mists would form and droplets would stream down glass. Some walls would actually pour. You passed through a shop, then an indoor forest. Bypassing the colossal main room we made for the relative shelter and genuine good vibes of the side room. We passed a few friends and faces in there and stumbled through to the largest of the two side rooms. Even the back room here was bigger than most venues. Some large events are run with military precision; indeed, many are better run than smaller ones. Because they have to be. Not Manumission, however. You had to look after number one in there. Despite 'manumission' deriving from the Latin for 'freedom from slavery', everyone there worked hard for a couple of millionaires – a very common theme in Ibiza.

However, in Manumission even the DJs were paid fairly poorly, which is unusual in this business. Ironically, this usually happens with either the very biggest events or the very coolest, but always with the ones that are big *and* cool. The cooler Ibiza brands tend to think they're doing you a favour by booking you and that all the money should go to them, and in some ways they're right. It's caught on these days, working for 'exposure'.

I weaved through the almost stationary mass of people to try and squeeze a couple of free-drinks tokens. If you find all this a bit silly, don't worry, that's only because you are correct. When you're used to everything being on tap you genuinely do forget to do things like take lots of money out with you when going to work. Usually everything you need is right there, but here it was a different story. Or maybe I was having a meltdown. Bit of both perhaps. I gave up and went to the bar and paid more than what I would usually spend in a week for an armful of drinks. Ibiza is *fucking* expensive. I stood there and purposefully drained them all. I was approaching something like normality now, surrounded by heavily inebriated strangers on all sides, oppressed by the volume, as if I were deep underwater, and swaying slightly as the booze started to get busy. It's a weird sort of job where you have to do this just to get involved. A surgeon dons gowns and scrubs up. We dress down and get high.

Don't get me wrong. There are plenty of DJs who operate completely sober. True, they tend to iron their socks and be dreadful human beings, but it does happen. Most of us have a few drinks and perhaps a small dose of something to lift the energy. It's not merely an excuse or 'cos it might actually be fun. When you're at a certain level you're constantly travelling and on the verge of collapse. The performance-enhancing substances aren't to win the race; they're just to achieve a semblance of normality. You have to understand that I'm laying it on thick in this book to entertain you, but most of the time there are no wacky sidekicks, it's just toil. Solo toil.

After a few years of it you can get very isolated, and walking into a party every night starts to feel weird. So you get weird too. You're often two, even *three* times older than most people in the room, people who are having fun, perhaps for the first time ever, with an enthusiasm and energy to match. You've arrived straight from an airport, usually alone, having just done the whole thing somewhere else. And somewhere else before that. And somewhere else before that. You're arriving to compete effectively on an energy level with people who are literally experiencing the highlight of their lives. Being in the VIP section of the biggest club in the world is literally the best thing that has ever happened to them. Or ever will.

I mean, look at her over there. She really seems so very normal. She's looking about furtively 'cos she knows she isn't supposed to be in there. She's slightly intimidated. For all she knows all these frankly amazing-looking people could be *famous*. She's playing it cool. She really hopes that man sidling up to her is famous and not horrible. She feels a bit like it's a dream. She'll tell this story to anyone who'll listen for the rest of her life.

She's overwhelmed, excited, *alive* – the opposite of my disease. Hoping that what I do makes people happy is the only thing that keeps me sane. *She* is the only thing keeping me sane. Christ, I hope it really is the best time of her life and not a few moments away from something hideous. I really need some drugs.

I will spare you the rest, plucky Pilgrim. I played a few records and some people danced. I endured it rather than enjoyed it, and that's about as much as you can hope for by this point in your career. The hours flew by, and as usual I was so hyper and augmented by the nervous energy of being alone in front of so many people that I barely noticed the prodigious amounts of drink and drugs I'd put away, and as usual as soon as I stopped it all hit me like a hammer. One of those big two-handed sledgehammers. A steel fist forged out of forced fun and desperation.

A door opened somewhere and it was blazing daylight. How that happens every morning I do not know. It hits you physically like rocks. You're a living souvenir of the previous night, so people see you as a totem to hang on to. In the vast sloping car park they all wanted to know where I was going. Small parties had started around cars with their sound systems on. I call this point 'the vortex'. It's a bit like the water rushing around a plug, a whirlpool or the nimbus of doomed light around a black hole, everyone milling around looking for the best bet. Some with no patience will split off immediately and sit around a radio in a tiny kitchen with six other people, sharing one wrap of drugs for the next eight hours. Many tend to shoot off to get a shower, change and, refreshed, look for the next party. Some experts even get some sleep. Not the DJ, though. Everyone is looking to us for direction. Fuck knows why – most of the time we don't even come from that country, never mind that town. Often a smart party-planner is ready to scoop you up for a relatively well-put-together afterparty. Mostly the organisers smell money and don't want anyone else capitalising on it, so they have their own official events. In the case of Manumission, this meant Space.

Space was one of the world's most prestigious clubs, while Manumission was so vast that its afterparty was bigger than the main event of most clubs. Did I mention it was a Monday night and now it's Tuesday morning? Yeah, Monday is the biggest night of the week in Ibiza. And you wonder why I'm fucked up. I was bundled in a car carrying about eight other people, like sausage Jenga in a can, and probably driven by a teen drug addict who could see out of only one eye. I have done things like this so often it chills the blood.

A note on being intoxicated on the job. A new stratum of DJs has emerged of former professionals who faded into the obscurity of real life some time ago, then decided, aged forty-five, that they're now DJs again. Many of them emerged from the shadows of the sidelines of the industry. They have deified the DJ process, fetishised the equipment – and vinyl, of course. *Always* with the vinyl, these boys. Yeah, always male, naturally. So in order to make themselves superior to professional DJs, they've issued rules. A DJ who uses the wrong format is not 'correct'. If you're drunk, you're not *professional*. You can imagine the rest. Of course, none of them do it for a living, travel daily to do it or lose sleep over it.

They are fanboys, no different to the nerds who obsess over science fiction. Every one of them would piss his expensive imported Japanese denims and cry for his mummy if he spent one week on the road with a pro (that's not hyperbole by the way; it happened once). Quag Allurgie does more drugs in a weekend than they'll ever do in their entire lives. No, I mean *really* – I've counted his average intake. One dose of what Tour Manager takes hourly would kill them. I'm not being artistic with words – I mean that if they had a weak heart, they would *die*. So tell me *all* about how heavy the things I carry round the world should be, talk to me *all night* about how to do my job, write little notes about what constitutes making people happy and post them to me so I can read them while I do something you only observe from a ridiculous remove. These are the same men who obsess for hours over professional sportsmen running around and then sit on their fat behinds and loudly criticise what the pros did and what they should do in the future. Family guys, men with good jobs and a steady income. Good citizens. Civilians. They're reading this right now harrumphing because I'm not describing the 'correct' venues and I'm not being reverent enough. Because despite never having done it, they think they know better than me. I guarantee it. Sounds bitter? Try dealing with the fuckers at the centre of one of their online circle-jerks, then talk to me about being nice.

Anyway, en route to the afterparty the Guardia Civil pulled us over just outside Space. I know some Spanish, so it was hilarious to hear them argue with each other that they had seen someone stuff the drugs in a novelty Afro wig they were busy tearing apart, while I was palming the gear in my hand the whole time. Yes, they don't just have observation posts but also plain clothes officers driving around in tall SUVs to look into your car full of idiots. They're not men to be fucked with, but then again, I've been doing this all my life. The guy who made the call was getting a verbal kicking from his boss as they let us pass on into the car park. We were lucky this time, and not just with the police. In a couple of years some brainiac conservative politician would decide that tackling the problem of hundreds of thousands of people from all over the world bringing money to the island needed addressing. So one genius move was to close all the humongous clubs at exactly the same time and pour every one of the idiots into their hire cars at exactly the same moment all over the island and loose them on the roads, at exactly the same time as all the local citizens were going to work and taking their kids to school. It didn't go well. You were lucky to arrive at an afterparty alive that year. If you're reading this and wondering at our stupidity, believe me when I say it's matched only by those who claim to be our leaders.

7 a.m. Time for the next shift. I say 'shift', but they didn't pay us! One of the longest, best-kept secrets in the industry is that 99.9 per cent of DJs will do it for nothing. Since working that one out the biz has been in freefall, mainly due to the thousands of new DJs working for free. People had already formed a queue outside the venue; some had probably been there since 6 a.m. As well as shambling monsters from last night there were party pros who'd just woken up. Ibiza is the global hub of what we do and there are people who will get up, go see their friends in a club, have a bit of a dance and then go to work, totally sober all the while. Insane, isn't it?

It is entirely possible to live *completely* in the dance music bubble. You have dancing friends, and *only* dancing friends, who you meet in dance halls that you choose from your dance magazines, while wearing the dance fashions you bought from the dance shop, with the whole thing soundtracked by your favourite dance music, and you probably dance all the way through the entire procedure. And you wonder why we worship DJs? No church is this immersive, no day of worship so fervently celebrated as ours.

You enter the hallowed booth of the Space Terrace and meet some DJs you've never seen before in your life, as Manumission is so large and apparently unconcerned about its DJs it can have as many as ten, twelve or even fifteen playing on any given night. They aren't billed or named anywhere, so who is 'working' at the afterparty is a lottery. An endurance contest too.

Some of the DJ fanboys reading this will be sneering so hard they look like stroke victims. While certain things are, unfortunately, measured in terms of money and power, many more are measured in 'credibility' (the inverted commas signify my disdain there, in case that wasn't clear). It's a very modern thing to immediately assume the polar extremes of everything we engage with. In a complex modern world we oversimplify everything. We have to, or else we'd go mad. We wear silly beards and workwear because we wish the world was simpler and more 'authentic'. We obsess over the past. Most of all we dismiss, polarise and generalise – 'You like this, therefore you like everything similar to it,' etc. Ergo some DJs reading this will be thinking, 'Aha! I'm better than him because he's playing at large events with little credibility.' Son, you don't get to work with the big dogs unless you've already done a minimum of ten years at the coalface of cool. More like twenty, if we're being serious. True, some DJs seem to suddenly appear out of nowhere, and many 'producers' are being crowned as DJs after barely a few months on the job, but for the purposes of the narrative we're going big. It just so happens it was these clubs at this point in time. You'll have to trust me when I say that I've played everywhere. Believe me, if we did the cool journey you'd be comatose with boredom by now, and more importantly so would I. This ain't no history textbook about vinyl and who did what when. But if it makes you feel better to think you know more, please, be my guest. Who knows, maybe you do and you will write an awesome book one day.

Stop interrupting me anyway. Where was I? Yeah, I was out of my mind, through the night and into the next day. Playing records again. This time in the sun, which, very much like eating, is *so* much better outdoors. I had finished work now, and in order to avoid the inevitable crash I was looking for more substances to stave it off. Thank fuck Bobbie Baluga arrived.

'Aaaaaayyyyyyyyy! Ayiyiyiyiyiyiyiyiyi!' Either some Middle Eastern woman was mourning the dead or Bobbie was making his entrance. Perennially sober and inappropriately fresh as only Americans can be in the middle of Ibiza, he was my saviour. As usual he had an entourage. In Ibiza, usually Italian boys.

'Oh baby, where you *been* all my life?! Don' yo *worry*, mamma's here!'

At this time of the morning there was still enough room to breathe on the famous Terrace. Bobbie came strutting over, while one of the Italians trailed after him shouting disconcertedly, 'Oh Baahbie, Baahbie! Don' tell me you are a-gay!' One of his entourage was wrestling with the fact that one of the world's biggest exponents of an art form invented by gay men, for gay men, was in fact a confirmed homosexual. He was visibly distressed.

'All day and all night, baby!' replied Bobbie.

Bobbie was a force of nature and just being around him was a shot in the arm. People started to notice us as we milled around on the edge of the legendary dance floor, gradually accumulating a small crowd. The inevitable gang of party pros were forming ranks for more, while the amateurs went home.

While we were doing the old 'where next?' shuffle, I was discussing our recent trip to New York and Miami with a stranger, when a random American guy in the group started loudly claiming I was full of shit, as he knew Bobbie 'personally' and he didn't know me.

'You mean *this* Bobbie?' I replied, stepping to one side to reveal with a magician's flourish Bobbie, slightly hidden among his circle of Italians.

'!' replied the random angry American.

'It's OK, dude. My life is pretty unbelievable. Get it all the time.'

'Sure, my apologies, man. Here, you should try some of this . . .' He was dosing out a measure of powder on the back of his hand. It looked like every other slightly off-white powder my face had met and I dutifully sniffed it without question, as I pretty much always did.

Yeah, that turned out to be what they call A Bad Idea. To this day I have no idea what it was, but the effects were more akin to a large dose of jellies. If you know your drugs, and a pro *really* should, you'll know all about the benzodiazepine family. Their effect is similar to ketamine: fairly calming and floaty if a small amount, absolutely zombie if large. All I knew was I was walking and talking and things were happening, but I was simply not there. It's scary because there are pictures and stories told of our exploits that day but . . . nope, no idea! There's a photo of me and Bobbie semi-buried on the beach, in novelty masks and asking passers-by if they will help dig us poor people out of the sand.

There's pictures of the gang dancing on the same tables that innocent holidaymakers are trying to have lunch off in their very poorly chosen venue of a beach club full of ravers. If this was a film, there would now be a montage of stills of ascending idiocy.

All I can be sure of is this: I was experiencing an entirely new drug. The American guy was pissed off and had spiked me. Or maybe he genuinely thought he was doing me a solid. Who knows? I remember I was the King of Everything. And also that there was a fight. Fights never happen in Ibiza, but a random had said something homophobic about one of our gay friends, and I didn't like it. I seem to remember taking off my beloved Paradise Garage T-shirt for the fight and Bobbie being genuinely offended that it was found in the dirt.

I'm not a reliable witness for much of this bit but I do

know one thing: I can't have been great company because eventually I found myself alone and barely able to walk in a straight line. I also had two huge flight cases full of records and two large bags. If only I'd employed an adult to help with the bags and transport thing. Oh, right, I already had. I wasn't entirely sure where he was, or indeed where I was either.

I went out onto the road and started to try and flag down a cab. There seemed to be plenty. For some reason none of them would stop. Maybe it was because I was semi-naked and covered in blood and my eyes were swivelling independently – I can't say for sure. I had a flash of idiot logic and used the four large items of luggage to form a sort of jury-rigged road block. Eventually, after many cars had swerved around and honked, a cab pulled up and the driver wound his window down, looked me up and down and simply said, 'Hospital?'

'Manumission Motel,' I answered.

'Ahhhhh . . .' he replied, nodding sagely. Suddenly it all made sense to him.

Manumission had rather cannily converted a fairly grim roadside brothel into a 'motel', which meant no hotel bills for its millionaire owners. I didn't care, I needed sanctuary, and even a tacky waterbed with a zebra theme was better than a boiling-hot piece of roadside. I felt very wobbly, even though I considered myself something of a machine at this point. I was youngish, physically very strong and pretty macho. To this day I can probably drink you under the table; back then I would actually have wanted to. However, despite this capacity, I was definitely at a crossroads here.

I'd never felt so out of my mind before. There was no room service or water and the 'motel' was actually on a small traffic island. Besides, there was no way I was leaving this room now, so I decided a shower was best. My internal thermostat had gone. I had no idea if I was hot or cold, but everywhere I stood I left a puddle of sweat.

Shower.

Dreams of insects on face. Endless insects crawling.

I woke up with the shower at full blast on my face. That explained the insects. I was collapsed face up on the cubicle floor and resembled a wrinkled pink starfish. Nothing was funny any more. I looked at the bedside clock. I'd been in there for nearly eighteen hours. I'd become death, destroyer of worlds.

I dragged my carcass across the island to try and find His Tourmanagerness, eventually finding myself in exactly the same place where I'd left him some days ago. My phone rang.

'Hello! It's Chudleigh here! I've been looking for T-Man, but he won't answer!'

'Hiya, Chud. Yeah, I remember you called him, but you know what he's like. He was looking for whizz.'

'Yeah, that's the thing. You see, I was given some and I don't know anyone who takes it, and I heard he was here so . . .'

'Meet me at his room in thirty minutes. Texting you the details . . .'

Chudleigh was very smartly on a scooter, cutting through the insane Ibiza traffic far faster than me, so by the time I arrived he was already there.

Tour Manager looked like a corpse at the best of times. Liz's nickname for him was the Transparent Man: as he approached her on the beach back in Miami with the setting sun behind him she swore blind she could see through him he was so white. With a strong backlight he looked like a walking cardiovascular system, and several days of motionless stewing in his personal comedown juice hadn't helped the overall look. On top of that, he was the easiest target for mosquitoes ever conceived, so he was covered in vivid red blotches, adding to the overall 'Thriller' zombie effect. On the plus side, he was stood upright.

'I've been eaten alive,' he said in a tiny voice.

'Literally the only time in your existence anything with a pulse would consider your flesh a tasty dish. I'd consider it a compliment,' I countered. 'Have you done nothing but have a hideous comedown this entire visit?'

'Well . . . Quag Allurgie came here and mumbled at me for ages about me taking his promotion into my club.'

'Hope you didn't sign anything!' I joked. 'Anyway, at least you have your medicine now.'

'He did it all in one go!' said Chudleigh, perpetually amused by life and cheerful as a cherub. Tour Manager went to attempt a shower.

'I can't help but enjoy the irony really, Chud. You were literally the only person on the whole island with the drug he wanted, and from the moment we arrived you were trying to give him some for free. He was so withdrawn he wouldn't even answer the phone properly to someone genuinely trying to help him.'

'He never answers the phone anyway.'

211

'True, but I'm enjoying this far more than I should . . .'

'RIGHT!' a steaming apparition bellowed from the bathroom door, looking very much like someone had blow-dried a poodle and gene-spliced it with a dandelion. 'Where are we going out? I feel great and I look *amazing*!'

'Going *out*? You're leaving, mate. Your flight back is in about two hours.'

'FUCKSTICKS!'

Chapter 9

Festival of Shit

Festivals. Urgh. At one of the worst ones a plucky sewage truck was dispatched to try and suck out the excess water from the soggy and newly enlarged dance tent. It was a deeply Christian idea that might have worked if someone hadn't flicked the switch to blow. In a matter of moments a quivering bunch of weedy children were coated in raw sewage, suffering the festival full house: acute *shit-shock*. Was this biblical brown shower upon the dance tent God's judgement on our festival scene? I think theologians should be telling us straight. If God wants to bum flush the show, then us mere mortals should be warned. It's not like he has no history of smiting; it totally fits his modus operandi of Old Testament ferocity, back when the God of Love hadn't been invented and we still had the Right-Wing God of Austerity: pillars of salt, plagues, locusts, dead first-born children . . . right through to today's whirling heathen dervishes showered in cold shit. Even if you don't believe in Him, you *have* to admire His work.

At the risk of taking the scatological route well-trodden, when you stop to think about it, it really is all about poo. Festivals always have at least one new generation of pampered twits experiencing actual human faeces for the first time in their mewling existence. We've become so divorced from our animal selves and so dainty we experience defecation as some sort of abstract concept that only ever happens to other people. Naughty, evil, smelly people. Or bad dogs: 'Oooh! Pick that shit up, *bad dog*!' We're absolutely petrified of it despite it firing out of our fun holes twice a day, all of our lives. Yet take us out of our sterile homes and plonk us into a field and it's like the potty years never happened. It's youngsters that are the worst; obviously they've only recently come out of nappies. It doesn't help that some of them are so simple they have to shout constantly to know which end to shit out of. Every year we're treated to random human pyramids of festival virgins puking up their own ring-pieces and then spitting these brown hula hoops at the nearest innocent grazing animal (and at a festival there are thousands of them, if not entirely innocent). A veritable sea of children who can barely read trying to erect tents is like chucking a technical Lego set into a box of cats, except the cats don't think they're all TOTALLY AWESOME, YEAH? and look BARE WICKED. Actually, maybe they do, now I think about it.

Watching any festival transaction is like buying a continent off some primitive natives with beads, bangles and buns. Suddenly Jack coming home with some magic beans in exchange for the family cow doesn't seem like an unbelievable fairy tale. No wonder Jack's imaginary mum went spare. Rather than thinking for ten minutes in advance and bringing outdoor essentials, festivals are riddled with people paying £10 for something that's 10p in real life. I once knew a girl who went to a festival with a bikini and wet wipes and nothing else. Not kidding. Mind you, she had her bearded walking wallet with her.

Girls are a different species, though, especially at a festival. Where else can you be mid-conversation with one of the opposite and fairer sex, only for them to suddenly squat, shit and puke like very bad garden gnomes, their arse spraying mayhem all over the shop, before they stand and carry on as normal?

And it's understandable, all this badness. Being bereft of walls and ceilings to tell them which way to point themselves, people get disorientated. It properly freaks them out. It's existential. On a deep level they *know* that we're the dominant species on this planet. That dominance came about over 10,000 years – spent mainly on the Earth's surface, though, not in rooms. We've totally lost that command of our external environment, to the point where we don't even know how to shit any more, as confused as some lonely and deranged zoo exhibit gnawing its own paws off. The reaction to this deep and profound species-shame is clearly seen at a festival at night, with lost children shuffling on their own in a lonely dark corner, fist-pumping to nothing and trout-pouting to themselves like a mad badger waiting for the cull.

The only relief is to helicopter in huge-toothed, overpaid American EDM DJ shit-plinths to aurally smash us into oblivion. *Thank you for the pain!* Sweet welding-volume ear pain to obliterate all sense of nature, the music going *donkdonkdonkdonk* at me forever to remind me how civilised I am. See, EDM DJs do have a point: they're the world's most minimalist philosophers. Mind you, even they don't do the outdoors well, 'cos I mean nothing aids the ancient art of stagecraft like wellies, a thin crust of shite and

215

a look of defeat previously only seen on German infantry walking the 1,377 winter miles back from Stalingrad.

So, good luck, plucky campers! Welcome to the outdoors you ran so hurriedly indoors from just after the last Ice Age. I have to go now, I'm off indoors. I may be some time.

Festivals. So much fun the first two hundred times. My favourite was an unnamed festival that was fairly new and, let's be frank here, deep house in every way. I'm not against it. I play deep house as well as deep house. I like both. I like being paid and I like seeing young people enjoy what I do. (I'm just setting the scene.) With me was a 'House Legend'. It was a good day for me because for once I wasn't the oldest person in a ten-mile radius. It was him. He'd never done a large festival before. He called me beforehand and asked me what he should wear. I told him to expect knee-high mud. When he laughed, I had to explain that I wasn't kidding. He talked about the good weather report, and I had to patiently explain that hundreds of thousands of people, like cattle, can churn up fairly dry ground into a morass in a matter of hours, indeed in minutes if there's a bit of rain.

It rained. He arrived in the best outfit ever: almost dayglo bright preppy golf wear ('It's outdoors, innit!'), a pair of bright-pink, box fresh Hunter wellies and a see-through cape over it all. He basically looked like a middle-aged mum on a day out at the races, the epitome of someone who literally never left the city. I loved watching his face as it pulled disgusted look after Victorian stage shock after cringing terror at what unfolded before him.

As we got deeper into it (in both senses of the word), the ground became treacle, then soup, then liquid, while he turned into a sort of overdressed Bambi, his legs shooting out in different directions as he flailed to stay upright.

We weren't getting very far, so I turned and asked him, 'Listen, don't take this the wrong way, but do you want me to carry you?'

For as long as I live I'll never forget the look on his face. Then, in a tiny voice, he replied, 'OK.'

As we got towards the centre of the whole quagmire, he went, 'Stop! Stop! Put me down. Listen . . . listen . . .'

'Listen to what?' I asked.

'I can hear the same record coming out of two different arenas. Do you think if we wait here long enough they will beat-match?'

'Mate, in a festival like this, if we wait long enough we'll hear it coming out of every system all at once, like when you wait for a room full of pendulums or metronomes to eventually all sync up. I call it "terminal knob velocity".'

'Are those children over there *shuffling*?!' he exclaimed. Shuffling was a new dance craze.

They were. Again, I've nothing against it. I'm 100 per cent in favour of people dancing to dance music. But it did seem odd trying to do it knee-deep in beastly ooomsch. Like one of those toffee-pulling machines or a fairground candyfloss maker, their little legs were straining against the brown doom, while a slight foam formed in a circle around them. It's hard enough to shuffle on a shiny, waxed dance floor. Why they were attempting it semi-submerged was beyond us.

Festivals are the polar opposite of nightclubs. I get that people think, 'Ooh, loud music, wang it in a field,'

217

but I just think clubs should be clubs and raves should be raves, but festivals should just be special things where we keep the middle classes under observation. You know, the kind where girls waft about wearing ill-advised bindis and Native American headdresses, and every other converted van sells beards-in-a-bun, while forty-five-year-old men who work in an office all year become DJs for a day, thousands of them all at once. But this wasn't one of those festivals at all. This was more like the ones where kids destroy everything like a plague of locusts and everything smells of burnt plastic, as people who barely qualify for the sapient part of the species attempt fire for the first and last time, failing miserably with the simplest and most basic technology known to us humans, then leave everything they brought with them scattered everywhere for someone else to deal with.

Suddenly we weren't the oldest people there. My mum and dad had arrived. Neither of them had ever seen what I do. They were vaguely proud of me 'cos they'd seen me on the telly once. Job done. But they had no contact at all with my world, which was best for all concerned. There was no getting away from it here, though, as the festival was about five miles from their house. They'd spent all week in the village very proudly pointing my name out on posters to the locals. My mum was recovering from an illness, about twice as old as House Legend, and had a pot on her recently injured leg. She steamed past us straight to the bar, while I held House Legend in my arms like a baby. She is from the countryside, though.

Next time I saw her I was working on the stage and

she was at the front among all the kids, shouting random epithets like, 'That's my son! He's a DJ!' and 'I've got a pot on, you know?' to kids of about nineteen. My dad, meanwhile, was stood next to me on the stage, the grand onion in the custard. Every now and then I'd look over to him and give him an enquiring thumbs aloft, and he'd reply by taking his fingers out of his ears as fast as a gunslinger to reply with his thumbs up, before whipping them back in his listening holes as fast as I've ever seen him move.

I was performing in front of thousands, my mum moshing at the front, my dad stood next to me on stage with his fingers in his ears, while House Legend was pissing himself laughing at me for the next two hours, in front of everyone. It was nearly as bad as the time I was playing on the Space Terrace in the morning while the resident DJ, having just woken up, stood inches away waiting for me to finish, yawning massively, eating an egg sandwich and reading the *Sun*. Maybe this look was worse. Hard to say.

When we finally got far enough away from the noise for my dad to be able to hear anything, House Legend asked him what he thought of it all, being new to it and all that.

My dad thought hard for a while before he spoke, something no one does any more.

'Well . . . it's a bit like World War I, isn't it?'

'World War I?'

'Yes, lots of noise, petrified underage kids covered in mud that all need sending home and . . .'

'And what?'

'I think I have trench foot.'

'I love the deep house!' shouted my mum.

Cheers, Mum. So do I. Both kinds.

🎧

We'd been deposited there by Tour Manager. He was mortally afraid of festivals. And people. And travel. In order for him to come he'd demanded that we 'bring a busload', which was his personal slang for lots of girls. This was a slight problem for me as I didn't really know any. By now I had hardly any friends and none at all from outside the industry. I've never been much of a ladies' man anyway. That whole thing seems slightly preposterous. People often say horribly gauche things like, 'You must beat them off with a stick,' which sounds pretty nasty. If you only knew the sort of disappointment that comes with a drooling, panda-eyed, quadra-spazzed nitwit throwing themselves at your job description at 4 a.m. on a Sunday morning, you'd probably rephrase your statement. This isn't a comment on womankind, you understand. I personally believe that only women running things and enforced atheism can save us as a species. It's just that my job *severely* limits who I meet. I've always wanted to meet someone normal, but sadly that dream slid off the table and smashed into millions of tiny pieces about twenty years ago. These days I'm barely awake before the crack of lunch and am just getting up to speed when nice normal girls are getting in from a long day at work. Anyway, boo hoo. T-Man wanted women and I didn't know what to do about it, but there was no way I was going to a festival on my own.

I eventually had a brainwave of scamming the festival for six tickets (for 'press') and running a competition online, with the winners coming with us. Then I rigged the competition so the handful of people remaining in my life who happened to be female all won. It was a weird busload. Tour Manager was happy, though. Most women found him hilarious. Which wasn't really what he was aiming for precisely, but he was happy to settle for it.

T-Man was obsessed by big tits, my theory being that it meant both he and the person attached to them were as far apart as possible. I think my generally being chemically sterilised and he being the de facto point of contact for a well-known DJ suited him really well. He wasn't just much older than everyone else, he was also culturally miles away: wild-looking, hairy, eccentric in a truly natural way and weirdly dressed long before it was fashionable for everyone to look like that. Indeed, we're the generation the hipsters watched and copied. Some kids instantly rejected us as improper and alien, but many loved the fact that we were so odd. After a few years my crew started to gain a bit of a 'look' too, and Tour Manager joined in with a vengeance, becoming by far the hairiest and weirdest of us all. But nothing could hide the fact that he was from a different generation. *Two* generations sometimes.

He was always overjoyed to be taken for one of us – a DJ or performer, I mean, not a human. Just after I finished working the festival set, he was stood by the side of the stage when a young girl came running up to him.

'I'm sorry to ask, I just had to come over and see . . .' she started.

He began to puff up like a chuffed pigeon and waggle his vast eyebrows like the mandibles of a stag beetle.

'Yes? Can I help you?'

'My friends made me come over and ask . . .'

'It's OK, my dear, you can ask.'

It was clear she thought he was one of us just coming off set. He was even carrying some of the record bags for once.

'It's embarrassing, but are you . . .?'

'Yes?'

'Are you . . .?'

'You can say it.'

'Are you our coach driver?'

'COOO-OACH DRIV-AH?!' he exploded.

I think it was one of his finest moments. He was like Lady Bracknell in *The Importance of Being Earnest*, sounding both like a boiling kettle *and* managing to turn two words into about eight ascending syllables.

'Dude, you're wearing string-backed driving gloves and a hat that says "Driver" on it. Plus, you're the oldest person in here by some distance,' I explained.

'That child is *clearly* simple,' he declared and flounced off, huffing like an early steam engine.

He'd only just recovered from laughing so hard at me accidentally burning the clutch out of the bus we'd hired he was nearly physically sick. In his battered logic, this made him the victorious king of all drivers – and, in fact, today an *actual* coach driver. And yet he was somehow simultaneously mortified that anyone would actually mistake him for one.

Once again I was doing all the work. He was getting good at avoiding his duties.

'Your butler is a bit mental,' said my mum, as she barrelled past surrounded by her new friends, still getting more traction than anyone else despite having one leg. My dad shambled behind her, looking highly oppressed by it all, the only innocent man in Gomorrah.

I was starting to think I might get out of this morass alive, when someone from the festival came charging over, all flustered sweat, rattling passes, wristbands and radios.

These poor souls had the unenviable task of dealing with all the 'artists' and pandering to their various insanities, and they answered to their equally insane promoter superiors. I had nothing but sympathy for them. They were the only sober people here, apart from my dad, some medics and two of the security.

'You need to come with me, please. Your friend is being arrested.'

'What friend? I haven't got any. Took me years to achieve.'

'Tall man. Looks like a tramp. Talks like royalty.'

'Oh God.'

'Yeah, looks a bit like Him too.'

As I approached one of the 'backstage' areas (essentially the grass behind a very large tent, where the staff who can't be bothered with the huge queues for customer toilets go to piss), a drama was unfolding. Not unusually I saw Quag Allurgie slinking away, as was his wont when trouble reared its head. An omnipresent force was that man. No matter where you turned, there he was, causing fun, making things 'interesting'.

'Tssurr Munnuhur's bun hurrstud,' he commented unhelpfully.

'I know he's been arrested. Can't you help?'

'Nurd muh prublum.' Quag Allurgie wasn't really the helping type.

Tour Manager was looking very distressed. He was surrounded by both the police and the gigantic club-wielding criminals that passed for security here, and looked very irate and, unusually, quite slight and vulnerable, like a poodle surrounded by Dobermanns.

'Look here, I'm an innocent man!' he protested.

'Look at his driver's licence,' I pitched in. It was usually all that was needed before some inevitable forelock tugging and semi-bowing started to happen.

'I'm sorry, sir, but in my experience, which is *considerable*, a person of your advancing years at a place like this is always some sort of high-level drug dealer.' The copper had one of those unfortunate voices that sounded like a small-engined motorbike straining at too many revs.

'You are very much mistaken, sergeant! I'm a very keen follower of . . . this one's . . . er . . . things,' T-Man said, gesticulating vaguely at me and clearly racking his brain for something authentic to say. 'Yes, and . . . er . . . very fond of . . . *many* things . . . here . . . in this . . . field of disco and . . . DEEP HOUSE!' he bellowed, almost deafening the officer. 'Yes, a huge, *huge* follower of . . . deep house *hits* and . . . er . . . other houses. *Species* of houses!'

He wasn't ignorant about electronic music at all. Quite the contrary. For someone of his age and background he could shame a professional DJ with his knowledge and appreciation. It was just that, like some deep compulsion, he nearly always said completely the wrong thing at the wrong time, particularly to anyone in authority.

Once, back at his own club, I was waiting for him to finish up. It was the middle of the day, not a time you want to be anywhere near a working club. At night a club is an ephemeral nebula of light and love. During daylight they all look like the inside of a cancerous lung, like an elderly transvestite caught in the sun with her make-up sliding off: working lights, black paint everywhere, the stink of the sweat of thousands and, despite it being years since they were banned, ancient cigarettes. Without warning three full-regalia police ambled into T-Man's place. Police have a way of parking their cars diagonally and walking into places that screams casual arrogance but is entirely deliberate – 'You thought this was your place? It's ours now.' T-Man staggered into the huge room and immediately started blithering at a hundred words per second, the problem being that not only did they represent authority, one of them was a fairly attractive woman – a double-edged sword for our plucky knight in rusty armour. They were investigating a noise complaint from a neighbour whose dear old daddy was a lawyer. Every venue in the world has one of these neighbours. You know the type: mum and dad bought them an apartment in the middle of the city as an 'investment' and then they immediately start attacking everything that's been there for a century. They're 'investing' in a 'vibrant' culture and yet also demanding it all ends on their whim, thus, along with their developer chums, slowly sterilising every city in the world. We have a specific term for them in the industry: 'cunts'.

Police generally prefer to do actual police work than things like this. I know because they've told me repeatedly. Sadly, the rich squeezing the poor means eventually they have to get involved, being the de facto long arm of the politicians. Suffice to say, there's always a slight air of resignation about them when they come a-calling on trivial matters such as this. There's something about the world weariness of experienced police that produces some of the best sarcasm in the world. This met its match, however, in the blunder-vortex that is Tour Manager at full steam.

In clubs the daytime is for cleaning and maintenance. Sorry – 'cleaning' and 'maintenance'. At T-Man's club this meant splashing around some bleach and rummaging in the attic for pointless artefacts. The venue had previously been a gay club, a garage and even a boxing ring, so T-Man loved finding old decor and other objects from its previous incarnations. He received the police covered in cobwebs and wearing a tiara.

First up was the foxy copper. She was in charge. After some simple preliminaries about sound levels, she asked T-Man the most complex question of all:

'And what is your name, please, sir?'

What followed was two minutes of pure nonsense. T-Man had just had one of his doses and was extra-verbal, a state wherein only one in five words made any sense and his brain formed sentences that his mouth couldn't achieve in time. This was accompanied by his eyebrows gesticulating wildly for random emphasis. When he thought he was being charming and/or making advances to a completely uncomprehending woman, they started working overtime.

'Real name stroke title and/or *nom de guerre*? Ahaha, yes, yes, *titular* [*waggle-waggle*]. What's in a name, indeed!'

At times like this, when he was over-refreshed and also nervous/aroused, he resembled the pianist guy in *Shine*.

'Just your name please, sir, so we know we are in the right place.'

'Ah well, you see, there's my God-given, then the old title, then there's a list to choose from . . .'

'What is it you do here, sir? Are you the owner? Manager?'

'Haha. Well, owner or manager? Manager/owner? Owner/manager? Manager or owner?'

'Yes, which one?'

'Which indeed!' (Waggle-waggle.)

When he was in this state – the one known as 'raging speed horn' – he would find a closed door arousing. A woman in uniform was almost too much for him, so he started waggling and winking almost at random. He'd say things he thought were charming, but his face would be too late. Then, in the midst of some unconnected phrasing, the features would catch up and start gurning and leering in completely the wrong place.

'Can you just tell me your name please, sir!' She was losing the will to live.

'Tour Manager. My name is Tour Manager.'

'Can you spell it for me, please, sir?'

'"T" for "terrific". "O" for "Oh my god". "U" for "undercarriage". "R" for "rrrrrrar" [*waggle-waggle*]! "M" for "*massive*" . . .' He went through his whole name and title using a fictional phonetic alphabet based upon really terrible sexual innuendo.

Forgot to mention, the other elephant in the room was Hitler. Not in person, you understand. T-Man had just found something else in the attic. Part of the old decor was a giant painting featuring a full-sized Hitler with his *hosen* painted bright pink and 'MIEN CAMP' written in huge pink Gothic script next to him. For extra comedy points the artist had also spelled '*mein*' wrong. T-Man had just found it upstairs and brought it out, and was overjoyed at his discovery. The police had entered with it propped on the wall behind them, and for the entire discussion it looked like Hitler was stood in their midst. The other two male police officers constantly shared glances and nods at it, and at T-Man's tiara. I think the fact T-Man also had a T-shirt on that said 'Hitler World Tour 1939–45' was completely and genuinely accidental. He loved novelty T-shirts, the more shocking the better.

Eventually, once the cops found out who he was, and more importantly who his uncle was, everyone had a nice cup of tea and shook hands. To this day I always imagine them walking out of the building saying, 'Those gay Nazi fellas were all right really.'

☊

At the festival, things with the police were far less cordial. Festival security, indeed all private security, is kind of hit and miss. Some are very excellent professionals. At the other end of the spectrum are quasi-paramilitary gangs of the right-wing persuasion who use festivals as a way of making soft kids miserable and dominating all the highly lucrative drug sales. Some operate very closely with the police, for good or ill. Guess which type of situation we were in the middle of?

'Look here! I'm a pillar of the community!' cried T-Man.

It was all going a bit dark. In our town we had some juice. Knew people. Even in Ibiza and New York we knew people. In this shitty field it was being made clear we had no friends, least of all the organisers, who were nowhere to be seen. Our friends were very notable by their absence. Some were clearly observed actually running away, in particular the boss of the whole thing, who had pressured T-Man into bringing him loads of horrible stimulants. For free.

To be honest, I never minded when things went weird, particularly those of your own making. You have to own your shit, as they say. Here we were knee-deep in everyone else's. Surrounded. Betrayed and abandoned. Wading in a literal mire. By now I was too dense and blunted to appreciate any poetic justice or irony. If you have any survivor's knowledge of drugs and general decline, you will recollect that everything is awesome until eventually it isn't. Then everything is a problem, and until you realise the common denominator at the singularity of the brown hole is *you*, you will never get out of its gravy-well.

Even T-Man's get-out-of-jail card wasn't working today. Ironically – and it's SO ironic I've used a capital 'SO' – he didn't have anything illegal on him. It was back in the van

I'd burned out. Yet he was still getting hammered by the law. Proof, if ever you needed it, that all you have to do is be in the wrong place on a cop's bad day and things can go south faster than a migrating flock of bastards.

I didn't like it here in the soupy, filthy Middle Ages. I wanted to be back where the sun always shone, ideally in the twenty-first-century Mediterranean. Who doesn't?

♩

Tour Manager was not happy. When someone on powerful stimulants is not happy, what happens is they relive the bad mood in a constant loop. They're incapable of breaking out of it until they finally, eventually crash. After a couple of hours of hearing T-Man drone on about the injustice and indignity of it all, I had to get away. Maybe find my old folks, who were likely experiencing the dangerously extreme polar opposites of the festival. Spending too much time with T-Man was like being trapped in the worst episode of *Doctor Who* ever. And being a sidekick is never much fun.

A sudden shower of nasty-smelling globules woke me from my reverie. A famously punky electronic act had found one of the backstage quads. Half golf buggy, half 4 × 4, they were for important people only. The group were having a high old time rampaging around the backstage area and deliberately spraying anyone within a few metres with mud and faeces from the spinning tyres, all the while giggling like girls. They were one of the headline acts and as such could pretty much do whatever they wanted. They definitely didn't have to worry about security or police. By now the whole place was beginning to reek and hum. I had had enough. I was going home.

Home is my old folks' place, never where I'm currently living. Always will be. It was just down the road. Literally. However, I wasn't storming off there for a warm shower and slippers. I passed the production cabin near the exit and secured a new vehicle pass. Someone was going to pay for my mood, and the quad riders were the chosen ones. You see, I love engines. I love cars, bikes and trucks. I love anything mechanical. I love my beach buggy. I went to get it.

It didn't take long to find them skidding about, shrieking. Mine was much bigger than theirs, with stupidly huge tyres driven by a modified engine that sounded like a gang of bikers approaching. This was more like it. By the time I'd done the thirtieth doughnut in a tight circle around them and they all resembled crying turds, with sods of grass for green hair, I was nearly back to normal.

I gathered up my folks. My dad couldn't wait to leave; my mum was over the moon and demanding to stay. My mother misheard T-Man's name on the way back and called him Tube Hangar for the rest of his life, which was a sort of strange justice. But I was done with festivals. I was due back in Ibiza the following day, and this time I wasn't planning on ever leaving.

Chapter 10

The Man Who Disappointed
Himself to Death

I'd done all my gigs in Ibiza and was greatly looking forward to a whole winter there of blissful tumbleweed (I say 'winter', but at its worst it can barely manage half a day of rain). T-Man came along for a couple of days, then left the island. For some time afterwards there was a hideous smell in my apartment. It transpired that in our staggeringly inept attempt at normality in the supermarket on our previous visit he'd taken the wrong bag at the checkout. He loudly refused to acknowledge it at the time, as that would have involved trying to communicate with normals. Upon returning to my rented apartment he found out that instead of buying his usual of cornflakes, sugar, milk, fizzy pop and cigarettes, he'd taken someone else's bag. A bag containing some sort of hoof, the entire foot of some kind of ruminant. This being Ibiza, these odd bits of animals were quite normal in a supermarket. His response to this error was his standard reflex of having a large panic, then hiding all the evidence – this time behind the air conditioning.

As anyone who has lived in Ibiza will tell you, the heat is no joke. Electrical blackouts are regular. Turn off the juice and within hours any fridge turns from a chiller to a form of sealed oven. If you've been away for a few days, opening a switched-off fridge is half horror film, half science experiment, all filmed like a Frank Zappa claymation video. Suffice to say, a hidden trotter left in a room for a while in the Ibicenco heat goes *very* ripe, very fast. It took me about a week to work it out. I called Tour Manager.

'T-Man, I can say with some authority, and with all due affection, that even after you leave, the stench of death still lingers.'

'Thank you very much!' he chimed, seeming to enjoy the thickly veiled compliment.

'How are things back over there?'

'I'm in dire need of a holiday!' he complained.

'Yeah, all that work must have been exhausting for you.'

'Sarcasm is the lowest form of wit. I am contemplating a short break on the Broads with Quag.'

It always worried me that he was the only person who didn't use Quag Allurgie's full name. It seemed blindingly obvious to me that Quag Allurgie was a rogue, to put it mildly. T-Man was worldly in some ways, but mostly massively naive in all the others.

The idea of them both on a narrowboat in Norfolk amused the hell out of me, though. T-Man's ancestry, as well as being hugely aristocratic, was naval, and he fancied himself as something of a salty sea dog, even though he'd no experience at all of the sea. Mainly he loved the idea of it, and this manifested itself in frequent boating trips of the most primitive and simplistic kind there is: narrowboat breaks. Principally because you didn't need any experience or qualifications to take one out. Or any sense of direction at all. To navigate a canal only a few feet wider than the vessel.

'Hey! From Ibiza to the Norfolk Broads! Haha!' I said. 'FROM IBIZA TO THE NORFOLK BROADS.'

'No need to shout itineraries at me, I'm not a real tour manager!'

Unless Tour Manager was cracking the joke he wasn't really interested in humour. His brain operated so quickly that anything anyone said to him immediately resembled a distant memory, rather than current affairs.

'I hear you had a typically successful journey back?'

'FUCK OFF!' he bellowed into the earpiece.

I'd been reliably informed that he'd arrived twenty-four hours late for his flight, having got the date wrong, had then bought a new flight that arrived in the wrong city, and then managed to get a lift in the middle of the night from that wrong city to another city that wasn't his, until the total time from leaving my company to his getting home was something like three days. He was a special person, no doubt. I was beginning to think he wasn't entirely suited to the role of tour manager.

'Well, enjoy yourself and for God's sake don't do any business with Quag Allurgie.'

'I'm not an idiot! Question: what's dead cool and hangs up on wankers?' he chimed in his usual sign-off, always managing to slam the phone down before I could. At fifty-one years old.

Not long after, I got a call myself from Quag Allurgie. I will spare you the incomprehensibility of it all, but suffice to say, it was an offer of business. In this case, he was representing one of the biggest nightclubs in Ibiza, if not the world, and not his own tiny regional disco. It was definitely interesting. This would mean weekly appearances for strong wages in the most high-profile sense and, most importantly of all, he was more of a broker than employer. It was a risk worth investigating. Quag Allurgie was uncannily good at getting what he wanted. The biz is full of them, Pilgrim. Nothing but promise and charm, neither of which you can take to the bank. Your agents and managers might make things appear unnecessarily complicated, but work outside of them at your peril, Pilgrim. If you take nothing from this book, take that morsel at least.

We're entering the brown period here. Every career has one. Not quite black, but on its way. There will come a time in the game when the shine wears off. It's very much like a motorbike. It's chrome. It's glittering excitement. It whispers promises of travel, glamour and freedom. It's sexy as hell and faster than anything else on the road. People point and stare as you cruise past them. It's also just a matter of time till it kills you. And the fun goes out of it pretty much the first winter. After that you wish you'd bought a big, slow, comfy car.

For the longest time I saw the thing I do as an almost *political* act. No, stop laughing, really! For many years I was in bands, and playing records before or after the show was for fun. I was lucky enough to be in the music business as the DJ thing exploded, and while technically I was always a DJ, in the sense that I played records to people in public, it became a 'thing' parallel to my general career in music. So very gradually and over many years I played fewer instruments and more and more records. Kids ask me, 'How do I become a DJ?' And I usually say,

'Fucked if I know, son.' It happened *to* me, not because of me. Promoters saw the costs for four guys and all their kit and the cost for one guy and his box, and the rest was mathematics. Don't get me wrong, people have been paying me to play wax for thirty years. But for the first ten it wasn't a thing, and no one got paid more than the guy collecting the empties. And rightly so!

Then, acid house, about which there are *plenty* of books. Suffice to say, many of us fought with police, danced in warehouses and in fields and really, 100 per cent thought we were changing the world. But all we did was create another revenue stream. Hippies are not to be trusted, and we were nothing but the 1980s version of hippies. Like those of the 1960s, the minute any of us got a chance to make a packet or get some girls or have smoke blown up our behinds, we ditched the lot and became entrepreneurs. Me included. When asked, 'Can you feel it?' we resolutely failed to.

Drugs you see. Drugs are the problem. Let's talk about drugs.

My generation is the greatest sociological experiment of our entire species' time on Earth. Sure, people have taken drugs throughout history, but never have so many done so many at once as we have. And the thing is, you can't tell *anybody*. No one in power wants to admit what's going on. The fact that they're as bad or worse than us doesn't help. These days, at least publicly, drugs are a thing that only happens to other people, despite everyone being on them. *Everyone*. None more so than those in the music industry, which actually depends on personal collapse and its manipulation. Our biz is entirely about supply and demand: supply the drugs, then demand everything. Drugs are the grease on the wheels of the machine. But no one will admit it. When it pops up, it's 'personal problems'. It's similar to institutional racism in the police: everyone knows it's there, but nothing ever gets close to dealing with it effectively because the institution never progresses past the denial stage. The cancer is enfolded around all the major internal organs. All we see in the media are 'isolated incidents'. An entire society's problem is presented as a personal one. And to cap it all, now that we've dispensed with truth, fact and science, we can't seriously hope for a solution. A cynic might say our betters are quite happy about this – there's big money in cures, policing and punishment.

Nowhere is this better illustrated than in the comical laws our venues operate under, in a global prohibition that makes the dry 1920s look like a soaking debauch. There's no personal responsibility any more, ironically. No one is to blame, so for some reason the building is penalised if someone gets hurt due to something they did to themselves. Says a lot, doesn't it? Governments close down venues and imprison poor people, but none of them ever seem to check the toilets and bars of their *own* seats of power. Until it is accepted that nearly everyone is at it, there can be no real governance or solution. Who wants to be watched when the watchmen are as bad, if not worse, than we are? It's hypocrisy and lies that are killing people as much as illegal substances. It's the dabbing of the eyes with a hanky and thanking Gawd above and the Baybeh

Cheezis at the awards ceremony, then going straight to the toilet for more drugs and being truly thankful to yourself. It's the pressure to be 'normal' and 'good' when things are neither normal nor good.

Every arrivals, every checkpoint, every customs I am a villain, fugitive, enemy. On paper? Nothing. A good citizen and valued guest across the globe, yet riddled with guilt and red-hot shame because I'm a part of that transgressive evil called drugs. DRUGS. Shout it out loud. Whispering about it clearly isn't working.

🎧

For me the 1980s were speed and acid, poor man's drugs. I didn't drink, though, so my debauches were very sporadic. Drug use sparse, experimental. Counted in single days and random hours, rather than months and years. Then a move into THC, delivered via weed and hash, although I didn't smoke tobacco, so again it was now and then. In the 1990s booze and coke ruled, with weekend MDMA. The smoking became weekly, then daily. I was still 'recreational', though. Or at least that's what I told myself – my recreation could have floored most people. Then, by the 2000s, everything. A blot. A blur.

Then the high-powered stimulants came along in earnest. I was never truly in trouble until I started to self-medicate to deal with the comedowns. This is the real danger sign. You have big weekends and they start encroaching into the week, and so you start drinking and smoking to 'chill out', which is, let's face it, just more legal and/or illegal drugs to counter the others. Then you take more at weekends to counter the tiredness from the downers taken during the week. It spirals into an arms race in your guts thereafter. By this point *any* true rock 'n' roller – and by now, Pilgrim, *you are a rock 'n' roller* – is on the old Go Faster Stripes.

Speed. Whizz. Meth. 'Phet. Base. Call it what you like. Hard stimulants. Let's start at the top and work backwards. I will assume for the sake of forward motion that you understand we're talking about an *occupational* hazard here. I'm not talking about your wacky weekends spent at a house party in someone's kitchen. I'm talking about passing through different time zones daily. I'm talking about the sort of sleeplessness they use as torture. I'm talking about getting on it at breakfast. I'm talking about staying awake for several days straight every single week for a lifetime. You think that sounds over the top? You have no idea. I'm talking about not having to pay for any of it, and it being handed to you wherever you go. And it's a pretty small group that experience this reality. Taking. Drugs. All. Day. Every. Day.

Most performers have a mayfly existence. The music industry is geared towards disposability. Not many actually make it for more than a few years. Three years? Four? Then they *burn*. That can be physical, mental, social . . . familial. People either wake up and get a life, or life wakes them up the hard way. This goes for the punters too. Every two or three years I see new faces in the discos as the old ones fade away. Clubbers have their moment in the light and then pair off, get jobs, have kids . . . get a life. But I'm still here. Always. An ageing outcrop of rock slowly being weathered away. A retreating glacier. Ten, fifteen, twenty, twenty-five, thirty years on, here I am, an obstinate lighthouse winking warnings at you from the dark. You think you know shit 'cos maybe you lived The Life for a bit. *A bit*. You don't know. It's a very small club in the veteran's lounge, Pilgrim, and you ain't in it yet.

☊

Thirty years too late for northern soul, speed is the drug of the professional worker. Nurses, taxi drivers and strippers are on it. Night people. *My* people. It's the only drug with which I've had what could be called a real problem. I think that your poison is very much decided by the area you're lacking in. 'Slow' people go for stimulants, 'hyper' people like depressants. I'm generalising but I believe it to be true. A habit condenses all your myriad personal issues, old and new, into *one*. One great big but so easily solvable problem. Imagine everything that makes you feel bad – the mortgage, the spouse, the job – *all* of it can go away in one dose. Ironically, it simultaneously shreds your life and, strangely, uncomplicates it too. It's a clear-out. No more mental clutter. Just one big problem that you don't need therapy or big bucks to salve. One cheap, easy fix is all it takes.

This is addiction as science or politics knows it. Looks simple, right? *Wrong*. To end up in this loop, there is a point in the middle of the cycle of your week where all the weekend's excesses and the comedowns from them cease to be peaks and troughs and blur into a constant long sine wave of flat misery. To be a pro at drug abuse there's no boom and bust recovery cycle. Your use is constant. It's a very slow process. It really is just for fun to begin with, but to end up at a point where it's daily and the cost of stopping is way too high? Takes a lot to get to that point. Can be a lot of time, can be a lot of sudden and rapid badness. Can be both. But you do everyone, including yourself, a great disservice if you underplay it. We'll never conquer it as a species if our leaders dismiss it as either weakness or chemistry. It is way, *way* bigger.

I'd long ago gone through any pretence of it being about fun. By now I *had* to do it. A truly vicious circle. Once I started on a serious drug daily, which ironically was to get me through the night, my fate was sealed. Familiarity was also a huge part of it. After all, I have stronger and longer relationships with some substances than I do with any person living or dead. There was no way for me to stop because, first of all, I would have to admit it was a problem.

There's also the pressure of performance. And I don't mean going up on stage. I mean the constant impression given by our Americanised media that you're competing and have to be 'better'. Yes, you could do your job stone-cold sober, but you have to be *more*. You have to reach higher, 'cos by implication what you are isn't good enough to make it.

Every minute we're bombarded by images of the star-spangled *Übermensch* – male and female fantasies of success, the zenith of physical perfection – while simultaneously being told that we're sickly and lacking. There's age too. You know what they say about policemen getting younger?

241

Imagine what it's like in a business where everyone around you is stupidly young and pretty. Pressure you would not believe! Not merely pressure working on you from within, but pressure from the people you work with. They're the ones sending you to an airport with fifteen minutes to make a connection, while sitting at a desk in an office thousands of miles away on a comfy salary. They're the ones saying the photos need doing again, but not saying why exactly. They're the ones who need you to work harder to make them more money. The pressure comes from inside and out, and you're a thin membrane in between, a delicate bubble. The parents of the bastard are ambition and isolation. We're told to exceed, and yet in doing so we find ourselves utterly alone. It's not the jape advertised.

Compared to meth, cocaine is *fun*. When I see 'slebs spinning out on coke it makes me chuckle. It shouldn't, but it does. Tell me *all* about your problem with 'painkillers' while I'm bleeding out of my eyeballs. Cry me a river about your issues with alcohol. Write me a memoir about your coke problems. These are the things pros take for the good times. They're the fun extras. Pro loons take *everything*. All. The. Time.

Cocaine was ruining my life ten years before we even met. It was killing the vibe in clubs, harming socialism and murdering bank balances on the periphery of the music biz (and many other bizes) long before I got to the party. Cocaine deals in *certainty*. That it isn't used more by churches has always amazed me (then again, it probably is). Meth is almost the opposite – overthinking masked by repetitive action. If meth is the daily grind, coke is the reward for a day well done. For me it's no good on a day-to-day basis. It's too expensive and its effect is too short-lived, and as a result you waste too much time and money up and down and dosing.

You know cocaine is trying to tell you something when you start to bleed out of every hole. Nosebleeds are fairly obvious and, indeed, inevitable, but when you start seeing blood on the toilet paper it could not be a clearer message. Ironically, the smarter you are, the better you are at fooling yourself, never mind those around you. My theory is that it's something to do with the part of the brain that regulates portion control. I have the same problem with, say, pasta or chips as I do with weed or coke: when I apportion them, I go large without thinking. Fast-food places understand this to a scientific decimal place. So do online casinos and people who make episodic television. If we're not already natural gluttons, we're sure as shit encouraged to be so. Even porn is stupidly exaggerated and based on greed. There's no 'off' switch on me, anywhere. Never has been. I've never had just one of *anything*, unless you count women, and even when I fall in love I *totally* overdo it. This is my doom. In another time we'd have been chieftains. The kid that can never be full grows and takes over everything like a chubby virus. In our DNA it's all about being large to survive in the wild. In this era we're merely slobs.

Even when you give up you're only one bad day away from starting again, a bitter 'Fuck it!' on your lips. And we all know another bad day is a matter of when, not if. How low did I go? Not sure if there's an exact moment, but you know you've bottomed out when you're using your diabetic dog's needles to inject meth into your arse cheeks.

Party drugs? No matter how bad things got there were fun times too, and that's what MDMA is all about. However, the phrase 'no such thing as a free lunch' was made for these substances. Way, *way* too powerful to be taken daily, these are the ones that really wreck your brain's natural set-up and mess with your emotions. The amount of times I see people snapping, crying and shouting on a Tuesday after a big weekend and then loudly claiming you're a rotten bastard for insinuating it's down to their weekend's excesses . . . well, let's just say it's a *lot*. And that's just in a *professional* situation, never mind a domestic one.

While we're here, let's talk about the most insidious substances of all: coffee, cigarettes and booze. Holding death in an elegant pose a thousand times a year, your cigarette is hundreds of chemicals, many of them secret, fucking you up the slow way. And I don't just mean making you cough. Your brain is who you are, and if you're someone who's under the gun with more obvious, more powerful substances, thinking smoking and drinking are innocent is plain stupid, my friend. Nothing has messed with my life more than the midweek 'chill out'. You think this is the quiet time, but instead of being 'off duty' you're merely fucking with yourself even more. And, Pilgrim, you don't need an official drug habit to feel this monster fuck with you. There isn't a person out there who doesn't know what the daily drink and smoke is doing to their lives or a loved one. Even if you don't want to know, you *know*. And you think I'm a bad case? At least I *know* what I'm doing to myself. I don't pretend my poisons are harmless. I don't tell anyone else they're fine, and I sure as shit don't sell them to the public as such.

The thing about the legal drugs is they *really* mess with your sleep patterns. So far, so *duh* . . . but even good old friendly booze means you don't sleep correctly. All of you going, 'Oh, I can't sleep without wine or a smoke' – well, yeah, you think that's true, and it may relax you to a point where you start to sleep, but once you nod off you just aren't doing it right. You're sleeping drunk/high/weirdly/incorrectly, and there's nothing more destructive than messing with your sleep because – *newsflash* – it's the only thing that can fix your brain naturally. And not just your brain: it's been shown that bad sleep messes with your gut flora and increases the risk of obesity and type 2 diabetes. If anything is fucking you up, it's that right there, Pilgrim. I would say as a layman that my lack of sleep was actually as bad if not worse for me than the intoxicants. The way to come down off a weekend's excess is to exercise, sleep and eat well. There's just no getting away from it. You're not fixing things by giving yourself downers 'cos, dude, they're *still drugs*! And then you are on the merry-go-round of up and down and up and down, and, Pilgrim, you're *this* close to spinning right off the carousel.

If you're a civilian reading this and saying, 'Oh hoho! Not me, Mr Crazy Man! Not *my* life,' let me help you get your head around this. Look no further than your caffeine, your daily tea and coffee. Many of you have a 'handle' on it – or you think you do. But your beverage doesn't give you a 'lift'. It adds nothing to your system. It just deprives you so that you feel tired and therefore relieved when you get your fix.

The irony is you do not *need* caffeine or booze. If you spend two weeks getting off the stuff, your energy levels will skyrocket and your brain will give you a standing ovation, especially if you're exercising. This is pure physical addiction, your brain chemistry demanding something. See how easy it is? All you have to do is remove the stigma of drugs and they're as common as caffeine. And as mundane. Come on, reach with me here! Imagine!

But it's not that easy in the post-truth age, is it? It's the hypocrisy and ignorance of our leaders that simplifies it to 'chemistry' and, therefore, something that's 'solvable' through the rigorous use of science and hard law. Yet we've never even *approached* a solution. Why? Because there's a secondary addiction. It's known as 'behavioural addiction', but I prefer to call it 'cultural addiction'.

Drugs don't add anything to you. You aren't an empty vessel that is suddenly filled with a magic powder called cocaine or heroin, or alcohol. All that happens is they fool your brain into producing more of its natural substances. They effectively milk more out of your mental udders. You're asking too much of a limited resource. You're a microcosm of climate change up there. Same thinking applies to your brain's resources as the Earth's. But then again, we don't really want to know, do we? We always happily ask, 'What?' and 'Who?' and 'Where?' but hardly ever 'Why?' Why? Because we really don't want to think too hard. About anything.

What are my whys? Why do I take substances? What

are the cultural pressures? You can attempt to analyse all you want, but I've already analysed the hell out of myself so you don't have to.

At the start it was *entirely* for fun. A hint of genuine experimental curiosity too.

Then it was for work, but I thought it was still for fun. Then it was definitely all about work.

Eventually it was a joyless routine and I had no idea what it was for. I was too busy on the spin cycle to self-analyse about anything.

Then I *had* to do it because I couldn't do many things without it, like have fun. And if you get to that point and you're still at it, *you're* an addict too, my friend.

Addiction. What is it? Isolation and a direct reaction to the alienation of modernity. It's not weakness. We drug battery chickens so they can endure the coop. Surely it follows that the millions of us living in tiny apartments and watching screens need tranquillising too.

○

My own personal hell was to start in earnest with prescription drugs. You may remember the hype around Prozac. It was certainly the first time I ever saw a prescription medicine in the style magazines. In my lifetime prescription drugs have gone from things that are dealt with quietly, by professionals, to something loud and public and very, *very* amateur. It's an altogether American phenomenon: create the disease to meet the new 'cure' – the 'happiness pill'. Well, as a drug connoisseur I *had* to try it. I mean, it looked like *fun*, right? All I had to do was pop into a doctor's and say I was a bit sad. Bingo. Packet of free drugs.

Take one, nothing happens. Take two, not a sausage. You don't know they're supposed to be accumulative. You don't know they're slow-release. Your experience of every drug both legal and illegal has always lead to some sort of semi-instant effect. Am I an idiot? Absolutely. Are the dangers of these things made known? No, they're not.

I was in the bank – you know, in the days when you still did things in the real world, in person. The entire pre-internet banking system hinged pretty much on one thing: the end of the transaction required my signature. The teller refused me. My John Hancock wasn't up to it. I wasn't who I said I was. Fast-forward a couple of weeks and it was a scrawl. Eventually I couldn't perform small acts of dexterity at all. I pushed the wrong buttons and resolutely failed to do up zips on clothes. I would miss the brake and mash up the clutch. I'd reach for a cup and push it off the table. And in your stupor you gloss over it. Mainly I thought I was 'overdoing it'.

So I cleaned up.

It wasn't that hard. I wasn't in the grip of heroin or crack. Cleaning up had never been something I'd *not* managed to do by this point in my life. In fact, before I got on the meth daily I used to take one week out of four off without fail. Unlike many of my peers I exercised and ate well, and I was never a big drinker. Laying off ceases to be tough when you're scared. And I was petrified.

Three weeks later I was worse than ever, but clean. Four weeks and I couldn't hold a glass of liquid without spilling it. Five weeks and I had a constant, visible palsy, the shake of a pensioner or near-to-death drinker.

I needed help.

For the first time in my life I went to a doctor in earnest. Sure, I'd been once or twice, but in a very mundane manner – no fear, just routine. I was clearly a mess as I walked in the door. My neck was cramping up and I found it hard to look over my shoulder without swivelling my whole torso. I slurred all the time. Mumbled. I had strength in my first finger and thumb but not in the whole hand. I sometimes fell because my feet felt like they belonged to someone else. For some reason I kept looking at the ceiling or the sky.

Almost immediately, and unusually, the doctor personally drove me to hospital. It was a huge, spooky, Gothic pile. He seemed eager to leave, and I couldn't blame him. It was only after a raft of questions that seemed a bit overly personal that it dawned on me I was in a madhouse. I was losing the ability to control my body, and they had put me in the cuckoo's nest? Lucky for me, upon seeing the resident doctor the next day it was made clear that the problem was entirely physical in nature, but I couldn't help but wonder how many poor souls accidentally ended up there, some for life.

Looking back, I don't know if it was the stress of the situation or merely the condition but I rapidly began to lose the power of speech. The slur became a gurgle. The gurgle became a drone. My jaw was locking shut and my neck and head pulling back until my chin was almost occupying the space where my nose used to be. My limbs were moving of their own volition.

I found myself in an ambulance. The attendants took

one look at me and strapped me to a stretcher. Full restraints. They were picking me up from the loony bin after all. Then things started to take a very odd turn. Perhaps I was in withdrawal, because nothing seemed real. Maybe I was in shock. It felt like a dream, far more peculiar than any artificial trip. They asked me questions in the ambulance. When I didn't answer clearly enough, they simply stopped addressing me and started to talk over me to each other, as if I wasn't there. Arriving at the hospital I was wheeled into a corridor. I couldn't get up and I couldn't speak. I was definitely experiencing some sort of internal panic that wasn't helping either. All I could do was writhe about and make guttural noises, which really isn't very attractive. If anything, it seemed to make me invisible, which was *too weird*.

I spent something like twenty-four hours in that corridor. I wet myself only once, I'm proud to say. It was coming up to forty-eight hours since I'd last eaten. I felt very peculiar. I hadn't slept – the involuntary spasms wouldn't let me. Gosh, I was tired. I've said it before and I'll say it again: if you think drugs make you high, try staying awake and being exhausted, completely sober, for longer than twenty-four hours and you'll see why it's used by the CIA as torture.

Eventually there was some commotion and I was rolled away. During my time in Corridor Land people had passed me every few seconds, yet they didn't seem to see me at all. I gathered from the upset that the main reason I'd been invisible was there was no chart on my trolley. Apparently the chart is important, the person irrelevant.

No member of staff had addressed me directly since arrival, something that would continue for a good while. 'HELLO! HELLO! HERE I AM!' I would scream in my head, but nothing came out. The rear left of my head, neck and jaw was locked. My tongue seemed to be asleep. I rolled, locked and popped like a prone breakdancer. It hurt too. Constant sprains, strains and muscles pulled. Back arching. Spine crunching. It was petrifying because each new spasm seemed bigger than the last and I wondered if something was going to break. It was like some sort of sinister and utterly silent possession.

Eventually I ended up on a ward. I was manhandled into a bed and restrained again. No one said a word to me and rarely even registered my presence. There had been some sort of mix-up because no one seemed to know who I was, and I couldn't tell them.

'WHAT. IS. YOUR. NAME? It's no good, nurse. Absolutely non-responsive.'

Then the administration of the place kicked in and suddenly I was a star again. For the next couple of days I got all kinds of visits to see the mystery patient. Eventually someone even thought about feeding me. I couldn't open my mouth, which meant it was messy, unpleasant and *very* frustrating 'cos I really wanted some food. Finally a drip was arranged, and then some kindly soul thought it might be a good idea to knock me out. I was grateful for this more than anything 'cos the last few nights had been very, *very* long.

I woke to voices from the next bed, and when my head decided to thrash in that direction I saw a large group of people in the traditional, slightly formal, painterly diorama of visiting family around sickbed. In order not to disturb the other patients a curtain had been drawn around the thrashing man by the window. I could hear a strong Irish accent. 'Saw him come in the other day with me own two eyes!' said the patient. 'Huge, he was. Looks of a fillum star! Fucking vegetable, he is. Nothing there.' He indicated his temples. 'Properly fucked. Makes you thankful to be alive! There but for the grace of God go I.'

I was glad I was performing some sort of public service at least. I was very thankful for the bit of curtain, however thin.

The next step was me being rolled out of there into another ambulance. With concentration and application, I was starting to be capable of grunting sounds. I could form noises at the back of my throat like a sort of ventriloquist. Until your lips, mouth and jaw are locked, you don't realise just how much they're involved in the forming of words. There were strange advantages to this situation too. Being shut inside your own body was like wearing X-ray spectacles. People immediately revealed their inner selves to you in the manner they treated your condition. Most completely ignored you. Many shouted at you like you were deaf. Some baby-talked to you. Once in a while, rare as hen's teeth, someone addressed you normally. It was like a cool drink of water.

I'd been driven to a specialist neurological unit, a small hospital entirely for the brain. At least here they had a certain baseline of understanding. You weren't contagious, you weren't insane, you weren't dangerous, you weren't an animal and you may even be conscious and human. The restraints were taken away and a wheelchair came out. It was a blessed relief just to be in a sitting position for once.

The human brain is the last frontier of medicine in many ways. Frankly, we don't know that much about it. Ironically, nowhere is this writ larger than in a neurological unit. All human knowledge of the physical brain is here. It isn't much. Imagine there's some kind of apocalypse and for some reason you need to access your drained laptop.

How much do you actually know about computers and electricity? Even hackers who write code don't know how to make a processor chip. The people who make the DVD drive don't know much about what goes into making a touchscreen. Sure, they're all experts and know a hell of a lot more than you or me, but they're specialists. When it comes to the brain our best minds are like an astronaut, adrift on his own in the vastness of space, with only a small torch to find the keys to his ship, which he thinks he may have dropped a thousand miles away. The first problem is observation. How do they see what is wrong? It's not like a fractured thigh bone or a tumour that can be seen, felt and X-rayed. Another method of observation is to ask, but if the patient can't talk, then that isn't much use either. If the medics don't even know your name, they can't ask a third party. You certainly can't cut open a brain to look for the problem.

So began the very, very slow process of trying to find out what the steaming hell was going on with me. If this was a film, there would be a very predictable and terrible montage here. There's some suspenseful music as I'm wheeled about from room to room to specialist to specialist and gadget after gadget is applied. First there are prods and pokes, and hammers and pins are used to test if I can feel. I can feel fine, I just can't tell them. As time progresses there's a lumbar puncture. You may know of it as a 'spinal tap' – a needle so large that it has to penetrate your backbone at the base. It's so brutal they have to knock you out. It hurts for a long time afterwards, mainly due to your having been stabbed in the spine by a humongous blade. The samples go away to be analysed. More time passes. Then an MRI scan. It's early days for this technology: it's not the sleek futuristic thing you see now, but for me it's full restraints and several shots to try and stop the movements as my head is placed inside a machine that hammers and bangs like someone has put a steel bucket on my head and handed a hammer to a demented toddler. When the MRI doesn't work, it's knockout drops. Then I'm injected with liquids that are mildly radioactive, similar to barium, so they show up when I'm scanned. There's ultrasound, blood and urine, samples from every hole I have. Even something I've never heard of called EEG, aka electroencephalography, which I later have them write down for me so I can remember it. They even pump me full of some sort of high-powered muscle relaxant and video me trying to walk on it. The film probably exists to this day somewhere, which is a chilling thought.

I started to regain some speech after a while, enough for them to find out a few basic details from me. I was also shocked to discover over two months had passed in the two hospitals. For two months and three weeks no one knew where I was. What was also very disturbing was that no one in my life seemed to notice.

What has to be understood here from a medical standpoint is that symptoms are not the disease. If you have a cough, it could be that you've just walked into the heat from the cold, or it could be a virus, or an irritant, or any number of very minor ailments, and also any one of some very, *very* serious ones, the worst of which could spell death. But on the outside what you have is . . . a cough. I had symptoms, albeit drastic ones.

What was causing them was, it appeared, completely unknown. The creeping dread was . . . was it *unknowable*? You see, to a degree the shock of it all and the unreal quality started to wear off in the neuro unit. It was almost like a job, being woken up every day to start a new task. Slowly the stiff-upper-lip thing and trying to be a good patient started to give way to actually wondering what the fuckity-hell was going on.

You think that's obvious? Curiosity as to your condition is initially far more like a constant state of panic rather than an alert and specific mental query. As the fight-or-flight panic subsides you start to rationalise, and then as time passes you start to get even more scared – scared that it isn't going to go away. I'd reached a sort of plateau where I couldn't be any more hyped or alarmed, and I began to level out into a state of morbid resignation.

Worst of all, as the final results came in and no more tests could be run, it became clear that not only was the entire discipline of neurology fairly short of answers in general, they very specifically didn't have any at all for me. In short, they simply didn't know what was wrong.

Chapter 11

Happy as a Bastard on Father's Day

Once in the machine you're sausage meat. I was trapped here in the sense of not being able to either escape my own body or leave the place even if I could physically move. I consider myself to be above average in terms of robustness, physically and mentally. However, by now I was starting to lose it. Don't get me wrong, these people had *saved* me, they didn't want to punish me. They were merely doing their jobs, and doing them well. I was just beyond what our current medical capabilities are.

Here I must address the idea that any sensible legalisation of drugs would somehow have saved me from being there. In the absence of any facts I was left with only my own guesswork. I'd put myself there. My lifestyle had lowered me to the point where I was reduced to prescription drugs, but I wouldn't know for many, many years that it was they, not recreational pharmaceuticals, that had put me under. It's not that simple, though, is it? Spend enough time on a suitably long tightrope and it's just a matter of time until the wind blows hard enough . . .

The irony is that for the first time in years I was getting a proper amount of sleep. Also, because I couldn't feed myself, I was eating, by my standards, hardly anything; and no booze, of course. As a result I shed so much weight I was almost unrecognisable. Mentally I was as alert and healthy as I'd been since I was a teenager, but this clarity only served to make me see the staggering futility of the situation. I honestly think I would have breezed the whole vile thing if I could have smoked some hash and had a drink. We take these substances into us for a reason, right? Who wants clarity?

By this point I was what they call 'ambulant'. I could stagger about under my own power and with a bit of effort could pretty much make myself understood. I'd been in the system for a long time by now. I didn't want them to contact my family, though. Because of my job, long stretches could pass in my day-to-day life without my speaking to anyone. Something inside me didn't want anyone to see me like this, but was simultaneously perversely curious about what would happen when you effectively disappear. I can answer that one for you: not much. All the 'hopes and prayers' on Facebook and the 'thoughts are with you' are so much dust. They don't mean shit when not a soul seeks you out once the chips are down in real life. By now I'd got enough speech together to use a phone and had made a few calls. One was to a 'friend' who was also my landlord. He was mainly concerned about the rent he was due. A couple of others 'um'd' and 'ah'd' and gave the distinct impression they couldn't put the phone down fast enough. Others, like His Tourmanagerness, never answered the phone at the best of times. Gosh yes, Pilgrim, newsflash: you really do find out who your friends are in these situations. In my case, no one, it seemed.

Does that seem a little odd? A touch hard to accept? Take it from me, no one wanted to know. Mind you, if you think this sounds self-pitying, I have to promise you

I really didn't feel all that bad when I took a look around me at the other poor cunts trapped in this silent movie of a dead end. Is there more of a cul-de-sac than a hospital for people who have problems science cannot even *diagnose*, never mind cure?

I don't know his name because he never had time to tell me. He was a young Asian lad, far younger than me. Can't have been older than twenty-five. I'd see him walking around every day, and to all intents and purposes he seemed to have nothing wrong with him. He seemed like a visitor in a museum, taking a leisurely stroll, curious even. I asked one of the staff because it seemed so odd that this apparently able-bodied young fella was here. I was told to simply go and ask him myself.

He was sat at the end of a table, so I shuffled and shimmied over to drop myself in a nearby chair. I asked in my strange mumbling voice why he was here, and he cheerfully explained that he wasn't sure why but every seventeen minutes – and according to him it was exactly seventeen minutes – his mind completely wiped itself. Apparently there was residual memory. He remembered his past fairly roughly, but only up to a point. He sort of knew who he was, then one day there was some sort of serious problem or seizure and . . .

It gives me chills to this day to remember his face switching off. It wasn't particularly dramatic, but a light inside just *went*. One side of his face appeared to go slack and his head bobbed back a bit as if he was nodding off. Almost as scary was the look on his face when he came round again a mere two seconds or less later. It was a look of total uncomprehending fear. (To be fair, I'd seen that look fairly recently in the mirror.) Something about it was more chilling than any horror film. I'll never forget it.

Most of the other damned souls were bed-bound. This was a serious place, it wasn't a movie. Nearly everyone was catatonic. One of the others who was able to move was an older gentleman. Once I happened upon him looking intently at a large poster on the wall that was a cross-section of the human head and some of its contents. He called over a passing doctor. He indicated animatedly that 'this' was the place he felt something snap. He was absolutely certain of it. If ever there was a tableau of the futility and insecurity of the entire place, it was this, a brain-damaged layman trying to explain the inexplicable to a professional, one with extremely limited powers, via the use of a 1970s poster and his finger.

I may be a layman, but to live through drug abuse is to experience brain chemistry first hand. It's much easier to sit in the mind of a maniac or depressive when you have felt that colossal drain or euphoria yourself. It's much easier to understand other people's problems when you've actually had some fucking problems too.

By now I'd turned from plucky patient trying to make things easy for everyone to grumpy spastic who received pity like thrown acid and the patronising tone of lost experts a hideous cacophony of misinformation. By now I was, in the deepest irony imaginable, a stuck record, simply asking over and over again, 'What is wrong with me?'

☊

Privileged people should be automatically barred from public office. Without degradation you can never truly understand others because life is almost entirely misfortune. Privilege is the arena of the self, governance is the business of otherness. Those in charge of us never seem more out of touch and futile as when you're trying to explain to them something you're currently experiencing, like acute pain, debilitating symptoms or, say, abject poverty. I was getting tired of doctors. I was, in my amateur view, definitely depressed as well as physically fucked. Then it dawned on me: I'd been depressed for a long time. I didn't seek out powerful antidepressants for jollies; I needed them because something wasn't right with me on a fundamental level. To be fair, though, by now I certainly had something to be depressed about. It would be more than a decade before I discovered, purely by accident, that in some people it's the antidepressants themselves that can violently exacerbate the problem. However, at this point the most depressing aspect of all was the 'occupational therapy'.

I strongly suspect that very much like our schools, hospitals have to operate at a sort of mean average level of intelligence and activity in order to work with the broadest section of society, so even when I regained the ability to communicate I was still often treated like an imbecile. I'd also worked out that now we'd got to the stage of trying to teach me how to use a spoon and go to the toilet (yes, I had to be potty-trained), it was a fair indication that they thought I wasn't going to get any better. It obviously didn't dawn on many patients that things that cost money are always done for a reason. Yes, believe it or not, through all of this, I still thought it was all temporary.

As the months dragged on there was talk of discharging me. I felt a sense of massive existential panic: firstly, because there was *still* no diagnosis; and, secondly, because I had to start thinking about the future – something I was really, really, *really* trying not to do. Throughout the whole thing my mind was crystal clear, but everyone around me treated me like a simpleton. There was a rage building. I knew in my mind that I respected doctors and nurses, revered them even, but in the unit, and in my misery, I felt oppressed by them. I needed some external sanity to match my interior clarity.

Out of the blue I realised that I'd completely forgotten I had a career and a manager. I body-popped down the drab corridors to try and find the payphone on wheels, then to find my Asian friend to borrow some coins – he wouldn't remember lending them to me, which was a plus – and a nurse to put the coins in for me. Luckily my neck was now permanently crooked to the left, as if there was an invisible telephone there all the time, so the nurse merely squeezed it in there and left me to it.

'Aye? Speak!'

'Mmmk. Us mi. I cnt tlk prubberly.'

'Get to fuck, Allurgie! I've told ye a thousand times not to call me.'

'Nnnuuur! 'S nud Kwug Ahurlee! Us mi!'

'Fuck me, you simple cunt! Are you off your head somewhere? Where the fucking hell have you been, man?! What the fucking hell is wrong with your voice?'

The chat was long and difficult, but I managed to explain to Chib the gist of the situation. He was unusually sensitive and even moderately compassionate about it all. Sod's law, of course, that the person I would have put very low on the friends list was actually engaging with me, while those I actually called friends weren't. He reported to me that Quag Allurgie had, naturally, completely fucked up the Ibiza deal, so not only was I in hospital, AWOL, I had no work ahead of me even if I got out. Also, Tour Manager had gone into business with Quag Allurgie, which was terrible but less pressing news. Chib told me he would visit me tomorrow.

He arrived carrying two hundred cigarettes, a bottle of vodka and some spank mags. You had to love him. He even managed to hide the cigarettes under me when the nurses came to take everything away. He was the first person I'd seen from 'my life' in going on four months; I had no idea he would be the last for even longer. You're thinking, 'Ah, four months isn't that long!' – yeah, well, you're dead wrong. It's a season of the planet's turn around the Sun, a whole summer or winter, made all the longer for being spent in a form of solitary confinement. It felt like a year, especially as usually I rarely stayed anywhere on Earth for more than forty-eight hours. Even when I was 'at home' it was only for a few days at a time. Chib was highly amused that I found time to have a laugh with him even while deeply in the shit, and as he was leaving he said, 'You know, you should write a book one day, son.' And he was gone. I never saw him again.

They'd finally contacted my family. Things started

to change rapidly. For the sake of anonymity I can't tell you who my dad is, but suffice to say, he's a serious dude and something of a hero to me. He also had friends quite high up in the health service. All of a sudden everything changed. Nurses came in often. Some even talked to me like a person. I got moved to a room of my own. Doctors started to actually form small queues to see me. Like in any industry, if one of their own is involved, everything takes on a whole new level of serious. I wasn't a civilian any more, and if anyone fucked up, there would be hell to pay. A pro was watching. From above.

My old folks lived far away in the mountainous regions. It would take a while for anyone from home to get here. In the meantime, a relief package arrived and, best of all, some money – I hadn't had any the entire time. In anticipation of my family coming, visiting specialists started to arrive. My results were examined. Decisions needed to be made. That went for me too. A side effect of being from a family in the business is that I have more than an everyday understanding of medicine. I'm no expert, but I'm reasonably smart and have a passing grasp of the terminology. One of the results of being a basket case in the corner is that even professionals talk openly about you and your condition as if you're not there. I was fully aware that not only did they not have a clue as to the cause of all this, they were also narrowing down the possibilities through a process of elimination. Science is all about rigorously going through all the options until little remains but the truth. Within full earshot of me I heard one specialist talk to the other. I won't try and dramatise the conversation because I'm not a doctor and I've never wanted a court case out of it all, but let's just say they described my options, and therefore the rest of my life, as dependent upon two likely diagnoses: one was the likelihood that I was settling into a set of symptoms that were pretty serious and, in their experience, wouldn't go away; the other was the slow poisoning of my brain by my own body's traces of copper – yes, the metal – which would mean a dramatic worsening of everything and eventual death.

So basically vegetable or death. Bit agro-Gothic, but there you are.

I felt very clear for the first time in a while. A weight was lifted. Here, at least, was *something* rather than nothing. They didn't mean to, but for the first time someone had helped me in there. I had better get used to this condition or be ready to die. Sound a bit purple and dramatic? You've no idea, Pilgrim. None. This thing was so dark I never even think about it these days. I've told maybe three people about it, and writing it down for you has taken endless attempts. It's something that has long since been boxed, wrapped, covered in plastic and filed away in a box marked 'NOOO!'

So I was going to be like this forever, or else maybe die soon in a nasty way. I figured if I was going to be like this, I needed to see what it was like out there, I had to discover what it was like being this way in the real world. I was pretty mobile by now. I could stagger along at a fair clip. It was time to escape. I didn't have any clothes – what was on my back so many months ago had long been lost in the system – so I stole a large coat from behind the reception counter, took the bit of money that had been sent and shambled off into the night. I wasn't sure where I was going or even what I was doing. I didn't feel like I was running away. I wanted to see the outside, to place myself in the real world.

I wandered up the streets for a while, sticking to the main roads. There weren't many people about, though I'm sure being near a hospital they would have been used to seeing someone wearing pyjama bottoms and slippers under a coat. In the distance I saw the warm lights of a pub. Nothing beats a proper pub. I've always loved them. I'm the sort of person who could happily walk into any place they serve alcohol and feel at home. I'd also not had a drink for a *very* long time.

It was a bit like a western, the place going silent as the weirdo crashed through the doors. I'm not sure I've successfully described how I appeared. My arms tended to flail about of their own volition. I couldn't stop them if I wanted to. The hands attached to them were two claws that I barely had the use of and they rotated independently like I was playing an invisible piano with only two keys, a piano that was spinning around me like a fly – ironic given my previous occupation, don't you think? At a push, if I concentrated hard, I could do a few things, such as open a door or smoke a cigarette, but I would need help with much of the process. My head was the worst: it refused to leave my left shoulder and nodded and jerked constantly like I was agreeing with myself all the time. My jaw had clamped into a constant curling gurn, while my eyebrows waggled like a *Thunderbirds* puppet and my eyes tended to roll a bit like one too. Add a gurgling, honking voice from the back of my throat and you get a rough idea of what I was: human wreckage on the shore of excess.

I was stood at the bar for a very long time. It was about 8 p.m. on a cold midweek evening, winter-dark and only a few regulars in the house. The barkeep pointedly ignored the shaking, dancing figure stood there. I was bullishly not leaving until I'd had a drink. I had to grip the bar with my only functioning appendages: forefingers and thumbs around the first knuckle – my 'rave claws', as they've become affectionately known. This anchored me in place, so I effectively swayed on these pinions like a sail on its ropes, not dissimilar to a serious drunk, I thought. Perhaps that's what they saw me as.

I harrumphed loudly a few times. Even in my prime I was a loud person and never took well to being ignored, content to make a scene. I still am. The barman wasn't acknowledging me and the regulars were gawping. I attempted to say something along the lines of 'Excuse me', but what came out will have been unintelligible to them, I'm certain. But there was no escaping the fact I was there.

'I can't serve you, mate, you've had more than enough. Look at the state of you.'

I moved away from the bar and gestured to my lower half. Then I raised my arm as best I could to show the plastic hospital ID band on my wrist.

'Ahhhh!' he breathed out, relieved. He turned to the regulars. 'He's from the nuthouse down the road.'

'Give the poor cunt a drink, Dave!' said one.

'What'll it be, mate?'

I managed eventually, amid much laughter, to order a pint. There was no way I'd have been able to handle a smaller object. After a few botched attempts at drinking, again to much merriment, the barman gave me a straw. It was that bad. Four pints later I was definitely drunk; not so long ago it would have taken three times that amount. I managed to pay and left.

My excursion had shown I was going to be a laughable freak for the rest of my days. That much was abundantly clear. Next I found a shop and bought more serious booze, a packet of razors and some painkillers in yet another grossly humiliating pantomime. The handful of people on the street giving me such a wide berth that they actually crossed the road as I approached. I headed back to the hospital. I now knew what I had to do. It was *very* clear.

The only places with locks were one toilet and a bath, which was a huge thing more like a jacuzzi, designed especially for the disabled. For a few weeks I'd been saving up all the various pills they issued me several times a day, the purpose of most of which I had no idea. I don't think my avoiding the meds meant I was suicidal, I really don't. I think I was trying to achieve clarity. I wanted to stop being a passenger in my own life. I wanted control. Most of all I wanted forward motion, for good or ill. I wanted *out* of this situation.

I knew with absolute certainty that I didn't want to be here or be . . . *this*. Also I'd been in the system for so long I was tired of it all in a very fundamental way. I'd been a 'good patient'. Indeed, patience is what I'd displayed in spades, ironically. But I was pretty sharp and I knew that we'd reached the limit of medical knowledge. We'd done everything, and now they were talking of discharging me. Into what I didn't know. Being cared for at home by my parents again like a baby? No way. *Not* going to happen. The poor buggers had only just successfully got rid of me!

I'd only recently reached my peak. I'd clawed up through my teens and twenties and attained some sort of moderate success, but now it was over. Ostensibly forever. I wanted to go out on a high note.

Under the cover of running-bath noises and with a chair against the locked door I swallowed all the pills and the painkillers I'd bought, drank the whole bottle of booze, used the empty to smash the plastic razors and, after a couple of painful and comically botched attempts, managed to cut my wrists.

As the water went red I started to slumber. It all felt very peaceful. I'd had a pretty good run really. Nothing flashed before my eyes. It just felt like drifting off . . .

Chapter 12

There Are Some Mountains High Enough

Tip here for killing yourself, Pilgrim: if you're serious, a hospital is about the stupidest place to attempt suicide. And I truly believe I was *very* serious. Oh yeah, and if you can't cut up your own food without help, don't expect cutting anything else to go well. I dimly remember alarms and being dragged around, and voices complaining about the weight of me – even at my lightest a heavy man – with some grumbling at being disturbed, some even moaning that I'd be better off dead. I also recollect someone telling them to shut up and do their job. It was all very cloudy, but I remember waking up back on the ward in a bed, tied down again and heavily bandaged over hands and wrists.

It was funny seeing my old man arrive. To me he was my dad, a loveable, funny, infinitely smart man, fairly short in stature but huge-hearted. The giant striding down the corridors barking orders looked just like him. The entire place, sleepy as death and as beige as purgatory, suddenly leapt into action as he raged up and down the place. Don't get me wrong, I wasn't mistreated in any way, but I'd nearly died on their watch, and he was having absolutely *none* of it. Everything started to move very quickly then. I was out of there. I was going home.

♁

I don't have the space here to describe the slow process of recovery. It took years. I was back in my familiar childhood surroundings, going full circle, if you like. *There* was an irony. Here I was back in the role of a child, but something about it kindled a will to live. There's only one true no-strings love, and that's the love of your parents. To feel true love is the greatest thing a human can experience. Hey, listen, I'm about as hippy as a house brick but, if I know one truth, it's that one right there. Being at home made me want to come back from the edge, and you have to *want* to come back for the process to happen.

The will to live is in the mind, and let me distinguish this for you if you are one of those slow readers who can't tell the difference between psychiatry and neurology: the mind is different from the brain. The brain is the machine. It's the hardware of the computer, if you like – the metal case, the chips and the wires. The mind is the software – the operating system, the apps. Look, sorry if this is obvious and, yeah, if you don't know this, then you probably move your lips while reading and let me congratulate you on getting this far, but the mind – entirely who we are – is quite a thing.

On the day of his retirement, I said to my dear old dad that as a medic, 'It must be weird seeing people at their worst.' He answered, 'No, you are seeing them at their very best.' He then explained to me that after decades of healing, and in defiance of all science, he'd come to understand that it's all in the mind. He's seen people who were wheeled in riddled with cancer literally skip out the door. He's seen people with absolutely nothing clinically wrong with them die within weeks. The mind controls the brain, the brain controls the body. It's not magic or Jesus. It's chemistry.

The specialist who saw me through the convalescent period explained it best of all. I can quote his words pretty accurately 'cos I will never, ever forget them: 'We don't know much about the mind, but what we do know about the brain is that a lot of it is apparently empty. We've seen people who've had parts of the brain surgically removed relearn what those missing parts of the brain did using completely different areas. Our mental abilities can physically shift from one part of the brain to another.'

I used to be a pretty good musician. Jazz level. Can't do it any more. I can hold a beat, but all the nuance has gone. My handwriting is shot. It's a scrawl. My voice has changed a bit and my teeth have been ground badly. Small motor functions are a lottery and my hands are a bit weird. I have the odd spasm but I have to say that, after some years, I beat it. What it took was *time*. I can't go into the years of recovery – makes for boring reading. The trick, if there is one, is that you have to keep at it. Life, I mean.

Does this mean I'm saying that prescription drugs nearly killed me? Yes, I am. Come at me, take me to court, but you may lose because I'm not the only one. Is the open marketing of neurological drugs outside the closed doors of the medical world the most reckless thing big pharma has ever done? It's definitely up there. It almost makes me want to use crazy words like 'evil'. Sure, you'll hire the most expensive bastards in the world to show how I was the architect of my own demise. You may even 'prove' it. But I wouldn't be able to have this printed if there wasn't clinical evidence that these drugs produce horrific side effects in some people.

First there were two sticks to walk with. Then one. For a while I didn't socialise or go out at all. Later I did, and I didn't care if people were stupid and insulting because vanity had died a year ago. I'd looked death right in the face, quite literally closed my eyes on life without expecting them to ever open again. When they did, they opened *permanently*. I was like a cartoon kid who'd been given superpowers in a terrible accident. I can see right through anyone now – X-ray spex, full panoramic 20/20 laser-guided opticals, a peerless clarity of vision that comes from within. You'll be surprised to learn that one of the first things I did was carry on partying. I found out the hard way that dying is so easy and random, so there's no way on God's green earth I'm going to waste one more moment in fear. Oh yeah, I have a total lack of fear too, in all senses of the word. None. Zero. I'm not sentimental about anything now either. It would feel like a lie.

Disappointment, though, that's my kryptonite. I've a very, *very* low opinion of humans. Animals? Love 'em, can't get enough – even cats, which I previously thought were total dicks. People, though? Nah. No, thanks. This is the part of the story where there would be a dream sequence, maybe some cartoon elephants doing a Busby Berkeley dance routine, but you don't dream on meth. Imagine how fucked up you are if you stop dreaming. Imagine what it's like to be a performer who doesn't like crowds.

How was I going to get back to work after all this? I had no manager, no agent. After a few phone calls I found out that the players I had history with on the island had written me off. The biz has a very short memory anyway. Leave for two years and you may as well leave for good. The cycle of punters turns over fast too. People who would pay money to see you DJ in 2005 wouldn't necessarily do so in 2007, especially if they'd seen neither hide nor hair of you in the interim. Many simply didn't go out any more. DJs are not entirely like rock stars: we're a lot more disposable. I had no problem with relearning the technical aspects of the job. It's not in any way physically or mentally demanding to play records. The lifestyle is brutal, sure, but the actual task is easy – always has been for me anyway. Learning and playing an instrument is hard. If you stop playing the guitar, the tiny but very specific muscles and calluses you need to do it can go within a month. You really have to keep doing it if you're serious about it. It's much, *much* less so with playing records. And now, thanks – or not – to the internet, rarities and the things that can make a DJ excel are readily available from the comfort of your sofa. You don't even have to leave the house to get what you need to be able to perform any more. No, physically performing wasn't the problem. Getting back into the industry was.

I still had a name and therefore still had some gigs, but now it was a case of me making them happen. Nothing came to me, I had to go to it. Yeah, I admit it, it was begging. My earning power was gone. I went from turning gigs down 'cos it was physically impossible to do any more and working internationally maybe four times a week to eventually working maybe once a month, regionally, if I was lucky. I'd gone from living full-time in Ibiza as a star of sorts to being a child again in the home of my elderly parents; then, when I was able, moving to a place near by in order to be around to help them in turn. After all, what have they ever done for me?

The fees went down, down and *down*. I should point out that this was also due to a shift in the industry. The big dogs still got the big money, but the mid-range guys were getting less and less as more and more kids were coming out of the woodwork to try their hand at the world's easiest job. Turntables had been outselling guitars for decades. Come on, everyone you know is a fucking DJ now, right? There must be close to a million DJs who can call themselves some sort of professional these days. When I started you could probably fit every pro DJ in the world in one large room. Now you can fill stadiums with the bastards. Suddenly I found that if I called a club or a magazine, the person on the other end of the phone genuinely didn't know who I was. *Awkward*. Is there a worse phrase than 'Don't you know who I am?' – to say as well as hear? I could never bring myself to say it, but even if it went unspoken the embarrassment was the same. As well as the dance floor turnover and people leaving the party to have real adult lives, the turnover in our industry is fast and hard too. Every three or four years a magazine or venue or agency has almost entirely new staff. Very young staff. Rolling up to the offices of a major magazine is like walking onto the set of *Bugsy Malone* – just a roomful of kids in grown-up clothes (most of you reading this won't even get the reference).

If you're thinking, 'Dude! Really? A has-been in just

over two years? Come on!' I will merely say that you don't know 'cos it happened to me, not you.

Two years morphed into three. Three into four. By year five it was over. I was on welfare. And do you know what will do you in, even faster than drugs? Thinking you are owed anything. Why should anyone who was ten years old when your last record came out know *anything* about you? Why on earth would a fast-moving global industry stand still and wait for you to sort your weak shit out? I've seen peers and even a couple of friends lose their minds wondering why no one wants to pay them stupid 1990s money, or indeed *any* money, to play their horrible clattering old records at kids who've never even heard their name. Accepting the disposable nature of the industry is the key to participating in it rationally and painlessly.

I had returned to the mountains. It was where I was from. And to cap it all my old folks were sick now too. They needed me around. I was living halfway up an incline so steep that in winter no normal vehicle could make the climb and most people on foot had a lot of trouble. I lived in an ancient house next door to a country retreat for bad priests – that's how remote it was. I was getting into my mid-forties. I was irrelevant, friendless, hadn't been with a woman for going on ten years and my best and *only* friend was a dog. Awesome dog, though, to be fair to him. A real dude.

The few gigs that were left were often the grimmest affairs, gigs in a small town's only club. In order to squeeze a little extra cash from them I would charge for an imaginary driver and a hotel. I would then load up on meth, which was all I could afford anyway, and go to work. This meant leaving my remote location on a Friday afternoon and pretty much driving a couple of thousand miles over the weekend, usually without any sleep, rolling in on Sunday or even Monday, dangerously close to clinical exhaustion, having recklessly squeezed in a couple of gigs many hundreds of miles apart, arriving at one wired and tired, doing the job through the night, getting in the car and driving through the next day to the second one, the meth allowing it to happen. Some long-weekend-type bank holidays I could easily do two thousand miles over the four days and nights, with four gigs at all points of the compass and no sleep. It wasn't like the superstar version of the job I was doing before. Not at all. Sure, that was brutal too in its own way, but actually physically driving the miles yourself? That's a new level of difficult. To top it all I wasn't young, pretty and fit any more. I was a sickly, portly, ageing shambles. All I was doing was hammering my body every weekend working, then being almost paralysed during the week as I recovered. It was a sick parody of my former lifestyle. Instead of a party weekend as an honoured guest and the fun drugs, I was a sad old man, awake all weekend on nasty drugs that kept me upright. I needed them just to arrive on time, and it was touch and go if I would indeed arrive. The most likely way the drugs will kill you is a road accident, not your organs failing. If I think back to some of the night journeys I did, exhausted and wired, I truly shudder. Also at this time, instead of having the weekdays to myself to go to the gym, maybe go to the studio, make a record or have lunch with an agent or interviewer, I would be in bed for three days solid popping painkillers and downers by the fistful, dreading the weekend to come. I was still unwell too, but trying desperately hard not to show it.

Don't you pity me! Not an ounce of pleasure was to be had here, but who said a job was supposed to be fun? Boo-hoo, hold the front page: man has to work for living! I was lucky that for a while my job was any fun at all. Ironically, the twilight of my career resembled the early days of the career of a jobbing DJ. Unfortunately for me, I was now *way* too old for it. Running around like a blue-arsed fly is strictly for kids, plus I had already done it twenty years previously. I had a strong name but, like me, it was pretty old, poorly, and only getting older. Add to this peers and up-and-comers whispering and bitching online that I was past it and any chance I had was poisoned. Of course, only *they* were the real deal, not old dinosaurs like me. Guys like me were done. A lot can happen in my business in five days, never mind five years. Maybe I can make another joke about a Bowie song here? But I digress. It was, finally, plain uncool to mention my name. Pilgrim, let me explain something very fundamental here: you can become very cool, but you're fucked the day you are, because you have to *stay* cool. You can happily live your life and bum around *not* being cool; careers and whole lives can be lived and enjoyed without you ever being dunked by your ankle in the cool-pool. But if you're ever unfortunate enough to become *uncool*, then, my child, you're *fucked*. Game over. You're contagious. *Ding! Ding! Unclean! Unclean!* DJ Leper Fingas in da house!

It's bullshit, of course. You don't suddenly stop being good at your job overnight. Far from it. The whole thing is about being a tastemaker by nature. We're the sort of people who see everything first, who've always got one eye on the road ahead. It's who we are. And that never stops. So even when your star has waned you're always ahead of the game. Only now your rep is damaged and, Pilgrim . . . Rep. Is. *Everything*. Doesn't matter then what you do. No one is listening any more. To top it all, do you know the one thing that really, properly matters when it comes to being a performer of any stripe? It's *confidence*. It's also pretty important if you're merely expected to be a man. Once it goes, once you can't really trust your hands to do the things your brain tells them to do . . . well, you work it out.

What's the longest you've ever spent on your own? I don't mean outside a relationship, I mean the physical absence of any other people. I can tell you right now most people can't even *afford* to live on their own in a modern capitalist society. It's not possible. I'll take a punt and say only the very elderly know what it's like. If you live alone outside a town or city, you can go for some time without seeing a soul. I know I did. Once a week a venture out to get supplies, and done only most grudgingly. The irony of seeing no one at all for five or six days, then having five hundred of them all staring at you while you play records is a bit weird. After a while it becomes two weeks in solitary, then three, each time the shock and existential alienation of standing in the booth being gawped at becoming weirder and weirder. Did I mention Burroughs said *The Naked Lunch* was about the moment you see what is actually on the end of your fork? Yeah, a bit like that.

Do you understand yet what is at the centre of human

misery, self-abuse and addiction? It's isolation. You can have a *great* life on Facebook, be chock-full of *awesome* on Instagram, but it's all a filthy lie. You're lonely and you're miserable. You're not? Give it time, you will be.

One of the things the Chemical Generation will have to come to terms with is the fact that none of us know yet what the long-term costs are. I can tell you anecdotally and from thirty years of experience that at the age of fifty we have the brain chemistry of someone of seventy. You forget stuff, you stumble over words and, most of all, you get *angry*.

This fury thing is what I see most with my generation. We are the space monkeys who did it first. The drain of brain chemistry has left a stratum of very angry and reactionary men. And it's nearly always men; women are much smarter and stop sooner. This is not unique to my peers. Anyone at all who does drugs as regularly and for as long as we have will be like this: moody, disappointed, perpetually let down by everyone and everything, enraged at the world, completely and utterly incapable of seeing that we ourselves are the dark heart at the centre. The common denominator in all these disasters is me. Yet it's always someone else's fault.

I've noticed my own anger has increased. For me fury is present and *very* noticeable because I'm naturally quite jolly and cheerful, and was pretty much exclusively so in my youth. Rage comes with age regardless. It's why most of the truly massive global evils are perpetrated by ageing white men with more power than humanity. Their brains are calcifying and their happy-chems are running dry.

With drug abuse this can happen far, *far* earlier than it's supposed to.

I truly believe that more people than you can possibly imagine have been damaged by drugs. I don't mean bad-toothed, impoverished junkies on street corners; I mean from park benches to plazas, palaces to parliaments. And for fuck's sake don't tell me that after all this time booze, prescription drugs and cigarettes are not in the mix too: just look at the world spinning down the toilet – they've got to be a factor, right? There has to be a reason we're all still as stupid as cavemen, or is it just me? When your life has degraded to the point where you never go out except to work, never stop staring at a screen and ravage your body through neglect and active abuse, you have to ask yourself, what is the actual difference between being inside and outside of a prison? Geography?

So now you may ask, 'Secret DJ, how can you tell when someone you care about is in trouble?' Well, Pilgrim, I can help a little. There are lots of cartoon 'signs' that people are departing for the world of drugs: bullshit about holes in shirts and rings under eyes. But right there is your most glaring pointer – 'departure'. Let me describe the journey away from people and into the prison of the self in terms of my own experience. When I was in deep with it I told myself that I didn't want to talk to people because:

Firstly, I was 'busy'. The easiest lie of modernity, and the most depressingly common: important people are busy.

Then, I was 'away'. Even better: both a travelling success *and* geographically unavailable.

Eventually isolation was just a habit married to a lie: that cool and successful people don't answer enquiries, they make them.

Later I became convinced that people weren't worth talking to. I didn't hate them; it's just that, amazingly, each person suddenly came with a handy excuse attached that meant it was OK to ignore them. Tour Manager even assigned comedy ringtones to people he didn't want to speak to. How we'd laugh when his phone sang out the theme to Laurel and Hardy when some clown he was avoiding rang.

Finally, I couldn't *afford* to speak on the phone. Actually, I would have been able to if it mattered, but by now nothing did. The hypocrisy of the indignation I felt when someone would call or – *madness* – expect to be called back: 'Don't they know *I have nothing*?! Idiots.'

And ultimately I'd misquote to myself the greatest writer who ever lived – Bukowski (who else?): 'I don't hate people at all, I just feel better when they are not around.'

So I hate to generalise, but if someone you love is 'not available' – and by that I mean unavailable to pretty much everyone, not just you – well, they usually want it that way. And drugs are not far behind the facade of the excuses given. Don't get me wrong, I don't mean they're busy drooling on the carpet and dancing with fairies as the phone rings. It's a permanent form of unavailability, not a moment of them being 'busy' or it being a 'bad time'. Drug highs last a few hours at best, a day *in extremis*. If someone can't speak to you over a protracted period, it isn't because they're high, it's because they're low. The 'recovery', the lifestyle and, most of all, the hidden but ever-present

281

crushing *guilt* are the main event, not the fleeting high. A form of constant excruciating shame is also there.

There's a reason we hide our faces when ashamed. Enough shame and you hide your phizog full-time. Drugs isolate a person. No one wants a postcard from a sunny beach when they're in prison, no one wants to hear about fun things when they're wracked with guilt and self-loathing, so you cut off lines of access to this information. You also go into 'passive mode' and do everything on autopilot. You watch a lot of TV and read, but you have no ideas and no drive. You receive but rarely give. You confuse action with productivity. Life isn't a series of physical movements; it's full of emotions and thought, and reactions to events. I started to think going for long windy walks with the dog or gardening was living. By 'doing things' I was 'OK'. I'd substituted my imagination for sensation. The only time I was alive was when I was high. The rest of existence was nothing more than a precursor to it.

You know that feeling you get when a brown envelope arrives? When things are so claustrophobic sometimes just the sound of the letterbox can depress and even shock. It's the world knocking with a big metal fist. When you're wrapped up in yourself you make for a very small, sad little package. As well as the phone, eventually you don't answer email or even texts. In fact, the sound of anything from 'outside' makes you jump. Just the thought of something like switching your phone on or picking up the mail makes your heart sink. Pathetic, isn't it?

When it really starts to hammer you, you get a little window into what it's like to be very elderly. You're alone.

Your body doesn't do anything that it should. You have to push to piss, use objects to physically help you get up and sit down. If before you had no respect and understanding for the old folks, boy, you do now! Ultimately you work out that it isn't the drugs that are the problem, it's the isolation. You do the drugs when you're with people to try to connect. You do the drugs on your own to fill the yawning gaps in modern life's plasticity. The void forces you to action. I'm never more rabid than when bored and alone. Which is most of the time.

The interesting thing about experiencing normality, then fame, and then normality again is you get to see how society behaves in a way that most people can only conceptualise but never experience. You get to see at first hand that people favour celebrity over things that surely should have more value. No one reacts to your personality or intellect or even your art if there's no fame attached. Ask any struggling artist. It's as if people can only experience things through the prism of fame. It can only be valid if stamped with public approval. I still made music, played records and wrote words here and there, but now I wasn't well known, it was like these things didn't exist any more. But artistically I hadn't changed at all. One day people loved what I did, then they didn't. But the things I made were the same. Odd.

By now I was definitely stupider. Less considered. More reactionary. Worse. Call it what you will, the result is the same: a glacial lessening of the self. So do you see? My story is not unique to me. My generation *all* did what I did, to varying degrees.

Let's not forget it's also about self-preservation. I've

often wondered if my subconscious is dosing me, self-medicating to avoid the perils and pitfalls of modern relationships, hysterical political correctness and feral offspring, and the crushing existential disappointment at what normality has to offer. I won't lie, sometimes I think it's good for me. Some of us were just never going to be normal. Not ever.

Conversely, when I look at the news and at what we're saying online, I see a pattern: a general degradation of the species. Can I prove drugs and consumerism are behind it all? Not really. I'm not that clever.

'Oh, man! Secret DJ, you're on a *bummer*, man! This book was *way* better when you were funny! Waaah, boo-hoo.'

What am I doing about it? Well, Pilgrim, I would definitely advise buying a chainsaw, never driving unless you have to, living up a tall hill and getting a large dog.

No, I'm serious. I used to do a lot of manual labour as a youth, but my later life was very physically undemanding. I now lived far out in the country, so I bought a chainsaw almost as standard. I was surrounded by huge trees that sometimes dropped large branches in storms. I had a wood-burning fire. Makes sense. As time progressed I found that operating something so powerful and dangerous, in my condition, was really very sobering. It got me out. It reconditioned me physically.

It gave me back some dexterity and strength. Most of all, confidence. Sounds crazy and unlikely? In *this* book? Come on. I stopped driving because I couldn't afford to any more unless it was essential, and anyway, the dog needed a walk. A large walk. A punishing walk up and down a ridiculous hill.

Then one day I looked in the mirror and I was there. I hadn't been for a long time. Next I did something I'd not done in a very long time: I picked up the phone.

'Hhuuuz?'

'Hey! Quag Allurgie! How about replacing those gigs we lost out on? Dude, I worked for you for free so often you must have something for me as payback, right?'

'Wull, uzz bun uh vrrreh tuff cubbel uf yrz. Donut uf yz hd ah-bud thungz bud thd jzzzd nuthun gunnun un . . .'

'I'll take that as a "no" then, shall I?'

'Yuz.'

Out of every ten calls, nine were a waste of time. After a hundred calls, ten were promising. After ten thousand calls I was almost back in the game. Sounds easy? Imagine how long it takes to make ten thousand calls when you have no money at all and no one wants to speak to you. All those favours you do for other people over the decades don't mean much when you're on top. When things aren't so good they mean even less, and this time it's you that needs a helping hand. Never do anything for anyone in the expectation that it will be returned, Pilgrim. 9.9 times out of ten it never will be, and never more so than in today's society of graspers and takers.

In the process of making the calls one of my worst fears was confirmed: Tour Manager had gone into business with Quag Allurgie. The venture went under. Or rather, T-Man did. No matter how hard I tried, I couldn't get him to answer the phone. Through mutual friends I heard he was living in someone's deceased dad's house. The old man had sadly passed away, and Tour Manager had taken up residence there, mainly as it was free of charge. He'd lost everything, and he was a man who, unlike me, had a lot to lose. Over the years the combination of drugs, changing scenes and bad business had whittled his empire away to nothing. Well, not quite nothing. His last remaining relative, a lovely lady, had called me to say that despite living in this odd situation, T-Man actually owned a different, perfectly good house that someone wanted to buy. It would secure his future. A pension, I guess. He was refusing to acknowledge it was happening, apparently. Why he'd left this place to go live on a sofa, I wasn't sure. It was also a perfect excuse for me to break into his self-imposed prison and find out what the hell had happened to him. The relative told me there was a spare key in a tiny safe hidden outside the house. I would have to get in by myself as T-Man both refused to leave the place or answer the door. We'd been the best of friends for going on ten years now, minus one year of silence.

It was the festive period. I went to see my family in the mountains. I don't know about you but I get quite sentimental at Christmas. I message friends and think about people I've not thought about for a long time. Most of all, I feel for friends who have no family. It's all about family after all – that's why we make up tales of families of gods having kids in stables under trying circumstances. It's the winter family campfire for us as a species. After the traditionally huge Christmas dinner I asked if a plate could be made up for T-Man. I'd resolved to take it to him. I was going to track him down when I went on the road for New Year's Eve – without doubt, the DJ's busiest time of the year.

I can completely miss things like Easter and Halloween. When every weekend is a party, even things as large and ungainly as Christmas can creep up and mug you. New Year's Eve is always a particularly funny one. It's a weird time of year regardless of you having to run around like a man on fire trying to get as much work done as you can before everyone decides they don't want to go out for a month. At certain points over this period the only life forms on the streets are DJs, taxi drivers and foxes messing with bins. This particular New Year's Eve I only knew it was midnight because of the fireworks. I'd already done two festive gigs and was on my way to do more over the next forty-eight hours. I was literally the only vehicle on the biggest road in the country. It was quite surreal visually, driving down a vastly wide, dark path, with many little firework displays popping out along the side of the road at various points. Even the psycho truck drivers were nowhere to be seen. Which was a shame 'cos, like nurses, they always have the best, purest amphetamines.

It became apparent after some time that I was in urgent need of lightening my load. By now I was no longer drinking and was driving myself many thousands of miles. The jet-set lifestyle was long gone. These journeys needed a lot of pit stops. I felt the panic rise as I passed the third major service station that was lights-off and barricaded. You take fuel, running water and refreshment very much for granted in the first world, especially on our biggest highways. However, there's a small window once a year when even the motorway services close, a few hours annually when even our corporate masters cannot wave enough money to convince a spotty youth to stand alone behind the counter of a hideous brand in the middle of nowhere.

I didn't just need a shit, like, in a truly *medical* sense, I was also running low on fuel. The former was definitely a priority. It's one of those things like asthma: if you start to worry about it, it makes it come on ten times stronger. I really, *really* wasn't looking forward to trying to shit by the side of a motorway. I'd not reduced myself to the level of the psycho truck drivers just yet. I was, however, quickly losing the will to live.

Lo! In the distance was a dim light. It was as sterile as a waiting room and would have had tumbleweed outside if it was in America, but it was definitely not closed. That was a start. I pulled in to the huge empty space. You don't realise how big these places are until you see them like this. A service station that's closed is like a nightclub when the house lights are on: a sad, elderly tarmac diva with her wig off. By now I had Portishead, which is a DJ term for touching cloth.

I screeched to a halt as close to the entrance as possible and was mumbling a prayer as I waddled and staggered to the doors, which were questionably lit.

'*Hurrah!*' went the doors as they slid open. I skated into the darkened foyer and did a good impression of a car drifting around a corner as I made for the toilets. The place was clearly not open, but lucky for me it wasn't closed either. I crashed into the gents and just made it into a cubicle in time. Result. Then, rather oddly, I heard footsteps and the door of the cubicle next to me open, close and lock. It was most strange, as there were no other vehicles or people anywhere to be seen. Bit '*Woo*' actually. Bit 'No, ta.'

'ALL RIGHT, MATE!' bellowed a huge cheery voice almost next to my ear. I clenched, pinched and panicked. I was so scared it was like I was a brown tap that had been turned off. I knew all about psycho truck drivers – enough of the drug-addled maniacs had tried to kill me on the roads over the years. I kept silent. Maybe he didn't know exactly which cubicle I was in.

'HAPPY NEW YEAR!'

Christ, he was cunning. He'd used a festive greeting. I had to say something – it's the festive rules – so I grunted a reply with as much false cheer as a telephone salesman. An 'Oh, er, happy new year to you too . . . er . . .' sort of thing.

'AY! WHAT YOU UP TO, MATE?!'

'Oh, I'm . . . er . . . just . . . er . . . having a wee in a service station and stuff.'

'GREAT! GREAT! YOU COMING OUT? GO ON! IT'S NEW YEAR'S.'

'Oh . . . well, that's very nice of you. I'm actually working and on my . . .'

'YEAH, YEAH, YEAH, BLAH, BLAH. COME ON, DON'T BE SHY!'

I was tired, I was a bit alarmed and I was in the dark in the middle of a motorway on New Year's Eve, three gigs in, being propositioned by a wandering, diesel-fume-sniffing assassin who no doubt wanted to wear my skin as a catsuit. I'd had enough. I pulled up my pants, took a deep breath and hammered on the paper wall next to me with all my strength, yelling, 'FUCK OFF, YOU HAIRY-ARMED

CANNIBAL! I'VE GOT TO WORK! I'M A DJ, MAN! AN *ARTIST*! I CAN'T BE DEALING WITH YOUR FESTIVE MURDEROUSNESS, FOR CHRIST'S SAKE. I'VE GOT WORK TO DO!'

Then the voice from next door said in petrified, whispering tones, 'I'm so sorry, mate, I will have to call you back. There is a fucking lunatic in the cubicle next to me going absolutely *mental*.'

🎧

I never made it to T-Man's place that year. Twelve months later I did exactly the same thing: I had a sentimental Christmas dinner, got a plate made up for the absent T-Man and set off to find him.

It was a six-hundred-mile round trip. Part of my rehabilitation was to stop driving whenever possible and cycle instead, so I bought train tickets and dragged the bike from town to town, station to station. (David Bowie again! So sorry. Can't seem to stop doing them.) I remembered the details of T-Man's address from the previous year. A mutual friend had told me he was still there, and that the complex procedure for gaining access had changed a bit. What had not changed was the fact that T-Man wouldn't answer the door to anyone. I was apprehensive. I'd not seen my best bud for two years now. It was a freezing winter's day as I laboured across the city and up the steep hill to the rather low-rent housing estate. When I got there the key was in the exterior safe, as promised. I had the documents he needed to sign in my hand. Entering the kitchen I was confronted with a pile of green, used teabags that formed a pyramid two foot tall on the counter, nearly head height. It was like one of those TV programmes about hoarders. Crap was everywhere. In the murk of the front room was Tour Manager himself.

'Have you got any cigarettes?' was his immediate greeting, a voice in the gloom after years of nothing.

'Nice to see you too.'

I went to buy him some. Upon returning it was clear he was in no state to acknowledge the reality of his financial situation. What was also clear was that he had given up drugs. Nobody looks like that unless they've done years of stimulants and then stopped. His face had acquired the permanent look of the ghost of a Victorian kid who had had his hoop and stick taken away. Baron Munchausen was gone. Colonel Kurtz had replaced him. Maybe he thought the same looking at me, who knows? Against all reason he disagreed that there was a buyer for this last piece of his empire. It was clear he was depressed and he was happy for everything to go under, including our friendship and his future. I'd been depressed too, so I didn't take it personally. Still don't. I took the papers over to him and said all he needed to do was sign. Inexplicably he refused. I asked him if he wanted me to do it for him. He agreed. I did my best imitation of his signature and left. The next day I gave the papers to the agent and T-Man's future was secured. We've not spoken to each other since, although not for want of trying on my part. However, all the windmills remain resolutely tilted.

♩

To this day I've no idea how you can spend so much joyful time with another human and end up not seeing them again. I hope it's clear that this man is truly legendary. He overcame the horrific British class system, a victim of imposed values and an obsolete, brutal hierarchy. He had everything and yet decided to live a life of adventure instead of avarice. He didn't sit on his privilege like a fat dragon, he kicked it apart as if it were a pile of golden leaves. He gave, gave, gave and gave some more. He launched careers and helped many achieve success, and never asked for a thing in return.

Most of all, he was one of the most hilarious people you could ever wish to meet, and despite many off-colour tics and flavourful language, he didn't have a bad bone in his body. Uniquely, he was completely and utterly without guile, with a surplus of personality that lit up everywhere he went. I can't explain it further, except to add: drugs are a hell of a drug. We did them so you don't have to, Pilgrim.

♩

Why do it? Why do we dance? I see it as no different to capering round a fire in a cave. The monsters may be extinct, and the wars with other tribes suitably far away, but release is needed now more than ever. Only the oppressors have changed. After the victories of Reagan and Thatcher we retreated from the real world into a completely alternative reality of drugs, noise and the internet. Our most intelligent and promising children interact with the world almost entirely through simulations now.

And yet . . .

During my peak years, I spent a lot of time on dance floors when I wasn't working, thousands and thousands of lost hours. I think I was looking for something, some connection with others. I don't think I found it, but I looked really hard. We live inside the opposite of what passes for a society now. Consumerism, shopping malls and social media are not a connection; they're just a one-way valve between companies and our money. Connection, human connection, is needed more than ever and has been for some time now.

Shakespeare's main rival Ben Jonson referred to music as 'the one true rapture'. I didn't google that; it's a phrase that has stayed with me my whole life, one that I heard again when it was transposed and remixed into 'House Is a Feeling' in the late 1980s. In a world of lies it's a huge, unwavering truth. That truth is other people, a feeling of unity. Even a mere impersonation of solidarity is better than none at all.

Ultimately what we do is all about people, but in a good way. It's the opposite of theatre or the high street or even a rock gig. It's not a performance to be exchanged for cash, it's a connection with others just like you, maybe the only human connection there will ever be for some. It's a *feeling*, a feeling of absolute togetherness, if only for a while. When you pull away from humanity, bad things can happen.

It takes a step or two in the dark to truly move towards the light.

Epilogue

In short? Pay your taxes, don't take drugs, get a real tour manager and don't get your friends involved in any of your business, otherwise it will end very badly for everyone. Got that? Good. Not sure if I've got it yet, but I'll let you know. If I'd told you that at the start, it would have saved you the job of wading through this nonsense, right?

DISCLAIMER:
The events in this book all took place in front of my very eyes. However, for the sake of actually having a narrative, a beginning, a middle and an end, some of the characters are composites of two or three people, otherwise the book would be longer than *Lord of the Rings*. Also, some of the events have been shuffled chronologically to be more pleasing to my overlords. What I will say more than anything is: don't *ever* cry for the superstar DJs. Those guys earn millions, they can wipe away their tears with some of those bills.

So many of us suffer now from what I call the 'King's Disease'. Look at old portraits and you're looking at those who could afford to have them painted – the rich, the royal. They're fat. They never walked anywhere; they were carried or they rode. They died of the diseases of the indolent and privileged. And are we not all little princes and princesses nowadays? You need only spend five minutes on social media to see it. Think that the internet doesn't represent reality? OK, spend another five minutes travelling anywhere. Roads packed with little emperors, seats on trains for lapdogs and baggage, hissing headphones and tinny smartphones capering and jestering in tiny fiefdoms of noise, everyone cashing in on the invulnerability of youth, in debt to an old age they have no concept of.

That's me now: physically pretty fucked and mentally not too sharp either. Still better than most on my worst days, but hey, you should have seen me *before*, Pilgrim. It's not all bad, you know. I've seen some things most people could live a hundred lifetimes and never experience, not least of which was seeing most of the world, what it offers, and everything in between.

If I regret anything, it's seeing how we went full circle from the innocent joy of acid house to the post-truth era. That is *truly* sad. Ironically, those of us who started this whole thing are the most precious guard dogs of it, grumpily barring newcomers, totally forgetting its message of joy and inclusivity, jealously hoarding and judging, betraying our past with nostalgic parodies. Bad form.

Wrestling with the post-truth era? Think of it like a man getting married to a woman. He may think he's OK with it in theory, but on day two realises that he's entered an entirely alternative universe, one where consensus no longer exists and everything you do and say is wrong. I'm more than prepared for the post-truth era. I've sat there while a woman berates me for having the nerve to point out that her car's tyres don't last forever and urgently need replacing.

I've been in the hot seat while she explains to me at length why I'm in the wrong for mentioning it, how I'm borderline abusive in my never-ending quest to undermine her so she doesn't die in a screaming ball of fire and metal. I understand the post-truth era because I've been married.

Don't hate me, girls. I'm sure you've experienced the same. It's not unique to either sex. No matter what your orientation I'm certain you know what I'm talking about. Anyone on any side of *any* relationship knows exactly what it's like to be the wrongest thing in the universe, and no amount of facts, patience, correctness past or present, Zen, goodwill or negotiations can dent the situation because there's only *emotion*. Emotion does not deal in the rational. It is what it is, until it isn't any more. The only thing that can dent it is duration.

'Taste' is a major piece of kit in the cult of the individual. We use it as a weapon of superiority. It doesn't matter if I've spent longer in this industry than you've been alive, if you decide the records *you* like are better than the records *I* like – and people *always* choose the records they like – then you are 'better' than me and I need to shut up. All the arts are driven by a cult of superiority, a pyramid of opinion that puts the teenage child of a powerful executive above a genuinely experienced artist. Therefore, Pilgrim, if you and I happen to disagree on matters of taste – say, for example, you like drum and bass, and I like techno – then nothing either of us says is valid. Look at it like this, I urge you: in the armed forces they salute the rank, not the person.

The post-truth age is merely an extension of this belief that our own tastes, thoughts and opinions are the only valid ones. It's spreading outwards. I first noticed this in politics: people treated political candidates and stories as if they were fashion items. They would round on something merely because it was popular, or loudly claim to be the first who followed something, as if it was a record or a pair of shoes. Then it moved into the realm of science: in the same way a bedroom DJ truly believes themselves to be superior to those doing it professionally, soon everyone in front of their computer believed they knew more than our scientists. The common denominator that runs through it all is the internet. By democratising everything from music to information and making it available to all, we've destabilised the expert and enabled the amateur. For good and for ill.

Ultimately the internet has delivered the most precious and valuable thing to anyone who wants it: an impersonation of fame. Doesn't the 'sex tape' say it all? Fucking for fame. And we applaud and reward it.

The absence of rationality is not simply emotion, however. The description of the post-truth era as one of a 'lacking' is false. It is, in fact, the opposite. Nothing's been removed per se, it's just the emphasis has now shifted away from forms of mutual agreement into a sort of selfish, shrieking siege mentality. Facts and the exchange of information haven't disappeared, it's just that our ability to hear them over our self-interest has been obliterated by the parts of us that deal only in feeling rather than thinking.

It's very easy to confuse thinking and feeling, in the same way that incredibly well-educated and intelligent idiots don't understand the difference between information and knowledge. People confuse all inner processes for thought, when in fact it's just raw feelings. Intelligence and wisdom are not the same. Nor are impulses and calculation. Sure, both exist in your head at once, so I get that it's confusing, but learning how to recognise and separate these things is more vital to you than anything else I can talk about in this book.

Some kids will be reading much of this with utter incomprehension. They've grown up under the ridiculous farce of manufactured economic depressions and having to do their socialising online, stone-cold sober. They've grown up to be good Americans, no matter where they were born or live. They must think we're ridiculous dinosaurs for hammering ourselves with booze and pills when there's good money to be made, and totally idiotic for being so publicly intoxicated. Is there anything more futile than trying to glamorise being an ugly mess to the selfie generation? All I can say is, don't do what I did. You're right, we *are* idiots. Maybe your vanity will protect you. But, Pilgrim, we really *lived*! Perhaps we're the last true rock 'n' rollers. Who knows?

Nowadays I'm back in the game, in a modest fashion. It took a *long* time. Most people would have given up. Many did. The majority of those years were about overcoming gossip and a bad rep that was only partially deserved. A lot of it was spent realising no one owes you a living, and if you want work you'd best better go out and damn well make it happen.

I recollect a long time ago I was a little down on the whole thing, complaining about it all being a bit 'opium of the masses'. I said this to a buddy of mine who was a chef attached to the club I was working in at the time. He looked at me incredulously and said, 'Are you mental? Your job is to *make people happy*, man! You have no idea about the degradation and hammering despair some people endure in their weekly disguise. Those peak two hours on a Saturday night might be the best thing that will *ever* happen to them. You are a fool.'

I tell myself this almost every day now. I've never thought this job is particularly worthy, but it sure isn't worthless. It isn't the cure for cancer, but it might be helping a more widespread and sinister ailment in a small way. Or exacerbating it. I don't know any more. So much can kill you these days.

But, Pilgrim, listen up: if the devil comes to take you, and you really have to go, give him the finger and go out *dancing*.

Glossary of Terms

Aggro: Truncation of 'aggravation'. Trouble. An incident.
Amphetamine sulphate: Whizz. Speed. There are a lot
of names for what is a pretty basic drug. Far less euphoric
and more workmanlike than cocaine, booze or meth, it
exaggerates and energises everything, mental and physical.
It rarely intoxicates or hampers the user; if anything,
it provides clarity and focus. However, it borrows so
heavily from the body's natural functioning that most
people rarely take it twice.

Bangers: A kid's firework or firecracker. Not to be
confused with BANGER.
Banger: A particularly good tune.
Banging: The effect of playing a banger. Can also be slang
for 'good'.
Base: Base amphetamine sulphate, the purer paste that
the diluted (and far weaker) powdered form is made
from. Almost identical in effect to methamphetamine. In
America 'base' means 'free-based' smoked cocaine. But
this isn't America. Yet.
Bent: Not kosher. Illegal. Dodgy.
Blag/blagger/blagging: To succeed elegantly at
gatecrashing.
Booth wanker: A person who *has* to be in the DJ booth
at all costs and either considers themselves too important

to be down among the crowd or regards being next to the DJ the apex of their existence.

Bosh/boshing: The sound of hard/to go at something with high energy.

Chupito: A shot of the local Spanish firewater.

Dodgy: See BENT.

Door picker: The gatekeeper. The one with the list. They who must be obeyed.

Dope: In the US it can mean any drug. In the UK it refers to smoked depressants like hashish or weed.

EDM: The recent American rebranding of thirty years of European culture. A handy acronym for people who can't be bothered to deal with the rich variety of the many very different strands of modern music. Literally, Electronic Dance Music. Anything that willingly calls itself this is to be avoided at all costs.

Gak: Cocaine.

Go faster stripes: Lines of powdered stimulant.

Gurning: The bulldog-chewing-a-wasp face that people on good MDMA involuntarily pull, constantly.

Herbert, spotty: Nerds who favour logic over melody.

Hobnob: To socialise.

Jazz: Pornography.

Journey, the: Taking the crowd from one very clear point to another through the medium of sound. Also something of a trope to the jaded.

Lifted: Stolen.

Meth: Short for methamphetamine, which is composed of an amphetamine molecule with an additional methyl group attached to its nitrogen (amine) group. Slightly stronger than straight-up amphetamine, but if you can tell the difference between unadulterated whizz and adulterated meth, you're a better junkie than me.

Mongs: People incapacitated by drugs and alcohol.

Monitor: The smaller speakers that are near a DJ's head. This prevents a time lag as often the booth is far away from the huge main speakers.

Munter: See MONG.

Phizog: Physiognomy. Your face.

Producer: Someone who makes records on their own in their bedroom. Not to be confused with a Producer.

Punter: Customer or paying participant.

Quadra-spazz: Originally, to take four pills at once, producing a dangerous level of intoxication. Has come to mean 'a very large idiot'.

Quadra-spazzed: To be in a very poor state of repair.

Rainmaker: One who claims authorship of something that happened naturally.

Random: A person who on the surface behaves like an

old friend due to the positive effects of certain drugs, but is in fact a total stranger.

Shazam: An imaginary butterfly net for catching digital moths.
'Sleb: Celebrity.
Spank mag: Girlie magazine.
Spunk it: To fritter away.
Sync: A function on Pioneer DJing equipment that automates elements of the job. Akin to stabiliser wheels on a bike or inflatables to aid people who can't swim.

Tastemaker: One who is at the pointy end of things. A trendsetter.
Trance: A form of dance music. Arguably the enabler of EDM. Big, simple and unpleasant, a bit like me.

Underground: The opposite of EDM and 'commercial' music but often as unpleasant. Here be all the cool kids, loudly hating everything, including each other and ultimately themselves. The sound of the underground is sadly muffled by dirt.

Whizz: Amphetamine sulphate. Meth. Go-faster drugs.
Womble: A furry creature from ancient UK kids' programme *The Wombles*. Wombles were given their names by donning a blindfold and sticking a pin in an atlas, similar to how most promoters choose which DJ to book.

Index

Adam Ant, 84
Allurgie, Quag, 155–71, 178–9,
    180–5, 203, 211, 223–4,
    233–5, 262, 285
Angello, Steve, 193
The A-Team (TV), 102

Baccarat, 39–40, 42, 51, 63, 66,
    120, 131–42
Baluga, Bobbie, 120–4, 129–36,
    138–41, 154, 206–8
Bananahands, 51–5
Berlin, 94, 137
Bongo People (hippies), 181–2
Bosnia, 137
Brazil, 137
Bukowski, Charles, 281
Burning Bieber-Man festival, 126

Caribbean, the, 137
Chemical Generation, the, 51,
    196, 236, 279, 283
Chudleigh, 178, 184, 210–11
chupito (alcoholic drink), 14
*Close Encounters of the Third
    Kind* (film), 175

Daft Punk, 127
Debord, Guy, 194
disco, 125–9
    mega-discos, 188–9, 196–8
DJs (DJing)
    80s version of hippies, 236
    anxiety, 97–8
    assault on senses, 17, 20, 22
    disposability of, 273–5

DJ booth, 18–29, 72, 99, 190,
    205, 278
    'booth wanker', 24, 301
    fanboys, 202
    'gentlemen amateurs'
        (hobbyists), 90–2
    music industry, 46, 49, 69, 84,
        90, 92, 154, 168, 202, 204,
        236, 239, 274–5
    'Plastic', 189–96
    post-DJing high, 26–7
    'soul-crushing banality', 36, 49
    tunnel vision, 17, 22
drugs
    amphetamine sulphate (speed,
        whizz), 4, 13, 52, 55, 57, 109,
        210, 287, 302
    cocaine (gak), 7, 14, 46, 50, 52,
        56, 57, 63, 160, 242–3
    gurning, 42, 110, 175, 193, 227,
        302
    isolation of drug-taking,
        281–3
    ketamine, 7, 130–3, 208
    legal (alcohol, cigarettes,
        coffee), 244, 280
    MDMA, 6, 16, 52, 63, 124, 144,
        182, 184, 238, 244, 302
    methamphetamine (meth), 35,
        57, 106, 144, 239, 242, 272,
        301, 303
    mongs (munters), 7, 98, 303
    'party', 244
    prescription, 247, 256, 271–2,
        280

EDM (electronic dance music), 59, 124–8, 141, 189–90, 196, 215, 302
  DJs as 'world's most minimalist philosophers', 215
Es Vive (hotel), 13, 178

Fabric (club), 193
festivals
  likened to World War I, 219
  parents' visit, 218–19
  Secret DJ on, 213–17, 228–9

'Guillaume' (aka 'Stuart'), 113

Hans, 9–12, 13–14, 16, 27–29, 31
hedonism, 8, 121, 172
Hendrix, Jimi, 97
Hierbas (alcoholic drink), 15
hippies, 51, 173, 181–2, 236
Hucknall, Mick, 54–5

Ibiza, 3–16, 28, 31, 35, 94, 102, 117, 119–20, 172–212, 229–34, 262, 273
  Dalt Vila (Old Town, the 'strip'), 14–15
  'disco mafia', 173
  Domino Bar, 15
  Es Vive (hotel), 13, 178
  Hierbas (alcoholic drink), 15
  history of, 172–4
  Manumission (gig), 15, 187, 197–8, 202, 205, 209
  'pampered aristocracy', 172
  Playa d'en Bossa, 174
  Privilege (club), 187
  Rock Bar, 14, 15
  Space (club), 98, 202–3
  Space Terrace, 205, 219
  'strip' parades, 14–15
Indonesia, 137
Invasion of the Body Snatchers

(film), 169
isolation, 29, 41, 61, 242, 247, 247, 279–81, 283

Jonson, Ben, 293

Key West, 173
Knuckles, Frankie, 195
Krautrock, 124
Kuala Lumpur, 35
Kwowser, 16–17, 27

Las Vegas, 94, 119, 124
London, 16, 35–7, 41, 44, 50, 53, 62, 94
  Fabric (club), 193
  Met Bar, 44, 52, 62
  Metropolitan Hotel, 41, 44

Manumission (gig), 15, 187, 197–8, 202, 205, 209
May, Derrick, 125, 128
mega-discos, 188–9, 196–8
Miami, 142, 153, 178, 211
  Delano Hotel, 154, 167–8
  'the strip', 153, 161, 170
  WMC (Winter Music Conference), 142, 153–5, 167, 178
Miami Vice (TV/film), 154
Moby, 121
Monaco, 173
Moroder, Giorgio, 124
music industry, 46, 49, 69, 83–4, 90, 92, 154, 168, 202, 204, 236, 239, 274–5
  annual conference (WMC), 142, 153–5, 167, 178
  Britpop, 44
  streaming, 84, 86–7

Naked Lunch (book), 166, 278
New York City, 120–48

Paradise Garage (club), 123,
208
Norfolk Broads, 233–4

Paradise Garage (NYC club),
123, 208
'Pilgrims' (wannabe DJs), Secret
DJ's advice to, 43, 61, 79,
83–4, 95, 99–100, 118,
129, 137, 139, 172, 185,
187–8, 196, 201, 235, 239–40,
244–5, 257, 264, 292, 296–7,
299–300
Pioneer (corporation), 90, 304
Privilege (club), 187
Prozac, 247; see also drugs,
prescription

Rihanna, 88

St Tropez, 173
Scarface (film), 154
Secret DJ
advice to 'Pilgrims' (wannabe
DJs), 43, 61, 79, 83–4, 95,
99–100, 118, 129, 137, 139,
172, 185, 187–8, 196, 201,
235, 239–40, 244–5, 257, 264,
292, 296–7, 299–300
arrested, 171
breakdown, 248–55
copper poisoning, 264
diagnosis, 264
extended stay in hospital,
256–68
incapable of speech, 248–54
in specialist neurological
unit, 252–5
persona non grata, 274
physical effects of, 271
slow recovery, 270
suicide attempt, 267–8
near death in Ibiza, 175–6

on attitude to drugs, 236–8
on attitude to legal 'drugs'
(alcohol, cigarettes, coffee),
244
on big pharma, 271
on chemical vs cultural
addiction, 246
on club 'tourists', 140
on comical drug laws at clubs,
237
on dance music as 'immersive
church', 205
on DJ anxiety, 97–8
on DJs as 80s version of
hippies, 236
on DJs as totem for insanity of
capitalism, 94
on DJ fanboys, 202
on DJing in the Alps, 102–9
on drug use/abuse, 238–9,
240–4
on EDM (electronic dance
music), 59, 124–8, 141,
189–90, 196, 215, 302
on festivals, 213–17, 228–9
on France (and the French), 33,
106–7
on generation as sociological
experiment, 236
on Germany (and Germans),
9–12, 17, 28, 33, 57, 216
on how he became a DJ, 235–6
on humanity
degradation of, 284
disappointment in, 272
imprisoned, 280
on Ibiza's 'pampered
aristocracy', 172
on internet age, 298
on mega-discos, 188–9, 196–8
on music industry, 46, 49, 69,
83–4, 89–90, 91–2, 154, 168,
202, 204, 236, 239, 274–5

on need for sleep for mental
well-being, 245
on party drugs, 244
on perils of 'being cool', 277
on 'Plastic DJs', 189–96
on 'politics of fear', 128–9
on post-truth era, 296–9
on prescription drugs, 247,
271–2
on 'the queue', 140
on reality-TV-bred generation,
190
on Switzerland (and the Swiss),
107–9, 111
on train travel, 107–9
on the *Übermensch*, 31, 241
pool ritual, 4, 7, 12, 13, 32, 157
the taxman, 69–101
top tips for being a pro DJ,
94–100
Shine (film), 227
The Society of the Spectacle
(book), 194
Space (club), 98, 202–3
Space Terrace, 205, 219
Spotify, 84, 86–7
Status Quo, 93

T-Man (Tour Manager), 3 *passim*
aristocratic background, 9, 32,
39, 45, 48, 142, 233

arrested at festival, 224–30
business failure with Quag
Allurgie, 262, 285
cocaine generosity, 56–7
demise, 286
Mr T likeness, 102
need for sugar, 114
pool ritual, 4, 7, 12, 13, 32, 157
prostitutes, 165
Schrödinger's buffoon, 44
spoonerisms, 115–16
views on Germany (and
Germans), 9–12, 17, 28, 33,
57, 216
'terminal knob velocity', 217
Tibet, 137

Übermensch, the, 31, 241

Vangelis, 124

Waters, John, 134, 136
WMC (Winter Music
Conference), 142, 153–5,
167, 178

The X Factor (TV show), 88
Xenon, 39–40, 51, 63, 65–9, 73–8,
82

Zombie Taxi, 37, 120